Turn *Yourself* On

Marina J

GOLDEN
GODDESS
HOLDINGS

GOLDEN
GODDESS
HOLDINGS

Published by Golden Goddess Holdings Pty Ltd
PO BOX 1160
Terrigal
NSW 2260
Australia
Marinaj.net

Printed and bound in Australia

National Library of Australia Cataloguing-in-Publication entry

Creator: Marina J., author.
Title: Turn yourself on / Marina J.
ISBN: 9780994535498 (paperback)
Subjects: Self-actualization (Psychology) in women.
   Self-realization in women.
   Women--Conduct of life.
   Life skills.
   Well-being.
   Happiness.
Dewey Number: 158.1

ISBN: 978-0-9945354-9-8

Contents

YOU'RE THE
QUEEN
YOU'RE THE
POWER
YOU *Turn*
YOURSELF
On

This book is for you. I care so very much that you get yourself back.

For Paul and Maya, I love you.

Once you've finished this book, keep yourself high by using the detailed contents page to help you decide which part of you to turn on – Oh là là!

Foreword

If you're anything like me, I entered my 20s without the most important skill of all: Knowing how to heal myself from my biggest upsets. I think most women could put their hands up and say the same!

As a result my coaching practice is full of women who are stuck and frustrated with the men in their lives, *but mostly with themselves*; their life is not what they thought it would be by now...

I wrote *Turn Yourself On* to turn ON your power. To deliciously turn your life around and become Queen. To turn ON whatever you need inside to flourish... because your happiness is everything!

Turn Yourself On will also turn your innate healing ability ON. Did you know that your healing ability is in you right now just waiting with baited breath to heal you from your biggest upsets; so you can live that life that's waiting for you? And when you do? You'll have the relationship you've been longing for, you'll naturally become the woman you were born to be and you will live that life that's been waiting for you. Because for a woman like you? *Nothing less will do.*

This book is right for you if you want to say yes... yes... yes to flourishing!

It's the only way to live.

And.

This book is for you when you can't connect to this and you're downright *crappy*.

But this isn't about me telling you what to do, this isn't that kind of self-help book – nooo – because nobody knows you like you do, minute to minute, second to second. So, how can I or anybody else truly teach you how to turn yourself ON without intimately knowing you?

We can't.

That's why some things are hit and miss for you.

That's why some things work for you some of the time, but not all of the time.

That's why you haven't got *there* yet.

And make no mistake.

There is where you want to be.

Otherwise you wouldn't still be searching would you?

You wouldn't be reading this now.

YOU have diamonds at your very fingertips right at this moment to LIVE the life that's been waiting for you. Not a book. Not a concept. YOU.

Be greedy. Use this book to make great change in your life. And if you don't? You'll come away with a concept of *how your life could be.*

A boring option for a woman like you.

And so we're going to embark on this now. Set sail, if you will. For there is no turning back when you realise you deserve to turn yourself on, to get your fabulous BACK! And if you've never been fabulous? Darling you're about to be!

For you to outrageously flourish the way you are meant to? The way you were *born* to?

It's in your DNA. It's in YOU…

… And you *know* this deep down.

You ready?

I invite you to treat this book as your new best friend; one that will lift you up higher than you can alone and one that you can call on in the middle of the night when you have trouble going to sleep. It's here that you'll heal what's happened in your day as you learn how to successfully navigate *those* situations in life. Yes *those*. It's like having your very own fairy godmother – *shwapping*! Except it's YOU. Together, we're going to build a personal system for you to live by (that fits you like a glove) so you come out of *Dry-out and into a life that excites you and turns you on.

> *Dry-out = where you feel sucked dry by a part or all of your life.

So, I recommend absorbing this book fully now, and then dipping into it when you need it. This book is written so that throughout your day, you can drop into a chapter for whatever you need: Little things and big things; they can all get a woman down. A particular chapter will be relevant to you whether you've read it two times or 20 times before, because it's written as if I'm sitting next to you talking to you right now. (By the way I like what you've done with your hair.) Oh, and sometimes we forget, so we just need to be reminded again because all of us are surrounded by people who are not flourishing and some of them, have no intention of doing so.

By the way, if I say, "he" and your lover is a gorgeous "she" please play "she" in your head as you're reading this book.

The examples given are from real clients, and situations; some examples are made up of two or three different stories all rolled into one fat delicious one to sharpen my point. Names and details have been changed to lovingly protect the identities of these people whose stories are helping you now.

And remember this lovely woman; you are not alone, even if you feel you are sometimes. In fact, the more you read the chapter you need, the better for you and the Goddess within you who gets awakened each time it's read.

A little note about why I'm going to call you a Goddess from now on...

*Goddess = Choosing to have a divine relationship with yourself.

If you were born a woman, you already are a Goddess. And there is nothing you need to do, or to change about you to become one. *Rather, it's the way you think about yourself that needs to change.*

Chapter 1

You Are The QUEEN Of Your Inner World

. . . .

It wasn't so long ago that my husband left me and I became a single mum. It was New Year's Eve, with one hour to go until midnight. I heard the revellers outside shouting, "Happy New Year!" to each other and I knew it was the worst night of my life. Alone with Maya, my baby girl, who was sleeping in the next room, I dreaded what the New Year would bring. I had never felt so alone, so scared of the future. To make matters worse, my family were on the other side of the world, back in England; and in addition, four of my closest friends, who'd all been pregnant at the same time as me, were moving away. I had no money – only scant financial support from my soon to be ex-husband, and no physical support from anybody. I found out that night about true despair.

One night, soon after, I was still reeling from the shock but I was beginning to untangle myself, I made a conscious decision. I decided there and then that I would not go down with this ship, and I decided that Maya and I were going to have an amazing life. I made a conscious decision to take control of the course and nature of my life and shape it to my will. It was from this standpoint that I made all my decisions – if something was going to give us a shot at a great life, I did it – and if it didn't, then I turned away from it.

I decided to move back to the UK to be with my parents. Within 5 weeks of making this decision, I'd packed up my life and was on a plane with all of my belongings flying away from Australia with my little Maya next to me. I sat on that plane and polished off an entire family-sized Toblerone bar and as we drove back to my old home, and new way of living, the second giant Toblerone bar in my bag was deftly inhaled. It wasn't easy being back home. It was a lot of adjusting for all of us, but my parents were very kind and supportive of me, giving me the chance (if I took it) to step out of this huge crisis.

But which direction was I going take? Relax safely in the family home, or use all my time to get my dreams? How was I going to do it?

I realised that I had to be working in a job I loved. What dawned on me spectacularly one afternoon, as I was finishing up a conversation with my girlfriend, was that I'd had a running theme my whole life: I seemed to be the person everyone (I knew) turned to for help *almost daily*. After I helped them, they often joked at the end of the impromptu "session", "God – I should be paying you for this!" I came alive in those moments, by *guiding her*, this incredible woman, anywhere, anyhow: on the phone, at a party, in the playground, back to her brilliance again. So, with aplomb I embarked on creating my coaching career, so I would have a solid way to start a business when I returned to Australia.

This meant waking at 2:00am for weekly study calls and lying next to me would be Maya, propped up; pretending to read the dictionary, like mummy read her notes, only upside down. There were many smiles and many, many more tears. But mostly a grit determination. Nothing was going to ever get in my way again of having a fabulous life. Nothing. Not my past, not me, and not this. And so I began re-building.

When I returned to Australia, I hit the ground running. I rented a flat within 3 weeks, went on a job interview, and got a job. Then got another job, then got another. It was hard. The mechanics of my life were hard. I would drop Maya off to day care and work was a 4-hour round trip on 4 buses, daily. At the end of each day I would carry my tired mini me from the bus, shopping bags banging around my ankles, up the very steep hill to my flat, and then up three flights of stairs. My legs would scream. A constant knot lived in my stomach – made tighter with each painful situation my ex-husband unknowingly passed onto me. I had no regular practical support from anybody. My back ached, my head ached from the strain, but throughout these months my spirit remained bright because I fed it. I created an ethos for myself (although at the time I didn't know that was what it was) *and I lived by that ethos daily, whether I felt like it or not.* It's this system that forms the basis of the coaching program I now hold for women. It's the same system that took me from there to here.

When I got my 14-year-old car back (another story for another time) I used it to drive to Maya's day care, then drive back to the beach most mornings before work. This was part of my ethos. I would run up the beach, head down, almost always crying – the morning dog walkers wouldn't get their sunny hello – and when I would reach the top of the cliff, I would close my eyes and let my consciousness expand beyond my frustrations and closed doors. *I was not the sum total of what was happening.* Then I would walk back to the battered old car and talk to the love of my life – the husband I hadn't met yet – *all the way.* To make it more real, to visualise him, and us, I would talk out loud. I would share the coming day with him. Sometimes I would laugh because he made me laugh. I didn't care what anyone thought; my dreams and the emotions they aroused in me for those 15 minutes were the highlight of my day.

One day, I bumped into the lovely marriage counsellor I'd had three years prior. I would go into her mansion right on the cliff top that overlooked the sea and marvelled at her life, her husband, and the lovely little school her daughter went to that I wanted Maya to go to someday, if I could afford it. I told her how I was and then she gasped, *"Marina – how did you overtake me?"* I was stunned: how did I, a single mother, living week-to-week, renting a small flat *even begin* to overtake *this woman*? How would she think that? And how can somebody overtake another anyway? Wasn't that a weird concept? But by the time I got home, I realised what she meant: I was beginning to flourish inside, even though my daily life was still so hard, while she had not gone any further in the last 3 years.

Within 6 months my life turned around in a big way. I was thriving. I was confident, GLOWING, my daughter and I were thriving, and I had men asking me out.

Soon, I had friends asking me what exactly it was that I was doing because I had a light in my eyes they hadn't seen before. Sure enough, I noticed how much lighter and happier I felt than a lot of the people I talked to: people who in material terms *had way more than me*. What I had was a system, which took me out of my old life and into my new one very quickly, so very soon, I had a little waiting list of friends needing my help and people wanting to work with me. I don't know how to describe it. I just felt *sexy*. I just knew how to turn myself on: all of me and particularly, my happiness. My system made it easy and that was no mean feat considering how my life looked on paper.

Then another turning point came: my beloved grandmother died and had left me a bit of money. What to do with it? Do I get serious and get a proper full time job, and work towards buying a flat? Or do I start my own business? With the business, I could still be a mummy to Maya, but it was a huge risk. I sat on my bed and cried. What if my belief in myself was all wrong? I couldn't afford to make any mistakes for Maya's sake.

I decided that if I was going to do the business, I would begin it with gusto. If I wanted to create an amazing future that Maya and I could get excited about, then this was it. So, Marina J was born and my little business got created each night between the hours of 10:00pm–2:00am.

Following my system meant I knew how to turn on my ability to receive, and three years after talking to my "husband" on that beach, I was on a real second date running down that very same beach, side by side *with him, him!* Laughing my head off! Looking *at him, a real him,* wide-eyed, and knowing that I couldn't tell him what I used to do not so very long ago because it would totally spin him out! OMG it was really happening!

Eleven months later he proposed. (Oh!) And a week later it was New Year's Eve! I had a very different evening that night and it felt very poignant. And now, fifteen years on from the year my daughter was born, I live in the life I created with my gorgeous system that I treasure so very much. My husband is that man I dreamed of on that beach, my daughter has the father I always wished for her, and my days are delicious with helping women like you discover how to turn themselves on, so they get really, really happy and flourish. I help women who look like they have it all: rich and famous women, those "it girls," who have it *all together* but are suffering in secret; single mummies who want to create a future they and their kids are excited about after divorce; and women like you and me. Big stuff happens and then there are those tiny bumps in the road that seem so inconsequential, and yet can derail us. When an upset comes, how quickly can you heal it? Navigating our lives without a way to switch on the fundamental parts of ourselves and keep them turned on is crazy and yet that's what I see millions of us women trying to do each day.

And that's why I made another decision; to write to you and to speak to you, as if I am sitting next to you. You are a woman just like me. We might look different. We might want to live very different lives, but I know what it's like to be so low, and I know what it's like to rise up, and I know what it's like to stay here. I want what you want for you and so I've written this book for you.

And we start with YOU.

As we re-wire you back to the way you are naturally made, you will be able to create a life that turns you on, instead of living a life that turns you off. Hurrah! It's called FLOURISHING and you deserve it. And this is important because if you're not happy then everyone including you suffers and we don't do long term suffering here. Not on my watch. We're going to use whatever has happened in your day to heal, and to turn all of you on, so come to this book exactly as you are: frazzled from that meeting with your boss, or bloated because you've over-eaten again. It matters not to me. I just see you, and if you're reading this, woman you're ready.

So, I'm curious, why did you choose to start reading this book today? What made you open it?

Is it you and *him*?

Are you upset with yourself?

Is it *them* or *that* situation?

Or do you just have a feeling that this book is right for you?

And why now?

Whatever the reason is, I know you are a *beautiful, brilliant woman with outrageous talent*. I know this because you were born; all women are born beautiful, brilliant and outrageously talented. So you can't help yourself really...

But if you are not able to be this brilliant woman we both know you are, if you are not able to be her all of the time, or if you've never actually been her... not yet anyway and you know she's in there somewhere... and you feel like you're going through the motions most days – you're not depressed, but don't feel you have much to look forward to. No one knows it of course, but you feel it gnawing away at you, especially at night. You have a shelf full of self-help books but everything you've done up until now has only taken you so far, you're still not in that life that's waiting for you. *And you know there's greatness in you.* Then Goddess? We need to turn YOU on! To get your fabulous back! Before you turn off completely. Before you really lose yourself to what has been going on. Especially after upset with him, with her, or with life in general...

Because your happiness is everything! And, yes, you have the power to turn parts of you on that are going to make you SMILE from ear to ear for the whole rest of your life...

Say the next bit out loud... "Because Oh My God YES I'M WORTH IT!"

And oh my God, yes you are! When a wonderful woman like you feels stuck and frustrated with an upset that's been going on: either within yourself, with a particular situation or with your partner, husband, ex-husband, or children; these "things" have the power to dry your happiness out, *daily*. I call it Dry-out.

Dry-out = Sucked dry by a part or all of your life.

Sucked dry by him, by your finances, by your kids, by your job, by the house, by one part of your life, or it can feel like *everything. Because more often than not, it is.* You can be a millionaire and have it. And you can be the poorest woman in your town and have it. It has nothing to do with where you find yourself in life, and everything to do with the relationship you are currently having with yourself.

And the antidote to Dry-out?

Turn Yourself On.

Do I mean you sexually turning yourself on? Well, a little bit, but we'll get to that later!

Do I mean the tacky, trashy, cheap kind of turn on that ultimately makes us women feel um... *Yuck? No.*

Turn Yourself On = every part of you completely turned ON and ALIVE!

You gotta know how to turn yourself on to live that life that's waiting for you Goddess!

Which bits? I'm talking about you turning your effervescent light ON – no matter how dull those around you are.

I'm talking about you turning your self-love ON, so you can count on yourself to give beautiful you the BEST time right now, no matter what is or isn't going on in your life right now.

I'm talking about turning your self-healing ON, your receiving button ON. Your sensuality ON. The very essence of you; ON, ON, ON. Because you turning yourself on? *Is an inside job*. Why? Because you are the QUEEN of your inner world.

And yes, turning yourself on is your antidote to Dry-out. It's you YELLING out the window that *you're worth* turning on the parts of you that take you swiftly out of the old patterns of hurt, sabotage, and internal blocks to get *there*. Where is there? *There* is the relationship and life you've dreamed of. *Nothing less*. And you deserve it.

I'm going to teach you one of the most important skills a woman will ever learn: How to heal yourself from your biggest upsets with the men in your life, with yourself and with your children, career, bank account and *that* situation. Yes, *that one*. Because if you think about it – life can get a little bumpy along the way can't it? And if you know how to heal yourself from them, then you'll have a smoother ride by knowing that nothing has the power to set you back for very long. That's real power and that's YOU!

You're the Queen. You're the Power. YOU can turn yourself on!

To switch your power on, this book houses my universal healing system that thousands of women across the world use, just like I do and just like you can too. Each page is overflowing with an opulence of gorgeous tools, ideas and techniques that will turn your life around and get you your fabulous BACK!

What are the things that hurt you the most in life? We're going to apply this system to take you out of it and into the life you deserve no matter how much you think it's unmovable. It isn't. We start with this and then together we build your own system that is personal to you based on the details that nobody else knows, *but you*. This system you're about to learn gives your power BACK! AMPLIFIED! And that's why I love it so much. Because the power is in you. It's not in a counsellor or a coach, and it's not in a book. It's the power you were born with, because:

You are the QUEEN of your inner world.

Imagine that you're languishing on a majestic chaise longue with a swathe of silk draped along your body. As you lie back, you see walking towards you a waiter wearing a bow tie and tails holding a round silver platter up by his shoulder. What's on that first platter? Oh look, it's what you most want. What is it? Well, it's on that platter and it's being handed to you by this waiter. Won't you pluck it from that silver platter this very moment?

Do you know why you can?

It's because *you are the queen of your inner world*. You are the queen of each and every part of you, especially those bits of you that have been turned off completely because of the past. Like your confidence. Your self-belief. Your desirability. You can get them back because:

I'm the Queen. I'm the POWER.
I can turn on whichever part
of me I need, NOW!

What would your business, closest relationships and health look like if you lived from this power every day? Because it's in you right now, I can promise you that. It's just been lying low because you haven't had the proper keys to turn yourself on. And so parts of your life will remain stuck until you do. Do it now before it's too late, do it before *that situation* takes even more from you. Yes, you are the queen of your special ability to self-heal and you can turn this on any time you wish. You are the queen of your sensuality and the queen of your ability to decide what you don't want, so you can desire and manifest exactly what you do. So, what is it that you're wanting? Imagine now, there is a long line of waiters all walking towards you with exactly what you want on each platter. And because you are the queen of your inner world, you can have it! There isn't anything you can't have: a love affair for life, that problem gone, confidence, huge success from your true life's calling, a life you love, the feeling every day that you've become that woman you've always dreamed of, and the profound peace and sweet happiness that settles inside of you because of it. Yes you can do this:

It's Time to Turn Yourself On so You LIVE a Life that Turns You On.

The 10 Turn-ons are:

1. DECIDE WHAT YOU DON'T WANT:

Definition: What are you done with?

Why you need to turn this on: Your power returns.

Signs that you are in Dry-out here:

 ✳ It's an internal fight to let go of things that *you know* are not good for you.

 ✳ You've put up with stuff that hurts you for longer than 1 day.

 ✳ You're not living the fantastic life you thought you would be by now.

Signs that you've turned this part of you ON:

 ✳ You have an easy time letting go of things that hurt you – you're proud of saying no and damn you're so good at it!

 ✳ You are very clear: You cannot put up with stuff that hurts you for more than 1 day anymore; it just doesn't *become you.*

 ✳ You're honest with yourself, which can only mean making great decisions for your heart = you flourish.

2. DESIRE WHAT YOU DO:

Definition: Sit close to your desires.

Why you need to turn this on: You cannot have a happy relationship without it.

Signs that you are in Dry-out here:

 ✳ You are tired and know more about what they want than what you want.

 ✳ You leave it to the last minute to ask.

 ✳ You get angry at him regularly and he often feels criticised.

Signs that you've turned this part of you ON:

 ✳ You know what you want, so he knows how to make you happy.

- You love to ask because you love to receive.
- He has become your hero.

3. DETOX WHAT'S IN YOUR WAY:

Definition: The ability to self-heal.

Why you need to turn this on: If you don't have a way to heal what's happened to you this month, you're already sliding into Dry-out.

Signs that you are in Dry-out here:

- An area of your life is drying out your happiness every day.
- You can't remember the last time you felt really good consistently.
- You're stuck in a dynamic and feel tired, heavy, numb, angry, sad.

Signs that you've turned this part of you ON:

- This part of your life no longer drains you; you've used it to take yourself higher instead!
- You are the QUEEN of your inner world, so you know how to feel good consistently.
- Because you've turned your ability to self-heal on, you are no longer stuck in the same situation; you're free.

4. TURN ON YOUR SELF-LOVE ACTION:

Definition: The action of being kind to yourself.

Why you need to turn this on: Poor discipline to implement self-love always leads to Dry-out.

Signs that you are in Dry-out here:

- You don't like yourself.
- You abandon your heart daily.
- Others don't treat you softly or lovingly.

Signs that you've turned this part of you ON:

- You L.O.V.E. the good, the bad, and the ugly in you.

✻ You've been kind to yourself in the last hour.

✻ Others treat you with the utmost respect and love.

5. TURN ON YOUR BEST FRIEND WITHIN:

Definition: Become the best friend you ever had.

Why you need to turn this on: Create a new story to empower YOU.

Signs that you are in Dry-out here:

✻ You're not letting a lot of good things in at the moment.

✻ You disempower yourself and are your own worst enemy.

✻ Something in your life is triggering you to feel bad.

Signs that you've turned this part of you ON:

✻ Your new story lets in a whole lot of new success.

✻ Like a best friend, you empower yourself every day.

✻ You no longer let your old story of pain dictate how your day goes.

6. TURN ON YOUR RECEIVING BUTTON:

Definition: You are as open to receiving as you are to giving.

Why you need to turn this on: You've been created perfectly to receive everything you want, to block this is to live against your feminine form = overwhelm, unhappiness, illness.

Signs that you are in Dry-out here:

✻ You feel guilty and uncomfortable receiving more than you need.

✻ Nothing inspires you; in fact your mind is overtaken with lack: lack of time, lack of happiness, lack of money, lack of goodness in the world.

✻ You're not receiving everything you want.

Signs that you've turned this part of you ON:

✻ You LOVE to receive way more than you need = you can give way more than you used to.

* You're inspired, rich with time, abundant in money and over-taken with excitement at all the opportunities to add to this world.
* You receive everything you want easily.

7. TURN ON YOUR SENSUALITY:

Definition: Fully receiving the NOW with all of your senses switched ON.

Why you need to turn this on: You cannot enjoy life without it.

Signs that you are in Dry-out here:

* You are not present to receive the depth of the moment.
* You haven't got time for it; there's no room for it.
* You become mechanical during the day and feel unfulfilled.

Signs that you've turned this part of you ON:

* You deeply receive the moment and it turns you on!
* Sensuality is placed squarely in your day, every day.
* You are all woman, and so *full* from the moment you just had.

8. TURN ON YOUR PLEASURE:

Definition: Whatever gives you huge gratification.

Why you need to turn this on: You were made to live this way.

Signs that you are in Dry-out here:

* You run away from your pleasure like a pro.
* You haven't received much happiness or an orgasm today.
* Your life force is low; you feel tired and dull.

Signs that you've turned this part of you ON:

* You run towards your pleasure like your life depends on it (because it actually does).
* You love to be worshipped and know how to say yes, yes, yes to what turns you on inside the bedroom and out.
* You have a high level of energy and you're GLOWING right now.

9. TURN ON YOUR BEAUTY:

Definition: Approve and fall in love with the exact shape your body makes.

Why you need to turn this on: Unconditional beauty empowers us all.

Signs that you are in Dry-out here:

* You use makeup and clothes to hide your imperfections rather than to accentuate your astonishing beauty.
* You peer at yourself in the mirror looking for problems.
* You swing between feeling uglier than or prettier than the next woman you see. (God, look at her.)

Signs that you've turned this part of you ON:

* You are no longer a slave to makeup and clothes; they are now an amplifier to your beauty because you start off beautiful every day.
* You love what you see: Wowee!
* You love to appreciate the beauty in every woman because you can now do that for yourself. This is unconditional beauty and it makes your beauty heavenly.

10. TURN ON YOUR POWER:

Definition: A personal system you flourish in.

Why you need to turn this on: Nobody knows you like you do.

Signs that you are in Dry-out here:

* You question, "Am I right?" and go outwards for answers.
* You march to the beat of someone else's drum daily.
* They are bigger and more powerful than you; you are so small.

Signs that you've turned this part of you ON:

* You trust yourself to navigate your own life successfully.
* You march to your own rhythm and it ignites your life force.
* Your voice is the loudest inside of you; your power is back... FOREVER.

So.

Let's start.

Chapter 2

Turn off Your Dry-out

· · · · · · · · · · · · · · ·

OK, let's see where you are at today:

Mini recap: we slip into Dry-out because we haven't turned on the parts of ourselves we need to flourish. And once you're flourishing? You're on your way Goddess; you're on your way to *that* life!

So, what can make us slip into Dry-out?

- Unresolved and unhealed upset
- Not knowing how to receive
- Not making a decision on the stuff that hurts you the most
- Living to his pleasure level
- Not ROCKING your beauty
- Not living to your sensual and sexual potential
- Having a slack desire muscle
- Not loving yourself
- Being stuck in a story that disempowers you
- Not having a strong personal system so you flourish

Am I in Dry-out Today?
Checklist:

1. Everything is a chore.

2. You go from 0 – anger in 3.5 seconds, faster than any Goddamn sports car on the planet. Yeah... stick it up your Axxe Ferrari.

3. You don't ask for help when it's offered – *"I'm fine!"* You say. And you actually *believe it* at the time.

4. You crave chocolate, Hollywood gossip, anything that distracts you for 5 minutes before the next big "push".

5. You don't feel juicy anymore; instead you're overwhelmed with all that there is to do; you're tired and brittle. You feel less; you are numbed out by it all.

6. You are frequently annoyed by him and have these sit-down chats or stand-up yelling matches. Either way, nothing changes; *he still doesn't listen.*

7. You feel guilty for not doing enough, for not being a good enough mum/wife/success in business/healthy woman/fill in the blank.

8. You cannot imagine 2 hours in a row without compromise – unless it's a special event or you're asleep.

9. You never have enough time.

10. Sex feels like another thing to do on your "to do" list.

11. You live quite happily in Making-Do-Land. All your friends do it.

If you've felt at least one of these this week, Goddess, you're in Dry-out. The good news is you are reading exactly the right book to shake yourself free of Dry-out. How brilliant are you? (Well, we knew that already.)

QUIZ: HOW TOXIC IS YOUR DRY-OUT?

You might be able to tell me about the state of your marriage, relationship, or dating life, but how much can you tell me about the state of the relationship you are currently having with yourself?

Count how many yesses you get:

1. I over-eat, under-eat; emotionally eat. Food is not a pleasure to me; it's a constant battle between right and wrong.

2. I say yes to food and drink that hurts me; whatever, I don't care.

3. I often say yes when I mean no. (I often feel I have no choice.)

4. I say yes to situations that hurt me and don't add to me.

5. I like myself when I make *you* happy. (I'm alright, thanks.)

6. Because I don't listen to what my heart is yearning for during the day, I'm often irritable by 6:00pm and "over it".

7. I do stay in hurtful relationships and situations longer than I need to.

8. I often ignore my intuition and I regret it afterwards.

9. I put others first at my expense, even when I'm tired and have nothing left to give; still I give, but get more moody as the day wears on.

10. I don't take a break for fun or rest when I need to – have I really earned it?

11. When I see other glamorous happy-looking women I'm irritated – I mean, who has the time for that?

12. I don't take the risks that I need to, so I keep myself small and closed.

13. I don't trust myself as much as I trust what you think I should do. What do you think I should do?

14. I don't like or love myself that much. I think more highly of others. I feel kind of "under" you – you know, "less than".

15. I don't feel good enough.

16. I'm always wishing I could have done better as I walk away from you.

17. I often feel fat and/or ugly and keep my fat jeans for those special days.

18. I feel unworthy of anything good because of__(fill in the blank)__.

19. I delay my pleasure or don't plan any: my day dictates me.

20. I don't say yes to what I really want with the big stuff because there's never any time. And I'm always running late...

21. I don't say yes to what I really want with the small stuff either. I often leave peeing till the last minute.

22. I constantly interrupt my workflow, flicking to social media/e-mail.

23. I don't work on healing the stuff that hurts me the most in life.

24. I don't prioritise my priorities, but yours always come top of my list.

25. What do I do that takes away rather than adds to me? Add it here.

How many yesses did you get? Having a bad relationship with yourself is rather hurtful and tiring just to talk about it isn't it? It means it doesn't matter how clever you are, or how much effort you put into helping people – *until you decide to be good to you* – it's going to be hard to enjoy most of your days.

If you knew how exquisite you were would you treat yourself more beautifully today?

Having a dried out crappy relationship with yourself can only set you up to receive dried out crappy behaviour from others. Men who don't return your call. Men who don't listen to you, respect you, or genuinely put you first. Friends only call you when *they* need you, or want to borrow something. So, when a client comes to me upset that her husband of 20 years doesn't find her attractive anymore, or her children just don't care about anything, I know it has everything to do with her and nothing to do with them. Always.

Hurtful at first and then the best news ever! Because they are not responding to who she is, they are responding to something much deeper: her relationship with herself. And that is something she can heal right now, just like you.

Is your relationship with yourself right now giving you relationships that fall short?

No beating up of yourself if this is you – that won't work – you are too beautiful to have that kind of relationship with yourself! Just like she is!

Remember: in any relationship, there are two relationships at play: the one you have with them and the one you have with you. The one you have with you is the most important and luckily the easiest one to transform!

I mean, you could try and change others and sometimes it does work, and other times they JUST. REALLY. WON'T. CHANGE. BASTARD. So, the only person we know that can definitely change is you because YOU are in charge of YOU and you can heal this.

But, if you don't have a way to heal yourself of hurt this month, then you are already sliding into Dry-out. If you don't have a way to fully receive what you want (because you feel guilty) you are sliding... if you don't know how to enjoy asking for what you want every single day and actually get it (from men to pay rises to clients to the moon) you're already there doing uninspired laps. And if your past disappointment stops you from really going for it with your current project? Guess what? You're suffering from Dry-out. And it's impossible for you to turn your light ON, fully. Your happiness, fully. Your life ON, fully because you don't know how to get there and stay there. You have no system and so it will feel as if there is always something wrong.

And you know what? You could have cancer right now, you could be horribly alone right now, you could be struggling as a single mummy right now; you could be about to marry the man of your dreams, be running a million dollar business that is close to your heart; you could be staring back at the most beautiful face. Others may not show they care about you, but I do care, very deeply that you live the way you were wired to. Because that divine woman is everything to me. And it is actually everything to you, if you're honest.

You can create a day that turns you on in the middle of a lifeless hospital waiting room by bringing a homemade care package with you, by asking for hugs when you need them, and by allowing yourself to receive them fully. It matters not where you are in life.

WHY IS IT SO IMPORTANT THAT YOU CREATE A SYSTEM JUST FOR YOU?

Nobody can tell you your own specific code for flourishing. There is nobody on this planet just like you, just like you are right now. There is nobody just like you right at this precise moment reading these words in exactly the space you are in. Look around you. Nobody. So, there is nobody in the world that knows how you feel, minute to minute, second to second. There is nobody in the world that knows what you are thinking right now; so there is nobody but you in the world who knows exactly what YOU need, want to feel, and desire like you.

And make no mistake; not having a system to flourish in has dire consequences for every woman. Let's look at the facts. According to the leading organisation, Mental Health America, "Women experience depression at roughly twice the rate of men". Another leading health company[1] in the USA found that: "Boys and girls have the same rate of depression until they reach adolescence. Between the ages of 11 and 13, the rate rises sharply for girls. By age 15, girls are twice as likely as boys to have depression, a trend that continues throughout adulthood".

---

1   From Aetna InteliHealth (a leading online health information company in relationship with Harvard Medical School).

A new study[2] has revealed that the most commonly prescribed medication for Australian women is anti-depressants.

This makes me sad because right now, somewhere in the world there is a woman and we'll call her *Miriam*. She's a 55-year-old married woman with brown wavy hair and right now she is sitting on her bed, reaching for her anti-depressants (she calls them her "Aunty Dee's" but that's the only thing that's funny about them). Her "Aunty Dee's" live in her bedside table because – as she says – her husband of 30 years "Loves golf more than me." *Jenny*, a stay at home mum of two is reaching for hers because she doesn't know how she can keep going without them. Her husband *Jerry* is a nice enough guy, but he doesn't romance her anymore, instead he stares at other women when he's with her in the car and she thinks he might be having an affair.

Both of these beautiful women have two things in common:

1. They are following their husband's tone for a relationship where they are being ignored.

2. They are stuck in *what he is doing to them;* they have not created their *own powerful system* to downright flourish in and *beckon him in with...*

Men will always go where it feels good. This upsets us women a lot of the time, but actually this is a wonderful habit to get into. Most women I know have learnt to compromise this habit within them, which means we women reach more for our pain than our pleasure on a daily basis. There are millions of Miriam's across the world right now *making do.* The house has been paid off, life is comfy and she is free to do as she pleases... although if she's honest, she's never really LIVED. Why are we women more depressed than men? Is it in our genetic makeup? NO!

And I'll tell you why.

---

2   From a study by researchers from The University of Queensland and the University of Newcastle, and from the leading Australian Longitudinal Study on Women's Health (ALSWH).

Have you ever met a depressed baby?

No. Me either. That's because they don't exist. People don't arrive here depressed, they become depressed through something that is happening in their world that depresses them. Women are becoming depressed through something that is happening in their world that is depressing them. Are women, then, having more bad stuff happen to them than men?

Or, do women just put up with more bad stuff than men?

Yup, you just heard the answer. We women put up with more crap than men. Here are the gems I hear from the women who arrive at my office, which I call Goddess Central. What is said below happens at the beginning of my coaching programs, and by the end they often look at me incredulously and ask, "Did I really say that"??

She says to me:

"He looks at other women when I'm with him – no Marina
I don't bring it up afterwards because that's just men, isn't it?" (*Making* do.)

"He's so tired by the time he's home from work that I don't
want to put more on his plate by asking for help. I don't want
to push him away." (*Making do.*)

"Yes, our sex life is good I suppose. We do it 3x a week; he always starts
it. How does the sex make me feel? Good, Marina, good." (*Making do.*)

"I'm bored at work. I'd like to start my own plumbing business,
but I'm worried I won't be accepted as legitimate by the men in the
industry and I'm not sure I want the hassle it's going to bring."
(*Making do.*)

"I can't have the life I want if I'm still married to him, but I don't
want to lose everything we've worked for." (*Making do.*)

"It would hurt him so much if I left". *(Making do.)*
"It's OK, really. I'm *fine.*" *(Making do.)*

How do you feel when you read these? Do they sound sort of OK?
Do you hear this sort of thing coming from you? Do you hear your
girlfriends languishing in the Land of Making Do too?
Can you imagine a man saying some of this?

Darren – "Yeah, my girlfriend looks at other men when
I'm with her. No, I don't bring it up afterwards because
that's just women, isn't it?"

Arnold – "It's OK, really. I'm *fine.*"

Tom – "She's so tired by the time she's home from work that
I don't want to put more on her plate by asking for help.
I don't want to push her away."

Oliver – "I'm bored at work. I'd like to start my own makeup/
hairdressing/cooking/nursing/teaching business, but I'm
worried I won't be accepted as legitimate by the women
in the industry and I'm not sure I want the hassle
it's going to bring."

Hmmm, what do you think? Stop for a minute: *is he sexy to you?* If he
was walking towards you, what kind of man would he be? Would this
kind of man turn you on? How highly does he think of himself?

Realising that your average woman does think like this is enough to
make you feel short changed; we women are habitually *making do.* I want
you to want more for *yourself.* I want you to get very self-possessed about
all of this and to scream, "DAMN IT! I'm going to create a real life that
actually turns me ON!"

Men have been doing it for centuries. And now it's our turn because when we win, they do too. They are not the enemies here. We are. To ourselves.

I believe the second-biggest manmade disaster after the environmental disaster is that of us women:

We. Have. (Momentarily.) Forgotten. Our. Value.

We have forgotten who we really are and the damaging ramifications this does to our gorgeous gentle selves. From the mum who wakes up in the morning with nothing to look forward to, to a society that has lowered their standards for women so much, they think nothing of selling a 5-year-old girl into prostitution; We as women must stand up and value ourselves enough to have our own system. One that turns us on, so we flourish. It doesn't matter whether you are having the best time of your life, or are having one of the worst times of your life; finding what turns your heart on, is the most important thing you will ever do for yourself. You were put onto this earth to flourish. You are meant to flourish. Not later when you've got more time, but NOW.

One of my clients is a top model, another a successful actress; they are rich, beautiful, and have the world at their feet. They are not being sold into prostitution any time soon, nor are they facing a year in isolation with a 2-year-old, nor are they depressed. But they are surrounded by a world with a very strong ethos, that of which *you must look good at all costs*. A real turn-OFF. Being in that world without your own system protecting you means you will always be vulnerable. It means you won't flourish because their ethos is bigger and therefore more dominant than yours. It wasn't tailored to fit you, *it was tailored to fit them.*

> And you, just like them are too gorgeous
> not to truly flourish this lifetime.

Wanna BUST out of this with me? It's way easier than what you have been doing, I can tell you that. We're going to jump to the next chapter in a moment, but I just want to chat to you about your age and what I call domestic Dry-out.

Are you 35 years old or older? Whether you are or not, I'm going to educate your gorgeous self on a few little details that often get missed:

At age 35–40 years, perimenopause begins. Don't worry, you remain fertile for many more years well into your 40s, but your hormones start to shift and this is when stuff that never used to bother you starts to bother the crap out of you. You find that you get more annoyed, irritable, and brittle, sort of like an early version of grumpy old woman syndrome. You know, the old crabby women who moan all the time and never seem happy? "She's just old" you hear yourself say... although come to think of it... you've noticed that *you're* getting grumpier as time goes on. My Goddess, what is going on?

Well, you're meant to be quick to anger my darling. A good night's sleep is no longer enough to wipe the slate clean of you over compromising the day before. It's because you are getting older and can no longer fill your day with the Put Them First Code. It doesn't feel right, and actually you're not meant to! You are meant to survive and flourish beyond the age of 35 years old, and to keep to the old code is to dry yourself out. So, the next time you feel angry that your husband has left you to clean up the kitchen *again* whilst he *pops* out to the gym, the next time your boss asks you to stay back late, if you aren't feeling annoyed *something is actually wrong*. So, can we clink our glasses together and celebrate that you're feeling angry? It's the right thing to feel. What if you loved your irritable anger instead? It's guiding you to shape your life into one that fits you so much better. Like the perfect velvet shoe – voilà it can fit now!

DOMESTIC DRY-OUT

Too much domesticity will kill any good woman's spirit.

Most mums I know have these sorts of mornings: You wake up, see the clock and calculate how much time you have to get things done. Whilst brushing your teeth, you wipe the basin down from hair and toothpaste, and on your way to the kitchen pick up his socks from the floor and fling them into the washing basket. Damn, why doesn't he ever put them in, *is he blind??* As you're waiting for the kettle to boil, you put the dishes away from last night whilst fielding questions from your children, "Where's my sports top mummy?" And you're flicking quickly through your e-mails. Thank God for smart phones. As you eat breakfast with one eye on the clock and the other on what's left to do, you wonder if you've enough time to make a gorgeous green juice for everyone. Do I have time? You look outside, hmm it's going to be a sunny day, so it's a no for the green juice. You lunge upstairs to the washing basket and put a wash on in time warp speed, shower, dress like a maniac, and (if you've got young kids) herd them like bewildered sheep/little devils, into the outside world. *The day has begun.*

Who has left the house feeling nurtured and loved? Them or you?

You wave at the neighbour who is backing his big shiny car out, but what you really want to do is the crazy dance right there on your porch and yell IT'S JUST TOO MUCH! You are ANGRY. You are PISSY.

When a woman *feels pushed* into becoming responsible for everyone *she has* to become irresponsible with herself.

Because your mum did it, you are held to some sort of invisible code that's a right turn-off: PUT THEM FIRST. It's the Put Them First Code. Thou shall move at 100 miles an hour clearing up after them, thinking ahead for them, walking through rooms, picking that up, putting that down, making one journey from one room to another count. How much can you carry? I'll quickly clean the shower whilst my conditioner is in. You're like Captain Kirk of the Starship Enterprise, you're at the helm of it all, you're at the hub, the hub the hub a hub hub... but unlike Captain Kirk, you have no crew in sexy/icky skin-tight latex to help you. And because you're stuck in your old ethos of being OK with being turned off, *you* are not used to helping *you* either, yet.

Who on earth thought that you putting others first at the expense of yourself *continually* would be a GOOD IDEA? One made in heaven??? One that would benefit your boss, children, and husband??? One that would benefit your health? Who on earth thought this and then silently created an invisible code for all women to agree to? Does it matter? We'll never know. But, what I do know is that it doesn't work. Ever.

Chapter 3

DECIDE What You Don't Want

. . . .

Yes. At the beginning of *any* hurtful situation, we're most aware of what *we don't want:* so much so, we are often consumed by it. It's natural to call a girlfriend and tell her *all about it* – analysing the situation with the precision of a brain surgeon. Yes, it's here we start because it's *where you naturally start*; at *what is not* working for you; at what the bastard did; at why *it still* hasn't happened for you yet.

And it all begins with a decision...

Because everything magnificent and not so magnificent you did or didn't do in the past started with an innocuous decision. Shall I go this way or that? *I'm never going through that again.* Shall I go for a second helping or not? Will I lunge and kiss him now? I don't know what to do...? (This last one is an example of a passive decision – you are deciding *no* here.) Shall I surrender sweetly to my heart or go with my head on this one?

Once you naturally decide *what you don't want,* the power sits with you. Once you decide, not only are the cells in your body informed of this change of heart, everything else out there is energetically informed of your decision. *Whether you know it or not.* And this means you've given the universe the chance to align its power with you. Watch how other people around you respond when you decide with your whole body that it's a full blown NO to what hurts you. To when you've made a stand for yourself.

IT IS HERE IN THIS BOOK THAT YOU COME WHEN YOU WANT TO MAKE A CHANGE IN YOUR LIFE.

Is it safe for you to decide what you don't want? What answer comes to you? Why? Know that it is always safe for you to decide and – know that if it's right for you – *you will find a way.* Just sit with this for a moment and feel what happens to your body when you realise it is safe to decide. Do you breathe easier? Do you feel a lightness coming to you?

When the answers come to you to the questions below, speak them out loud:

What happens to you if you don't give yourself this gift of deciding no? More of the same situation you're not liking? How long do you really want it to go on for? If you never decide, where will you be in 5 years? Flourishing? Or worse off than you are now? What's the worst thing that could happen, if you don't make this decision for yourself? What will you look/be like in 10 years if you don't ever make this decision? And if not now, then when? There's never a good time to. You only have now.

See? I told you, you naturally *do know* what you don't want! Don't beat yourself up here, this is just your snap shot of where you are right now, and I know that you're ready for things to be different. Now let's you and I be brave and begin because you bloody deserve it! It's time to raise our standards, you ready?

The universe is here to support you and so am I. It is here that you begin; it's the first "D" in the 3 Ds ethos:

Decide what you *don't want.*

Desire what you *do.*

Detox what's in your way.

Self-love action.

When you apply the 3 Ds to a particular situation of your life, hold onto those gorgeous knickers of yours because whoooosh! The 3 Ds *will* take you out of Dry-out. Wahoo! And once you're out of Dry-out? You can begin to flourish: just like you were born to.

Cherie, a 40-year-old new mum decided that she *didn't want* her body to slide into Dry-out. If she didn't make this decision now, what would she be like in 5 years? A fat blob of 3 kids that no one would want to talk to? She made a list and reeled. She could see where she was headed and didn't like it. Once she decided with aplomb that she didn't want to slide into this depressing scene, it became so much easier to spring into what she did want.

So, what's it going to take? How bad do things really need to get to make the biggest decision for yourself – you know the one I mean: the one that's going to catapult you out of the worst stuff? What if you didn't wait for things to get so bad this time around; took a deep breath and decided right *now* that you are worth it? That you are worth making a stand for – not later, *but now?* What would this week look like if you did? Would your heart feel lighter? Would your Dry-out lift? Would you feel better all round? Would you get some of that energy back? Would you respect yourself?

Trying it will *add to you* now. Trust me.
Breathe. What you don't want starts with a simple decision:
Please stand so your whole body makes this decision: not just
your lil' ol' head. Repeat after me out loud:
I (full name) give myself permission to state what I don't
want. I am free to do so. I am fully supported
and safe to decide now:
Then stamp your foot on the ground to mean that you mean it!
And you do!

The next step is to ask yourself:
Am I living a truly fantastic life right now?
Why not?
What's in your way?

Grab some paper and list everything that is in your way Goddess. What is in your way of having what you want right now? Is it you? Is it him? Is it them? Lack of funds? Time? Support? Where you live? How you live? Go ahead and write it all out until you are spent. It's cathartic and you need to get it out. Full permission to be a "moany cow" right now. Mooo away babe! Moooooooooooooooooooooooo!

Now, look down your list and if you're having a bad time of it know that there are good things all around you this very moment that are made of solid pleasure. Somebody's smile; looking out into the deep blue; curling up in the comfiest bed.

Whatever is in your way of having a life that turns you on, *know that at some point you decided to turn away from it.* It's you who has *decided* to stop letting the happiness in because it's all around you, always. The only person who can stop you receiving is you. So, look at your list and if these things seem to control you like self-doubt, self-sabotage, some sort of habit, a person or a stuck situation. Umm...

No, they don't.

YOU decided to turn away from your own happiness a long time ago and decided to turn to "it".

"It" being whatever is in your way right now.

This is not the time to berate yourself for doing this. *This is* the time to be *really honest with yourself, because it's at this point that you can make the right decision for you.* And you're ready to!

OK, read back through this list. This is what is in your way of getting what you want. If you're feeling any emotion – good! Just simply let it be in you. It's been in you the whole time anyway; it's just that it's come up to the surface to be felt, loved, and healed. And you my darling are so deserved of this.

We women put up with too much dilution of the good stuff and it doesn't work.

So, what are you done with? Start with a fresh piece of paper and at the top write I (full name here) am done with... and then on each line write I am done with... I am done with... until you are spent. Here are some ideas I have collected along the way that you might want to add in if they fit you:

I am done with living in Making-Do-Land.

I am done with doing everything on my own.

I am done with always giving at my expense.

I am done with my crippling self-doubt.

I am done with not having the man of my dreams.

I am done with him not seeing me, hearing me...

I am done with him not putting me first.

I am done with me not putting me first.

I am done with feeling lonely.

I am done with under earning.

I am done with not being happy.

I am done with not receiving what I need to flourish.

I am done with not owning my own home.

I am done with not have proper regular orgasms that make me feel like I'm flying.

I am done with not succeeding.

I am done with over-eating.

I am done with feeling ugly.

I am done with feeling sucked dry and turned off by life in general. This is not how I was made and I am done, done, done!

When you have written it all out I want you to stand up and read it all out loud. Really feel that you are genuinely DONE. SO YOU ARE! The decision has been made. Good for you! You have decided.

Shhhh...
Can you hear that? Your body, your soul, and the universe are listening intently to you.

What to do next? Wrap this paper around a heavy rock and secure it with string (a bit like wrapping ribbon around a birthday gift) and throw your decisions into the ocean, stream, creek, pond, lake, lagoon, really, any body of water you can find, and throw it. Yell when you throw it, "Yaaaaaaaaaah I'M done!" If you're not near a large body of water, simply fill a bucket and plunge it in for a whole day and then bin it. Or, safely burn the paper in a ceramic urn, or metal sink.

Helpful tip: Make sure that when you find your rock it's heavy enough to sink your paper to the bottom of that body of water, unlike a darling client of mine who wrapped her done-withs around a light rock only to watch it float down the river in horror, "Oh no!" she told me later "I hope the ink ran!"

Itsy bitsy question:
What do I do if I undo my decision by doing the very thing I'm done with?

Repeat after me out loud:

"I did my best and I choose to forgive myself right now for not keeping to my new decision. I (name) forgive myself. I choose to love myself instead of hurt myself. I choose to make this mean that I need more love for myself. I renew my decision right now by deciding right here and now that I am doing this! Yes I am! Because every time I renew my decision I give myself the best shot at flourishing again." Hug yourself; this is that extra love for you.

And make no mistake. By making a strong decision again, on what you don't want speaks huge volumes. Now, in the rest of this book we're going to heal you, so your done-withs disappear, but if you find yourself doing them between now and then; keep re-affirming this decision, keep hugging yourself, this is your ode of love for yourself. The more you renege on your decisions, the more love you get to put on that hurt part of you *that so wants to be done with* this part of your life.

OK, only come to this part of the book when you have thrown your done-withs into water. Seriously, if you're anything like me, you read this sort of thing in a book and go, "yeah, yeah," I'll do that at the weekend; I'll be fine to keep reading. But, actually something happens when you take action. You start being turned on. You become deliciously ready for the next paragraph, which can 'pop' in you now!

OK, we're on the next paragraph – did you do it? It doesn't matter to me, but it will to you. So I hope you have Goddess.

Chapter 4

DESIRE What You Do

· · · · · · · · · · · · · · · ·

OK, the coast is clear. What you don't want is dramatically drowning itself in *that* ocean, river, bucket, so come with me; *we're going to dance and twirl* towards your desires and do your first ever Desire Pirouette!

We're going to take your decisions on what you *don't want* and use them to deftly pirouette 180° to what you *do want*. This is the second D in the 3 Ds ethos: your fabulous desire! And it lives deep within, pulsating...

When a woman first walks through the doors of Goddess Central, the first thing I notice is her life force. I can usually pick it: it's the unsaid thing about her but it usually screams at me. If her life force is low, I also know that she will know more about what she doesn't want than what she does want.

Tell me about the last conversation you had with your girlfriend. Did you talk more about what was each upsetting you? Or, did you fill the conversation to the brim with your desire and tell her at length with all the side trimmings about what you do want? Shaping it and drawing her in so?

As we agreed before, we women do need to talk it out. We love it! It's a skill and a pleasure we have honed to perfection! I sometimes feel like a balloon full of hot air, needing to call my girlfriend to just *tell her everything*. Afterwards I feel so much better. But, do you know what happens to you if this is *all you* do? You lose life force pretty fast, like air running out of that shiny red balloon, zeeeeeeeeeeou! It's like losing your muscle tone when you don't work out – you're not using your desire muscle so it gets slack. Yes, I see it as a muscle that was strong when we were kids, but got slack due to us women spending more time talking about what's wrong than what we actually want.

Let me ask you something. When you were growing up, do you remember your mum getting everything she wanted? Did she have massive desires and tell everyone about them and did she get them? Most of my clients cannot recall their mum getting everything she wanted. Most of my clients remember their mum and the women around them complaining to each other about the men and about what they weren't getting in their life. Did they inspire you? Did you cross your sweet little fingers, and hope and pray to live just like them when you grew up?

Desires are a woman's lifeblood.

Desire *is* life. Sit close to your desire and feel your life force rise!

To sit close is to allow your deepest longings, urgings, and the quietest whisperings of your soul to come up to the surface. To be acknowledged and heard. Without editing. Without apology. Without undoing them. Just as they are. Raw, pure, true, YOU. This is how you live a life that is true to you. By being honest about what you want.

Your desires are powerful. When you sit close to them, they ignite your internal power, *"You're on fire today Ginny!"* You nod in agreement, you're hell-bent on getting it done, so nothing will get in your way for long! And you know that energy don't you? Because you've been there before: determined, on fire, on purpose. This is what wanting does to you: it turns you ON.

What happens to a woman like you if you sit close to your desires? The first thing you'll notice? You'll just feel better! This is the first stage of turning ON your desire (and so you!) And if you got nothing else from this little experiment with you + desire; it's so, so worth it!

> "When I hear people say *oh I don't think I can do it.* I always want to encourage them and say, *yeah you can. It's one life, don't deny yourself.*"
>
> *– Actress Julianne Moore*
> *Interview with the Belfast Telegraph*

And when you don't allow yourself to sit close to them? Something in you dies. Ever noticed that when you say, "Nah, it's OK," something in you drops? That's your life force plummeting. Zeeeou!

So how close are you sitting to yours, right NOW?

Here's how to tell if you're sitting close to your desire and you've turned it on fully: Well, how big is your life force right now? By life force, I mean your life energy, aka Chi, Ki, MOJO, and so on. On a scale of 1–10, 1 = low, 10 = high. How high is your life force today? Pick the first number that comes to mind.

What did you get? Congratulations! Don't *ever* beat yourself up. Your number shows *you* how close you've sat to somebody else's desire at the expense of your own: how much you've been marching to the beat of someone else's habits, living to their beat rather than yours because if you were living to the beat of your own desires; right now you'd be at a solid 10. So, if you've come in at a 4, you know that 6/10 of you is living to the rhythm of someone else's desires; not yours, so *of course* you're not getting what you want!

WHAT HAPPENS TO YOU WHEN YOU DON'T LET YOURSELF WANT WHAT YOU WANT IN ONE AREA OF YOUR LIFE?

Answer =

- Depression.
- Tired, weary; won't want to try new things much.
- Relationships will become lacklustre over time.
- Have a lot of things you know you should do, but don't get round to doing them.
- You won't be living out your full potential.
- Won't be having big regular "O"s and you haven't yet reached the full sensual potential of your body (and you *so know* there's more to it than this!).
- Your self-esteem will be wishy washy; you won't be striding out there *getting right behind your desires no matter what.*
- Your progress is slow: Slow to fail. Slow to succeed.
- You will be full of reasons why you can't have what you want.
- These reasons will seem bigger and more powerful than you.

FIVE MAJOR SIGNS YOUR DESIRE ISN'T FULLY TURNED ON AND REFLECTED BACK AT YOU IN YOUR CLOSEST RELATIONSHIPS:

- You resent his freedom and their freedom.
- You feel angry at him in small doses, like *all the time.*
- He gets angry when you pull back and *give him less.*
- You find yourself getting cross with all the giving that you do.
- Housework sucks the life right out of you.

And it's a funny thing you not marching to the drum of your own wants... you'll find that you resent him and certain people in your life.

The *more you desire* and manifest for yourself, the *less angry you're at him,* them, and the world. So, desire becomes your sliding ruler between the two. Want what you want and give Madame Compromise a gentle, but firm shove out the door. Wooopsie – byeee! I notice a lot of women *unconsciously* begin to put their desire on the back burner "for the good of the family." It's boring, it doesn't work and will make your relationship sleep faster than you can... yawn... snore... I'm sorry did I just fall asleep on you?

Want to change this so you don't fall asleep again in your own life?

Because you'll find the universe will always respond to your desires even if they are weak with compromise – although you might find it brings you rather compromised answers on its way back to you. This happens because the universe finds it hard to bring you what you need when you are simply not sure. It's like when you ask a child at bedtime, "Do you want a hot water bottle in your bed tonight?" If the child doesn't know, what do you do? You wait for a while and then go off and do something else. That's exactly what the universe does. It goes off and helps those who have already made their mind up. Making a decision is a clear and bold step; and it is the first step in anything you want. You have to decide. Pick one of the following and say it out loud with as much desire as you dare hear yourself speak:

⋙⋙

"I (full name) now choose to create a life that turns me ON!"
Or
"I (full name) choose to live as the Goddess I was born to be."
Or
"I (full name) choose to *only* flourish in this (particular situation)."
Or
"I (full name) decide (this) right now."

⋙⋙

You can either complain about your wants not coming through, or focus on them as if your life depended on them. *Because your life force actually does.*

Let your wants energise you. They will give you purpose as you sashay down that street, making you feel ALIVE as you load that dishwasher for the twentieth time, waking you up and opening you up to possibilities greater than the now. What is possible for you Goddess?

If a woman's life force is low, I know that her wants are weak in her, that muscle has gone slackety slack and it's billowing in the wind. *Because somehow she has found a way to discount what she wants.* Do you do this to yourself too? Do you say to yourself, "I really wish this could happen, but then this will probably happen and so I can't?" Most women have minds that resemble a chessboard. "If I make this move, that will happen. If I make that move, that will happen." And so on. You become a mass of analytic data that dilutes your desires and your life force. And really, whoever truly liked diluted orange juice?

Show me a tree that desires to grow tall, but worries about taking up too much space up around the other trees and I'll show you a tree with a low life force that isn't growing.

Seen one of those recently? No, I thought not. They don't exist. *Because nature is built on desire.* And it is natural to desire. With no limits.

So a few years ago, I'm listening to this wonderful woman tell me about how she *always* finds four leaf clovers in the grass. *Easily.* I became a child instantly and my eyes got really big and saucer like. I'd heard they existed, but never thought they *really existed.* I had filed that in the *miracle cabinet* part of my brain, *not to be opened until serious proof.*

The next week, she dropped a white piece of paper on the table, "There" she said, "This is for you and your husband. I went walking and thought I'd find you one" (my husband was a non- believer of the four leaf clover). My eyes grew wide (again) as I gently opened the paper envelope. *No, it couldn't be... it was!* Inside perfectly oblivious to its own miracle was a four leaf clover! Four perfect little leaves – and yes, I still have it!

This beautiful woman *knew* she would find a miracle four leaf clover easily: she's found lots before. What if you were this sure about your desires manifesting? Would you allow this sure belief to permeate a harsh reality you may find yourself in right now? What if you believed that miracles do happen and that you'd like one now?

What if you truly allowed yourself to want it? I dare you to go past your disappointments; I dare you to go past your hurt. There are no limits to who you are, how far you can go, or how happy you can be because to limit yourself is to go against nature. When you choose to see that nothing is limited, not now, not ever, then I dare you to dream about the miracles that will unfold because you believe in them...

You can have everything you want Goddess. What do you want? And if you're not 100% sure if you do want something, then I want you to get your desire dancing shoes on and pirouette from what you don't want to the exact opposite.

So, what would your week look like if you didn't dwell in Making-Do-Land?

Would you have a cleaner at least once a week? Would you start your day at 10:00am after a beach walk and swim every morning? Have a man in your life that really see's you? What are your wildest dreams? You know the crazy ones? Want to triple your income this month? Move out of the city? Receive a deeply sensual massage tonight?

And how do you want to feel in your life? Truly, you adore the thought of a desire because you know it's going to make you feel a certain way. For that carefree feeling you imagine having endless money will give you, to that feeling of being loved deeply by your beloved. After all, if desiring to create millions of dollars felt awful, we wouldn't want it would we?

This is *your life* and remember; your desires are your life-blood, desires summon your life force and they don't just shape your day, or your relationship: *they shape your life.*

BE THRILLED BY HIM!

When I ask my clients what kind of relationship/business they want, they almost always fall short of telling me something thrilling. I interject and say, "How about he cannot wait to come home to you?" "Well yes," they say, "I'd love that, but..." and they'll drop down to the collection of their disappointments that have become their memory and guidance system. They don't believe it really could be possible for them.

So I want you to sit for the next 30 seconds and gently close your eyes, and answer this question: What would thrill you to find out about this guy that you're with or wanting to be with? *It would thrill me that he be an expert on my body and would know how to expertly give me long, hot, orgasms. It would thrill me to just lie facing him and to see him looking deeply into my eyes. It would secretly thrill me to know he had established secure savings.* These are your genuine wants. The ones that thrill you. You become soft and very, very YOU when you allow yourself to desire what deliciously thrills you. You flourish with a man when you focus on what thrills you. Aim higher than you have been, he wants to sit close to you and he can, ever so snugly and delightfully, when you really go with the desire that's coursing through your veins.

Let's get your life force zooming at full throttle! I want you to really hear this. This is a beautiful message from Abraham which Esther and Jerry Hicks produce, aka the Abraham-Hicks teachings. They have a massive following worldwide:

"Desire summons Life Force. If we must continue to be alive, we must continue to have new desire. You are not willing to let yourself outrageously want because when you outrageously want something that you haven't found a way of getting, it is too uncomfortable, and the risk feels too great. We're wanting you to hear that there is no risk at all! Fantasize and watch what happens."

– Abraham

Desire is the first place to start igniting your life force. If you're feeling flat and tired right now, this process will give you clarity, energy, and enthusiasm to grow upwards again. You cannot take appropriate action *today* in your business, job, or relationship if you're unclear about what you want. You will get muddled feedback from your clients, boss, and partner.

So… are you brave enough to desire what you want? This is the beginning of you getting your fabulous back and feeling better. Are you ready?

TURNING ON MY DESIRE

Take a workbook and write on the front of it "Want. Deserve. Desire." Or hop onto my website marinaj.net and download a prettily designed sheet called "Want. Deserve. Desire." Which we created just for you. You'll need the special code (TYOGoddess) to access it.

Write out everything you: Want. Deserve. Desire. Write out everything you *want to feel in this life*. Everything. Yes, you want it. And yes, you deserve it. Don't edit when you write, and don't make it nice and attainable. I am not interested in you just wanting what *you know* you can get. I am very interested in you *swallowing hard* as you write the BIG one down. You know. The one you think you *can't get or are too scared to get*.

And if you received all of this, what would you want then? Add these in too!

As you write, there is only rule, and it's this: Only write what makes you salivate! The more outrageous your wants, the more powerful your life force *is. The more tuned in and turned on you get.*

So, yours might start like this:

I desire an interesting man to strike up a sexy conversation with me this week.

I'm so happy I've found the right practitioner for my hip!

I want to feel really happy in my life by July.

I love my new Mercedes-Benz with champagne leather seats!

I'm changing the world with my BIG idea.

I want a pay rise of $75,000 by the end of this year, easily.

I want him to spend at least an hour turning me on in bed this Friday.

And so on. We know you *deserve* it, but go ahead and remind yourself by peppering your wants and desires with the word *deserve*.

After each want, you can write a date you'd like to receive it by.

LIVE as if it's already happening. This 'it's happening now' vibration? Living with this certainty? Makes you vibrate at the exact frequency the universe needs to bounce it back to you. So you can write it as a desire or that *it's already happening*. Whatever feels like the most fun! And the most powerful for you! Mix and match as above!

And what do you do if you don't know where to start? If you haven't aired your wants to yourself in sometime you might want to start with something small like, "What would I really like to eat tonight?" Start here and enjoy the not knowing. In the not knowing, you will start to hear the little trickle of your wants as they start to tumble out from within you. And once you write them, you may want to re-define them in the next day or two. There are no rules, only that you are satisfied that these are your desires NOW.

When most of my clients begin this exercise, they write things like, "I want our family to be happy and healthy." I had a client who started gently like this. After the first month, she revised her list and then revised it monthly, honing it down to the exact shape and size of what she wants. Now her list looks like this:

- I want to be passionately desired by him 4 times a week by May.
- I'd like to find the perfect pair of red satin heels this month.
- I want to double my earnings by the end of this year.
- I want to create a lot of fun memories with my kids, Ben and Katia, starting today.

Once you have written your desires out, I invite you to carry them with you daily to look at. If they're in a workbook, I invite you to carve out the book into sweet little sections of your life for you to add in your desires for each. My current "Want. Deserve. Desire. Book" has my current desires at the front for when I feel like writing them out in a batch and then I have these sections: My home, my health, my sex life, my life's purpose, my clothing, my spirituality, my healing, and so on. I just add my wants to each section and include pictures, e.g. of furniture I want for our house in the house section, and so on. This is my special book and every time I think of it, I get a flash of secret jubilation that I feel across my face. It's my book of happenings and I always get what I want! I like to carry mine in my handbag!

Get ready for yours! Each time you receive what you want? Wahoo! Write "thanks" across it in your power colour! Power colour you say? What's that? It's the colour you associate with your personal power!

It might be red, gold, green, purple, or pink! I also kiss mine, but that's just me! Once I had a client who didn't believe in any of this; she made me laugh because she reminded me of me when I first started! I invited her to do it anyway (because it does work) and you know what happened? She did it and by her third private session with me, she was disappointed it wasn't harder, "Marina, what now? I've crossed off most of my desires already, I can't believe it!"

And this can be you, too. You've been made to receive exactly what you want. Do you know how she got her goodies? She enjoyed wanting them! *Want them*, get turned on just by thinking about them, but *don't need them*. This is a much more natural way for you because you are a woman. Ever been in a biannual review at work? "Yaaah *Diana*, we are very impressed with you thus far, and so what are your goals for the next 6 months?" Ever felt like dropping your head back and snoring? Most women I know, fake their answers. Goal setting, and the way that men do it, charging after them all gung-ho doesn't inspire us, it feels sort of forced, and doesn't always work. And quite frankly, don't you have enough to do without that also? Most women I know find it too tiring to do it the male way, but do it because that's the ethos of their company and was the natural rite of passage from their school. It's how we grew up, but it doesn't work with our natural way of being, which is to attract our wants to us. And the best way to do that? Really enjoy the wanting stage.

And whilst you're at this stage? If you're guided to make changes in your life along the way that feel good to you? Follow them! This is your intuition talking! Knock on that door, make that phone call, but above all, know that you are finally in alignment with nature: That of *wanting* to *receive*. You're *meant* to.

I was explaining women + wanting to my colleague and she didn't believe me. I was standing in the shop with her where we both worked. At the time we couldn't have been living more different lives: I was a single mum living in a cheap rental flat (although I did love it) and she was married to the love of her life, owned a house in the most exclusive part of town, and drove a Mercedes convertible sports car.

And you know what she said to me? *Prove it*. So, I told her that my aching desire in that moment was to receive some red roses from somebody. I didn't have a boyfriend and nobody had bought me flowers in years, so I said to her I'd like someone to give me some! Sceptically, she shuffled off into the back room. Two hours later a man popped his head through the door: "Would any of you like some roses? Only I've just tried to deliver them next door and she's not having any of it." And then he whispered, *"I think they've broken up."* Excitedly, I looked down. *Oh, he was holding a long, fancy, turquoise box.* As I took it out the back, I opened it up. I gasped: a dozen red, long-stemmed roses! "I'll give them to you for $10," he shouted. "Done!" I shouted back. I hadn't thought to desire them for free, but I decided to stretch to $10 back then because I knew *I was worth it*. (And it was a huge stretch.) My colleague stood rooted to the spot staring at me. Then she said, "Prove it again. I don't believe you – that was a jammy fluke!"

So I asked her, "What do you want for yourself today?" And she said, "I'd love a hot guy to come in and flirt with me. I know I'm married, but just to flirt with, I'm bored."

OK, so here is what I did, it took me about 10 seconds:

- I simply wanted it.
- Saw it happening in my mind's eye.
- Got excited about it as it was definitely happening.
- And then let the needing of it go.

Sure enough about an hour later, a guy sort of stumbled through our door, as if he'd been dropped in from a spaceship, and his eyes darted quickly around the shop, "Oh" he said slowly, "So this is what you sell, I don't really know why I'm even in here" he laughed, "But since I'm here, you may as well try to sell me something!" He grinned cheekily.

My colleague whipped around and mouthed back at me, "Witch!" To which I whispered back, *"No! Goddess!"*

This is kind of like daydreaming as a kid. Remember doing that in class? Keep that, the teachers who told you to snap out of it, forgot that it's one of the greatest skills you were born with...

So when you want something, *feel it,* as you desire it, there must be emotion attached to it. Sometimes mini versions of your big desires appear first, but – don't be disappointed! Instead, this is your time to confidently tweak them to your liking, they are your Desire Signposts, which are simply telling you: You're on your way! They are not telling you this is all you're worth! Enjoy the wanting of them. Go window-shopping, make calls, whatever you're drawn to do and when you get your goodies? Say thank you! Your gratitude opens you up to even more abundance.

DESIRE: WHEN MANIFESTING I:

1. Freely want it.
2. Visualise and feel it.
3. Expect to get it.
4. Want it not need it.
5. Delight when mini versions appear.
6. Fall in love with my **right now** and enjoy desiring.
7. Be grateful when desire arrives!
8. Enjoy all of the above.

So I take these action steps:

1. Write the desire down.
2. Visualise 30 seconds a day; let it move me!

3. Know I always get what I want.

4. Attach to spirit for 5 seconds so I can let the needing of it go.

5. Don't get disappointed when mini versions appear: they mean I am on my way!

6. Love my now; love the waiting game; enjoy the act of desire.

7. Say thank you!

8. Have as much joy as I dare whilst in my Desire Cycle! (i.e. life!)

Love the Desire Cycle:
We are always in a cycle of desire – wanting, waiting, or receiving.
We are always experiencing all of these stages right now.
So, can you enjoy 1-7? It will give you a better life.

DESIRE DRY-OUT

In 1, 2, 3!

Yup.

As far as I can see amongst us women, there are three main types of Desire Dry-out that stop you and me from receiving what we want. Boring. I've definitely overindulged in all three – have you?

Desire Dry-out #1. You've stopped desiring most of the time to avoid being disappointed again. You find yourself thinking, "Let's just see what happens." This is classic fence sitting: You won't let yourself go for it, instead letting the situation set the tone for you. At a later date, you may have to argue yourself out of this situation, because you didn't have clear cut expectations of yourself and of another. This Dry-out actually leads to far more disappointment than any of the other Dry-outs: ironic isn't it? *And* it plays havoc with business agreements and friendship boundaries.

Antidote:

- ⚘ Set clear-cut expectations at the beginning of your time with that person.
- ⚘ "Does that feel good to you too?" You can ask to ensure they've heard you and are on board.
- ⚘ Hug yourself (that took guts).

Desire Dry-out #2. You find that desiring and getting the little things are easy for you; it's the big things that are still not happening for you. You don't put as much effort into the big desires *you so desire,* which would make a massive difference to your life, because what's the point? You're so *far away*. They never seem to happen for you.

Picture this: You're driving and need a park *like now*; so you do what you've always done; *you immediately desire what you want* without question by calling on the parking angels and voilà! A parking spot will always open up. It never ever fails you!

But wanting and receiving the big stuff that would take your life to amazing heights, like the love of your life finding you, wanting and receiving real wealth through your life's purpose, so you never have to worry about money again, desiring and conceiving a baby, your dream car, taking a year out to write that book, to travel the world, and work for charities abroad? All those big things that we've wanted forever that make us want to yell, "Is it ever going to happen for me??" Really. Hard.

How come? Well, let's say you're the sort of gal who prides herself on her fortuitous relationship with the parking angels. As you're driving about you desire a park, and there it is. *Rock star parking.* And if it doesn't come as quickly as it normally does? You get *annoyed*.

Hmmm... So, what's your mindset as you're driving and desiring that parking space? Think back. Your hands are on the steering wheel. You've desired it, you're wanting it, and you're probably talking to yourself at this point in the car. What is your process? Are you sitting right up close to what you want? Are you imagining which road you'd most like to find your space on? Do you get a rise at the thought of getting this rock star parking? Do you then leave it in the capable hands of the parking angels and not think about it because *you know* it's going to happen? You're just open to the signs; your attention and intuition are turned on, you see a car pulling out now from the corner of your eye. YES!

Do you ever question yourself, as you're looking for that parking space, *"Do I deserve it?"* "Am I really worthy of this?"

What do you find easy to manifest? Ask yourself, "Is this the same mindset I use for the big things in life that would make a big difference to me?"

And if it's a no, then how come? Why would you have two different approaches to what you want? *Because you are more attached to the big stuff needing to happen.* It's easy to detach from a little thing you want because if you do or don't get it, it's no big deal. But for the big stuff? It's a bigger disappointment, bigger fear, and bigger risk. So what do we do? We get all news reader serious. We stop having fun with our big desires and hang onto them for dear life *getting really down* when they haven't come yet. Hmmm... the universe isn't set up for you to be more attached to your future than the now. Imagine – we would have a planet full of people throwing *here* away. And we all know what happens when we stop being present *to what is.* We miss it. *All the signs and all the goodies.* So, what do we do?

We put our hands on our delicious hips and say "Enough!" We're going to be brave and apply the same mind-set that is successful for us with the small things towards the big things too.

And (this is the important bit) *we become more attached to spirit than to "it".*

GET YOUR SPIRIT FIX

And by spirit, I mean a higher guiding power that you believe in like God, Goddess, universal power, and so on. Remaining detached is hard when you *so want something,* so we're going to attach to spirit instead. Much better for you, and them up there prefer it too! They'd much rather you attach to them, instead of things. So, simply tell them for the next 5 seconds what you want. Tell them about any background, anything you're worried about, and ask for their help. Thank them. *There, done.* You just attached to spirit far more than to the material.

Let this attachment become bigger than any attachment you have to your desires. And since practice makes perfect, you can look forward to detaching from your big desires as soon as you start. You can look forward to being so connected to spirit that you're not scared anymore of *it* not happening, and in the absence of fear? You're empowered, secure, and in alignment. Just as you are when you find that parking space. This re-alignment of you back to spirit can be done on a train, plane, whilst you are standing in line. As soon as you imagine it, it's done. And as soon as it's done? You won't need to connect to anything, or anybody that makes you insecure because you are already confidently connected to spirit.

Desire Dry-out #3. You're already full, so you've stopped desiring because quite simply you don't need it. This is an interesting phenomenon I've come across from women who tell me they've desired and got what they've wanted; they got the lovely guy, they got that pay rise, they got the house, they feel really full – now what?

I want for nothing, darling! He's calling me every day telling me how much he loves me, I have a waiting list of clients, my bank account is full, and so my life is really easy. Hmmm... I call this Desire Dry-out because you feel that you've had enough. And in that moment, you actually have. So, is it right to keep desiring when you feel you've got it all?

YES!

Isn't that a bit, well, you know... greedy?

Yup! And I want you to be the *greediest person* you know.

Let me ask you something – I want you to think of someone famous you admire for their talent, be it in music, business, acting, whatever, or somebody who has achieved something that you have not managed to yet and they've been wildly successful at it, financially or otherwise. They probably have more established wealth than you, they probably make more money than you do, they probably have a bigger house than you do and have a career in the area that you want, that they love and that wildly loves them right back. They probably have more than you in at least one area of their life. As the artist P!NK sings, "I could fit your whole house in my swimming pool" in her song, "Cuz I can." Do you think she has stopped desiring? If the person you admire is already making millions, or is super-duper successful, should they really be desiring *even more?*

Oh YES!

If they're living to the beat of that inner pulsating desire *they were born with* – they are made *of desire* and to not desire anymore means their life force falters. Would you be disappointed if they stopped making new songs because they couldn't be bothered anymore? Would you want them to stop wanting to make crazy good films? What happens if they shut their desire off? Would you want them to do that? Do you think you'd like them as much?

So if you're in desire dry out #3 and you feel so full already - are you worried the bubble is going to burst and you'll lose everything? Goddess, your biggest life's purpose at its core, is to evolve into the most loving highest vibrating being you can possibly be by the time you die. If you do happen to lose it all, know that this world is always working in your favour, truly. When I've lost the most, I've actually gained the most in the evolving stakes. This world is always working to turn you on, losing outwards always means gaining inwards and when you look for it, you'll always find the gift in each and every situation. So, don't fear losing it, fear not desiring at all because then you really have lost all hope.

Sit in your desire and make decisions from this point. Wake up in the morning and decide – what kind of day would turn me on? What kind of breakfast would make me light up? What kind of dinner would warm up my family's heart? Do you see? You cannot stop desiring. It's so YOU!

If you find that you've got into the habit of worrying about things? We're going to use that worry of yours to work for your good!! Ready to twirly whirly with me?

Desire Pirouette:

When you worry, pirouette 180 degrees and turn that into a desire.

For example:

I'm worried about my back; it keeps going out. *Allow yourself to feel this. Don't ever negate your feeling.*

(Can you feel your life force as you say your worry? Does it go up or down?)

Desire the exact opposite:

I desire to find the right practitioner to heal my back this week.

(Can you feel your life force after you say this? What happens to the way you think straight after this sentence?) There... can you feel some of your energy come back even just by thinking this way for a sequin of a moment?

> **This is Desire Pirouetting: try it all this week; each time you worry, turn it into a desire.**

Do you see how not desiring is the same as lowering your life force? And let me tell you, it doesn't feel good for any man if you don't desire.

Imagine you're taking out your 8-year-old niece for lunch. After lunch you ask her, "What would you like to do next?" She says, "Ice cream!" You take her for ice cream. Then you ask, "OK, what would you like to do next?" And she mumbles... "I dunno," looking down at her feet. "Okaaaaay," you say, "Do you want to go to the beach? Do you want to go to the library?" And you get big fat nothing. She has stopped desiring. So, you take her to the zoo. Yup. Elephants... and she's looking down at her feet the whole time, obviously not wanting to be there, but not telling you what she wants either... how does that you feel for you? Pretty confusing and uncomfortable because you don't know how to make her happy because she isn't telling you! Well that's how men feel when you don't share your desires with them. And you? You are that little girl. Share your wants with those you love. Acknowledge them to yourself – it's often a relief!

Remember: Want. Deserve. Desire. It's your birthright.

DRY-OUT AND MEN

You cannot have a decent, let alone a magnificent love affair for life, if you are in Dry-out. FACT.

Why?

Because a woman in Dry-out will make him responsible for where she finds herself in life. For how shitty it all is. She will criticise him, tell him off, seethe, and wait for him to fuck up again, to try and get him to see the state she is in. *Look at me* she wants to scream, look at what I've become, look at what your *lack of*

- earning power
- attention
- help with the house
- inspirational leadership with the children
- ability to make me happy
- desire for me

has done to me.

You have to change!

And this will go on for years until he finds someone who puts her happiness first in this relationship, which means he has to. Dry-out occurs when you stop investing daily in yourself.

There are two tools you have to get really, *really, good at* using, in order to ward off Dry-out for the rest of your life – and for the rest of your relationship with him:

1. Daily, you must ask for what you want: *no matter how he reacts* and

2. You must stop 30 minutes before you *really* need it and *receive*.

When you get what you want, he gets what he wants. I'm serious! Does he hold back from telling you when he wants something? No! And I want you to learn from him. Women often have a very fine vision and the levels of pleasure residing in that vision are often far higher than what he can imagine. That's why women are muses and men aren't. We inspire. And can take them higher than they can alone. Ever seen what happens to a man without a good woman by his side for years? Enough said.

PUT A ROCKET IN YOUR KNICKERS!

Reading this book without implementing is like screaming to the world: "I'm not worth it!", "I'll do it later, I haven't got time", and "I don't feel like it." Go on look in your knickers, you'll find that great big skid mark – kind of like the skid mark you're making on your life right now. *Fleeting and frankly undesirable.*

Why is it important for you to read this book?
Where might you be in two years, if you don't begin
to turn yourself on?

The only reason women like us slide into Dry-out is that we've stopped implementing. We've stopped investing in ourselves daily, hourly, and we've stopped enjoying it.

Dry-out = poor discipline to implement self-love.

Feel that rocket up your derrière? Good. We're about to take off and you cannot get to your destination without that rocket. So, keep it in your knickers for the rest of the book, so you implement each time you breathe.

Now, imagine being a guy on a Friday night asking you, "What do you want to do tonight?" You say, "I dunno. What do you want to do?" And he says somewhat uncertainly, "Err... takeout and a movie?" You mumble, "Alright." He *cannot live to his blueprint because you're not.* He is built to produce, you are built to receive, but not this Friday night... well enjoy *that compromise* because it's not going to lead to anything amazing when neither of you really want to do it.

So, what happens if you really ask him for what you want and he says, "NO?" *Know that deep down he is questioning his ability to produce for you.* It's about his lack of confidence in HIMSELF, not his lack of love for you.

Sammy, a 40-something gorgeous blonde, believed in being an equal with her husband. She believed in teamwork. She would talk to her husband about what, "We can do to fix the bathroom" instead of telling him what she wanted in the bathroom. Her husband, *Jeremy*, only hears that she is unhappy with the bathroom, (and so him) but doesn't hear what *she wants* that will make her *happy* again. He just hears the long list of what is wrong and feels strangely controlled by her, "What about if we did this?" type of conversation, similar to a mum telling him what to do. *Sammy* turns most men's heads when she walks down her local street, but *Jeremy*? He feels a bit beaten down by it all. He can't put his finger on it, but he isn't turned on by *Sammy* as much as he used to be.

She tends to complain more and doesn't look at him like she used to. He doesn't know what to do to make her happy anymore.

Here's the thing: when you do the "we" thing, *it isn't working for you either if you're honest.* You are made to receive from him. He is made to produce for you. The "we" ain't sexy for either of you: it's a bit like what a mum says to her young son, "Shall we go home now?" I command thee to stop the *"we" thing* – forever!

Stop giving to him. Stop trying to make everything all right for him. It turns him off. As a woman, *you are made to receive.* And he knows it and will respond to you when you decide that receiving is important for you too. If you stop receiving every last drop of pleasure available to you from him, from your day, from that café you were just in... he *feels it* – and he turns away from you – to something else that wants to receive his attention: a woman, football, and fill in the blank. Because he's got to give his attention to something: *It's the way he was made.*

Major turn-offs for men in the area of desire are:

- You know more about what his desires are than your own, and often can pre-empt them before he's even thought to desire them.

- Your conversation is punctuated with, "I don't know" "I'm not sure" "Sorry, do you mind?" "Shall we?" "Are you sure it's not too much?" "No, it's alright, I can do it."

- You begin a conversation with: "What we should do with the house" and "Why don't you ever..." "I can't believe you would..." He won't hear your desire here, just your desire to criticise him.

- You complain instead of ask.

- When he feels criticised by the tone in your voice (he will pull away from you).

- You not being aware that the way you ask can make him feel criticised – *way more* than you would in the same situation. So, you don't take notice of his feelings and continue doing it.

Major turn-ons for men in the area of desire are:

- You know more about your desires (than his). You sit super-duper close to them, which means you are his woman to make happy, not his mum to please.

- Your conversation is punctuated with: "I so appreciate you" "I know you can get it for me" and "Thank you!"

- You begin a conversation with, "I have to have it" "I'd love you to" "I'd like to have..." "You make me so happy when you..." "I want..." I desire..."

- You ask in a neutral tone. You ask in a way that feels pleasurable to you and him.

Which sentences, from above, turned you on? Stick to what turns you on. It's way easier to turn a relationship around and get everything you want when you're busy turning yourself on.

Goddess, you are meant to desire. You thrive on desire, like all the trees, animals, and plants in this world. The desire to grow, to expand, and also to contract. Desire is life. Stop desiring and you stop life.

How do you ask for what you want?

Yes, how do you ask for what you want? Do you get squeamish at the very thought of asking, so you leave it till just before you really, really NEED it... and then when you ask, it kind of tumbles out of you, all ungainly and clumsy? You feel embarrassed, and hope he says *yes*?

Or, it's the end of the day, and you're asking your colleague for a favour. Gawd, you so *need this* and hope she doesn't say no because you don't know what you'll do without this. And the air is so loaded with you needing *it* that the person you're asking feels under pressure to say yes...

When you don't allow yourself to ask as much as you want, *you get needy.*

Many women I know have become so disappointed in the past that they now hate to ask and prefer to do it themselves. Does this sound like you? When you ask, have you left it to the last minute, so that if the person refuses:

A. It becomes a really awkward situation between you both. (This is why you avoid asking!)

B. The next hour then turns into a tailspin of trying to get other people to take their place and help. Not something you'd look forward to!

Now you have all your desires written down, how close are you sitting to them right now? Right up close? Can you feel their heat on your cheeks? Want to know an astonishing fact about you?

When you sit closer to your desires, he sits closer to you.

When you sit far away from your desires and say, "No, it's alright," he sits further away from you.

So that man you're thinking of, is actually wired to give you what you want, RIGHT NOW. Yes, that man in front of you wants to follow his blueprint, but are you sabotaging his natural inclination to give to you?

He is made to handle, love, and give you what you want. When you sit close to your desire, two things happen to him:

1. The producer in him wakes up and he turns his attention away from golf, away from externals and sits closer to YOU.

2. Your *turn-on* (to what you want) *turns ON* his confidence.

Why? When you are turned on by something and want it: for instance, more togetherness, his 100% backing of your dream, him putting the kids through private school, fixing the fence, or making hot chocolate for you tonight, you turn ON his confidence and the producer in him to give to you. A man will rise for you when you believe that he can, or fall when you remind him that he can't. See the strength in him. He can do it. You are not saving him from anything by not asking. Trust me.

When you directly ask him for what you want, what you're saying is, "I trust YOU implicitly, and I know you are the man for me." You allow him to become the man of your dreams and he will rise to the occasion, get on his horse, and charge after what you want with focus and pride. You naturally become sexier to him. You are more alluring when you sit close to your desire. Your desire is turning him on (to you) and when you are flushed with your desire, a man cannot help himself.

So, each time you ask him for what you want, it:

- brings you closer to each other
- allows him to become the man of your dreams; it expands him
- raises his confidence in making you happy
- makes him want to produce more for you and so he just will
- makes the world your oyster again
- swiftly takes you out of Dry-out, out of your old story, and out of being a victim
- re-aligns the world,

and it's all in the way you say it.

> The closer you sit next to your desires,
> the closer he will sit to you.

I want you to sit right up close, so you LIVE and breathe them. Something happens to a woman when she decides to sit close to her desires. When she gets turned on by something and wants it, the men in her life get turned ON by her wanting it – they don't get turned on sexually, it's their masculinity and confidence that gets switched on. He will sit closer to you and will do everything in his power to give you what you want.

So, the first delicious step is to *know* what you want.

The second step is to give yourself permission to want it.

The third step is to *tell him* in a way that makes you and him feel good.

I often say to my clients lamenting during a session that he isn't doing something – I ask them – "Does he have a crystal ball right now and if so, is he peering into it listening to what you are saying right now?" It makes us laugh, but they get the point. He isn't a mind reader and doesn't know. *He isn't meant to know.* Actually half the joy is asking him! This is what brings you two together, if you *know how to ask.*

This is a technique that I've adapted from the wonderful teacher and author Regena Thomashauer. I LOVE this! It's changed women's lives across the world, including my clients. Yet, it's so very simple. I remember my dad saying to my mum once during a heated argument, "If you just knew how to ask me, you'd get a lot more from me." She used to ask him much like you probably do now: sort of last minute, half expecting a "no" anyway so what's the point?

How to ask for what you want:

I call this "The 3 Amigos" because they'll become your best three friends:

1. Align

2. Ask

3. Appreciate

1. Align – positively or negatively with that person. So, this is where you jump into his shoes and make a statement that tells him, *I see you, I've taken in where you are.* So, you might say, "You know how I love that paella you make?" (Positive alignment) or "I know you're tired from work." (Negative alignment) Either one will work beautifully for you and him; you've connected.

2. Ask – this is one sentence where you simply ask for what you want. "I'd love you to cook me a paella tonight!" Make it a pleasure to say. Do not start your ask with "but". This informs him that you're apologising for asking such a thing and makes it seem like a favour, which it is not. For a man to serve a Goddess like you, it's always an honour. And if it hasn't been I would assert that you haven't known how to ask up until now. Wait for his answer – whatever he says, yes, no, or maybe...

3. Appreciate – thank him. "Thank you so much!" "I really appreciate that!" "I really appreciate you!" Genuinely *mean it.* If you're feeling too pissed off to say it nicely (because if he loved you, he should want to do this anyway and he's been with you *long enough, he should know* what you like) remind yourself that the more you appreciate him, the more likely he is going to want to make you happy in the future. Men love to be appreciated (like us) and are more likely to appreciate us back when we do.

What to do if he says no, or maybe?

Repeat the ask using his negative as alignment. For example, let's say you're asking your husband if he could help more with the kids, and he says, in effect – "No;" I want you to use what he says to re-align and ask again. Here's how it looks:

First ask:

1. Babe, I know how busy you are at work at the moment.

2. Would you take Marianne and Esther to school all this week, so I can finish off my presentation?

He says: "God, I just can't, OK? I'm up to my eyeballs in work this week and the big boss is landing Tuesday."

Instead of replying: "God, it's always about you isn't it? When was the last time I ever asked you for any help with the kids? It's always me that has to compromise *my work, my time.* How about it's *you* for a change?"

You reply:

3. Thank you for considering it anyway. (Say it genuinely.)

Two things happen:

His jaw will drop open; he won't know what to do or say.

He feels appreciated for saying no; so imagine how good it will feel when he says yes! Even better! He will be more open to saying yes next time.

So, you start again; don't miss a beat. Re-align with the negative.

Second ask:

1. I know you're up to your eyeballs in work this week.

2. I'd still really love you to take the girls to school all this week. Would you? (No justification or pleading here; don't breathe another word.)

Him: somewhat grumpily, "Oh, alright then."

3. Thank you!

A note about men who respond to you grumpily when all you're being is nice. It's enough to suck the sparkle right out of a gal!

If a man isn't used to being appreciated for giving in the way he is naturally built to, (his mother didn't appreciate him, his girlfriends didn't know how to) he will talk to you from his hurt self. Hurt selves come across as grumpy, fault finding, and picky. Because your happiness is everything, do not take it personally, but instead talk to the part of him that is happy to produce no matter how small, and see the reaction that takes place. Each time I asked the guy who was fixing our house up to do something, he would come at me with a shake of his head and, "I don't know if I'm going to have time to do that in the time constraint Marina. I really don't, sorry." "*No,*" I thought to myself, I'm going to talk to the part of you who wants to make me happy. So, I ignored his tone and set the tone with my own! "*James,* you're so brilliant at what you do, I'd be very surprised if you couldn't fit this into the time constraint – you of all people!" *James* found himself doing every single one of those things he couldn't do in surprising time. And when he got appreciated? He turned from the grizzly bear that had met me on the steps into the kind of man I'd want for you.

Still nervous about asking? Read this!

What we're doing here is getting you to turn your receiving ON. You have to know what you want to be able to receive it and you will have to ask for what you want for about 50% of your desires.

If we look at the women in our lives: is it fair to say that for most of us we definitely know how to give and do? It's fair isn't it? If we look at the men in our lives, is it fair to say that most of them do a pretty good job at receiving really well? Most men I know sit on the couch when they are tired and turn on the TV, so different to us women who will push on with a coffee.

So, if we women are great at giving and need to learn how to receive *and* the men around us are great at receiving then they need to learn how to give…

So by being brave enough to break through your own barriers and ask; in the bigger picture you're teaching men to nurture us and the planet. Do you see? We need to ROCK what our men are great at, they need to ROCK what we are great at, and we need to blaze that trail! And you may not want to, but if you look at your own life: what's going to transform beautifully *if you don't?*

Can you imagine those running the big businesses that are stripping Mother Nature day in and day out? Can you imagine if they had wives and women around them who asked for what they wanted? Who were so hell bent on receiving what turned them on that they were femininely powerful and set the tone with him? He would *have turned on his giving, nurturing side* and it *would then be impossible to turn that off* when he thinks and makes decisions about the environment.

Asking does not come from a place of anger, nor resentment, nor "You bloody well should bloody give them to me because you haven't ever and I bloody deserve it!" This just kicks in his masculine shield and he will cut off from you – no – if it's pleasurable for you to say it, then it's pleasurable for him to hear it, and then darling, the world just got a happiness makeover. Thank you.

And:

Know that when you ask for what you want, it makes the other person expand. He *needs* to be bigger than what is happening at work, he needs to think bigger and so will become a bigger person because of it with a bigger heart to look after you. That's you creating a hero.

For example, say you ask him to pick the kids up from school two afternoons a week. He needs to expand his resourcefulness at work to accommodate this. So, he asks his boss to come in on this project just on those days: the boss says yes. In saying yes, your man now gets more support than he would have done had he not asked. This in turn, expands his boss who now needs to receive more support in the office and so decides to get an office junior in. And so on. Do you see? When you ask, it expands you to receive more abundance, it expands him to receive more abundance (to be able to give to you – yaay!) It also expands his boss to receive more abundance because if he takes on a new employee, they'll give him more back, freeing him up to earn more money. So when you ask, you set off a whole chain of events that is in the best interest of everybody. I call it the feminine chain of enlightenment – expanding to become bigger than where they currently sit to receive more abundance. We want unity in this world and that's what asking does; it brings collaboration. It's the opposite of lonely and unsupported. It's the direction we want this world to go in: more togetherness and more kindness. Plus, that man you just asked? He learnt how to make you happy this week *and* is appreciated and noticed for it by a beautiful woman (you!). It's win/win. And for your children also (in this case!).

Asking = expansion = collaboration = more abundance = unity = happier people = makes the world go round ☺

And lastly – what happens if it goes wrong?

If you asking him turns into an argument remember, it doesn't mean he doesn't love you. It means he is questioning *his ability to produce* for *you*. This is a confidence issue on his part, NOT a confidence query about you.

Inspire Technique

This is just a gorgeous thing to do for the man you love or the man in your midst. Talk to the hero in him who wants to do a good job for you and inspire him into being his highest possibility. "Oh, but you're normally always so organised," and "You're normally always so gentle with them," "I love how good you are at not speeding, you're such a safe driver, thank you for that," and "That's not like you to forget my birthday" and so on. Inspire him with love and watch him *hear you*. A concrete assumption that he would normally do "it," but hasn't on this occasion means his confidence in his ability to produce for you rises and he will do more for you in the future. Far more fun than "I can't believe you've forgotten again you idiot!" Your unshakeable belief in him is everything. And it's way more fun if he rises for you in this way, in more ways *than just this one* – huzzah!

... ON DOCTOR'S ORDERS

I want you to imagine you are going into a doctor's office with the ailment of Dry-out. You're exhausted; she takes one look at you and prescribes the antidote:

Nitric Oxide.

You read the script again that she's just zipped off her pad – what? What's that? "Ahhh," she says, *"Nitric Oxide* is a gas that researchers found gets generated in your body when you do things for yourself that you find pleasurable. Like orgasms, helping out at an animal shelter, eating food you love that loves you right back, fresh air, and of course moving your body in a way that turns you and your delightful happiness ON!"

It doesn't matter what it is, as long as it gives you pleasure. And if it gives you pleasure? By definition, it must be good for your body because pleasure *could never hurt your body.*

And when you allow yourself more pleasure in your day? Your Nitric Oxide levels start to multiply on their own! So, when you wake up in the morning, you haven't necessarily just been to Hawaii on holiday, but you just feel great and you bound out of bed. Conversely, if you don't regularly do things that turn you on, your body produces less and less nitric oxide, which turns in on itself; till one day, you wake up and you're already rolling your eyes. Dried out by life. What's the point?

And because Nitric Oxide is a gas, it can't be stored in the body, so it doesn't matter that you did something lovely for yourself last week, your body didn't store it in your internal fridge – so on doctor's orders: your prescription *is* to receive pleasure, DAILY. Put your work down. What would turn you on right now?

Always have something to look forward to; it's just in a gal's genetics!

Make a 7-day pleasure plan for yourself, and pop in at least one pleasurable thing to look forward to each day. I dispatch this pleasure plan to new clients who are pleasure anaemic and need a passionate transfusion of pleasure pulsating through their veins before they begin the deep transformation. Healing yourself takes energy you know!

Christiane Northrup, M.D. says in her book, 'The Secret Pleasures of Menopause:' "In other words, taking good care of your body and fully opening yourself to receiving pleasure (thus boosting nitric oxide) does all of the following: Helps the process of healing, boosts immunity, and helps prevent chronic degenerative diseases – keeping you physically strong and healthy as you age. Improves not only your mood, but also your outlook on life... feeds your spirit..."

This is your antidote to Dry-out. Some might argue it's the antidote for an unhappy life/relationship/body. What could regular, *real pleasure* do for you?

Chapter 5

DETOX What's In Your Way

· · · · · · · · · · · · · · · · ·

This is the third D in the 3 Ds ethos:

Here is where we detox whatever is inside you that is in your way of receiving the desires you listed in chapter 4:

This is you self-healing and it doesn't matter if you're having the best of times or the worst of times, it's important that you get good at it. If you don't have a system to detox yourself of pain this week, this month, this year, you're going to slide into Dry-out. That's yummy mummies and their yummy lives, that's uber successful business women, hippy chicks, and everyone in between. We all require a way to self-heal. And you, beautiful you.

This is arguably the most important chapter of them all. This is where you come to when you're stuck, shitty, exhausted, and over it. There are special processes right here to powerfully transform your biggest, shittiest problems. Stick around whilst we start detoxing you bit by bit.

And the consequences of you not detoxing regularly?

 Being a pro at blocking those desires you've just written down.

 You'll have more groundhog days than not.

 Staying stuck, then sliding; the only way is down from here.

- ⟳ Ageing before your time = illness.
- ⟳ You'll get too tired to do the things you want.
- ⟳ You won't get the relationship or life that you want.
- ⟳ All the other things that happen to us women when we carry dis-appointment, worry, judgement, anger, hurt, confusion, guilt and shame, etc., around with us like the latest handbag. Yes, all *those* side-effects.
- ⟳ Plus, these common everyday afflictions that I've outlined below, afflicting you day after day for the rest of your life.

Do you recognise yourself in these six self-inflicted hurts below? They are so common and they stop you from living the life you are meant to. We're going to begin detoxing you of these because they can knock you out for days, like the common cold. The first one is in the shape of a pill. A pill??? Whaaat?

1. HAVE YOU TAKEN YOUR VALIDATION PILL YET?

No, not a Valium Pill. I mean a *Validation Pill*.

Read this when you're feeling weirded out by someone's reaction to you:

Imagine it's a Monday morning and *Suzy* walked into the office. Her co-worker *Jess* (who is normally friendly with her) is frostier than a frosty snow flake. The phone vibrates, and she sees a one line text from her boyfriend saying "Can't meet you tonight." That's it. *Why?* She thinks. No explanation, no usual sweet kisses at the end of the text. Then her real estate agent calls her out of the blue; it seems that the landlord is putting the apartment up for sale next month, so she has to move, or buy it. For a cool $2 million...

... Then her boss buzzes *Suzy* into his office and in an *even tone,* he tells her that he's moving *Suzy* to another department at the end of the month. No explanation given, just that "It's better all round." *Suzy* has no idea what the crazy old fool is talking about.

But *Suzy* walks away and feels... deeply unsettled. It's not what has happened, it's how all of this has made her feel. No one has validated her. No one said, "Sorry I'm a bit grumpy this morning, it's not you. It's just that I've had a hell of a morning, don't take me seriously, I'll be fine in a mo." No one said, "Sorry I can't meet you tonight, just know that I love you and can't wait to see you Tuesday instead." No one said that to *Suzy*. So *Suzy* is now working, answering e-mails, but her stomach has nervous shots running through it, she feels like she is having a sort of out of body experience, like she's here, *but not here.*

What's going to happen to her? She can't explain this to anybody of course; they'd think she was needy. She is so unsettled inside; madly, silently she asks, "What did my boyfriend mean? Is he going to leave me?" "I can't believe we have to move out of our apartment, what if he does leave me and then I have to find a place on my own to live?? OMG, OMG, OMG, what am I going to do?" "And why is *Jess* being so cold to me? I must have upset her, but how?? Was it Friday? Was it because I didn't invite her to lunch with the girls? But I couldn't find her in the office to ask her... I bet that's why she's shitty" and so on and so on.

Why does *Suzy* become so affected when people don't validate her and her feelings? When they don't go the extra mile to make sure she is OK? Well, *Suzy* grew up like most little girls around the world, with parents who told her off when she was naughty. "No Suzy, stop hitting your sister." She didn't want her mum and dad to be any angrier with her because it might mean losing something really important: Their love for her.

See, when you're little, it's all about survival and whatever might threaten that safety? You stop doing it *fast*. This is just how most little people think. Most parents will do whatever it takes to keep their little people safe. But, little people make everything about them and deep down *Suzy*, (and most women I know) still believe that how someone behaves towards her is because of *her*. It must be, right? She hasn't yet realised that how someone behaves towards her is based on two things:

1) On the relationship she has with herself.
2) On the relationship the other person has with themselves.

So right now, *Suzy* is holding on. She's at the computer fake smiling at everyone, and will not be able to relax until these people make it better for her with a spiritual Valium pill that just won't last. She can check her messages as much as she likes, but these are just Valium: their words of *sorry, I like you,* and *I love you* are just Valium. Because no matter how much they tell her, it's never going to be enough:

Which pill do you choose? The validation pill or in the end, Valium?

Goddess, the more validation you give to beautiful you, the less you need from all of them. And the less validation you give to beautiful you, the more you're going to need from them.

> Which kind do you choose? To take that pill, or to not and cross your fingers and pretty please hope for the best?

Do you want the kind of relationship with yourself where you already think highly of yourself? So much in fact that when *they* don't talk to you nicely, or shock you, you know it's because they've just fallen off their happy horse? That's all! *It's because they are in pain.* It has to do with *their* relationship to *themselves* and their life, and has in fact nothing to do with you. How could it? Are you in their brain telling them what to say? Are you in charge of their fingers on that keyboard?

No.

But, you are in charge of the relationship you have with yourself. And, that changes everything.

Never ever look to your outside world for validation of who you are. You are *WOMAN*...

... Who can unleash herself anytime, anywhere, and anyhow to create a magnificent day; regardless of, *who is in it and what they forget to say.*

When my daughter was little, I explained to her that when mummy shouted at her; it was because I was in pain. It had nothing to do with her because she knew at other times I would have a very different reaction to the same thing she was doing. This was her validation pill and in the tough times when I was a single mum, I told her often.

Pop that Validation Pill in *NOW!*

It's time to validate and approve of *all of you*. Yes, the very flesh you find yourself in, that very thought you had just now. Are you game to give this a go? Because when you approve of yourself, from every little thing about you and what you do, then the outside world can only follow suit. Because the outside world is your mirror to you. It reflects the relationship you have with yourself. Brilliantly. Spectacularly. And with all its love. It wants you to see what you're doing to yourself.

So, if you don't approve of you often, you'll find it hard to come by this commodity in the outside world. People won't approve of you much and you'll keep searching, trying to seek it out from somewhere. But, approve of you – and you'll have started a warm fire burning inside of you. You won't need that unreliable external approval – and you'll find others attracted to your warmth, wanting to be near you, loving, and approving of you. And you know what? You can now let them in. There is no shame in what you can, or can't do because you have a huge fire of approval inside of you, and so you give them permission to approve of you too.

Let's create that warmth inside of you and take your validation pill:

- Each minute decide to approve of the next thing you say, do, or experience.
- Silently say to yourself, "I love the way I..."

So it looks like this: I love the way I am sitting right now, the way my legs are positioned. I love the way I am reading these words right now; I love the way I spoke to him this morning, and so on.

What would your world look like if you loved everything you said, did, thought? Would your words come out in the highest way possible? Would you be more respected at work? Would you be confident and show up in the world differently? Powerfully? If you had internal validation, if you approved of yourself of every minute of every day would the world benefit from you? Would you have more of yourself to give to the world? Would you want to model this way of being for your children? Wouldn't you want that for them, too?

And so what if you come to a point where you can't validate what you did because it was wrong? You can't be right all the time... right? Wrong! Yes, you can. It's great to be wrong. It's oh so right to be oh so wrong. Can you look at each moment of being wrong as a learning opportunity? Instead of shrinking away from the world because you made a mistake, actually it was a stratospherically BIG sign to you, that it's time to learn something! Can you imagine this? You would approve of every single mistake that you make – you'd fall in love with them all – each and every stinky little one of them and give yourself a wry smile when amidst one. OK, what is there to learn here? This is exactly how the successful people in my life operate.

So what would this look like? Well, let's say you're just walking away from a conversation thinking you didn't come across the right way. And we all do this don't we? "Ooo, I could have said that better. Now, she'll think I don't like her..." and so on. It sounds a little mad when I write it here, but actually we all do this a lot, *more than we care to admit*. So, in this conversation the others said you were wrong to think the way you do, they invalidated you. You protested, but didn't want to seem "pushy or ugly" in standing up for yourself, so you just laughed it off.

As you walk home, you don't like how you feel – *um, angry actually*. So, let's take that validation pill, "I love how I came across" (no I don't, no I don't, no I don't!) When you don't love that moment ask yourself, "What part of me did I need to switch on?" "What do I need to learn here?" Suddenly, you can see that you acted in exactly the right way for the situation because you acted in a way that was right for your growth, which is your growth as a human being. Some say that the only reason we are on this planet is to evolve. So some would say that you just reached the best part about living on this planet.

So, thank the situation and approve of yourself – practise having internal validation. You are always doing the right thing at the right time, even if it doesn't feel that way at the time.

I know that in each moment I am always learning.
The situation is always right for me:

1. They are right for them at their level of self-love.

2. I AM RIGHT FOR ME at my level of self-love.

3. So, what is this trying to turn on within me? E.g. self-respect?

4. I act from here.

5. When I am turned on, I realise that I am bigger than everything else and nothing has the power to topple me, NOTHING. So, I go out into my day knowing this.

6. Hurrah! I just validated me!

The world is always conspiring to turn me ON by teaching me something.

What is this moment turning on for you?

Is it your resilience? Is it your ability to take yourself to a 10, when you're feeling like a 2? The world is always turning you on, so each moment is perfectly designed to turn some part of you on. When you realise this, you are free to fall in love with each moment. And this world needs you to turn *on,* so you can work for good, so you can do your life's purpose, so you can lift the vibration of this planet up, up, up! And that only occurs when you are turned on, on, on – so the world always works in your best interest. For example, the next time someone abandons you, ask yourself, "What is this moment turning on for me?" "My self-love?" "My 'fuck it, I'm gonna live an amazing life, just *you* watch' crazy arsed part of me?"

So take your validation pill. (Oh, it's so sweet!) And LOVE what you do, say, and experience. And when you can't, ask: What do I need to turn on within, so that I do?

Is it your softness? Your confidence? Your receiving button?

Try it, play with it all and see how much peace you can insert into your day.

Try taking your validation pill before bedtime and write 10 "approvals" about you that you can heap onto yourself tonight: both for things that you did do well, and for the things you didn't. Goddess you were made brilliantly!

2. STOP TRYING SO HARD!

We women are powerful. And so a large portion of our day is spent trying to do our best; trying our hardest to make sure things run really well at work and in life, and trying our hardest to do better. We want to reach our true potential this lifetime and I love that about you!

But...

It can back fire on us too.

See if you can recognise where you might be doing this to yourself in a particular area of your life. Your beauty? Your job? In the dating game? Just let the answer come to you as you read this example:

I was watching my favourite TV program the other night with Graham Norton. I love him! He interviewed three famous celebs on his wine gum couch. All extremely successful in their own right. The man seated in the middle of the couch wore a simple pair of trousers and shirt. He looked good, relaxed, and comfortable, because he was.

The other guests were women. I noticed each had put maximum effort into their appearance. And that inspires me, but on this occasion, I noticed something. Goddess #1 was on trend, a stylists dream wearing the right dress with the right shoes. Goddess #2 was wearing a dress so tight, she could only perch on the edge of said wine gum for the *entire* show. After she sang Graham had to come and collect her, by holding her arm steady as she tottered back to the couch in her huge platform shoes. The audience laughed with her as she gamely laughed at herself.

It wasn't the first time I've seen Graham do this. In fact, he leads most of his female singers back because *they can't walk in what they are wearing.* In addition, Goddess #2's hair must have taken her *hours.* It was elaborate with 5 huge curls balancing precariously atop her head. Big falsies batting away... in fact, there wasn't a part of her that wasn't *trying.* Her eye lashes were trying really hard to stand out, her hair was trying to be noticed, and her dress was trying to get all the attention in the room. She was trying so hard. But did she have to? Isn't she enough? Isn't her beautiful singing voice enough for us to love her? What a symbol for how we women have become pre-occupied with turning others on at the expense of our wellbeing.

Now let's bring this into your life. Is a generous portion of your day spent trying to write an e-mail or a text, then double checking it to ensure it conveys the right amount of warmth? With the right number of kisses? One for casual, three if you really mean it? It has to be *just right*. It has to convey the message and ensure that the person reading it likes you and thinks you're kooky and fun, or busy and important.

One of my coaching clients actually added up the time she spent double checking her outgoing communications. In her next session with me, she was embarrassed to report back that on average she spent longer checking *how her e-mails read* than actually writing them! I can tell you now; men don't do this. And have you noticed, we don't expect it of them either?

How many of you have doggedly hit the shops trying to find that perfect birthday gift for your bestie? Only to hand it to her with a wince *"I hope you like it?"* You hold your breath as she opens it... "Oh I love it!" she says. "Are you sure?" you say, "Because it was between the red and the pink and I wasn't 100% sure. Really, *it's OK*. You can tell me the truth, I won't be upset. Really, I have the receipt in my bag still, if you don't like it I can take it back for you..." Oh my Goddess! Would you listen to us trying so hard, and still we are not sure! We are still not sure *even when* she *says* she is sure! And after all those hours trying and slogging about in the streets in the rain!

... And yet you try so very hard, in fact you are always trying. Trying to make a good impression at work, trying to be a good neighbour, trying to eat right and, trying to lose weight, trying to be a good mum, trying to get that promotion, or client, trying to be popular on Facebook, trying, trying, trying.

It's *exhausting!*

Goddess, stop trying so hard!

When do we ever arrive?

A big part of every woman's day is actually spent trying to do this and trying to do that. So, I'll ask you again gorgeous woman, when do we ever arrive? Have you arrived, or are you still trying? Are you trying to be better at your job, get more sales, get more... When you go to a party, at what point do you feel you've arrived? In your life, at what point have you arrived?

STOP trying and just BE it already – it's waaay more FUN!

And what of my over-checking client? She's done! She could slippy slide into trying too hard with every single communication, but she prefers to write straight from her heart now. Easy. She's cut her work day down by a third. I kid you not.

3. DOUBTEDY DOUBT

Did you know that trying so hard goes hand in hand with self-doubt? It's one of the biggest suckers of life force for any good woman and you do it a lot more than you realise. You doubt that you look good in those jeans, and I mean *really good*. If your tummy was just a wee *bit flatter*... or "Should I go for something hot, cold, healthy, shall I just give in... not sure...?" you're even doubting what you just chose for lunch.

You doubt your beauty. You doubt that he still feels the same way about you. You doubt that you're good enough, that you've made the right choices. You doubt you *can do it*. Doubt is a nasty little habit I want you to drop like a hot potato. Because you doubting how you look, your talent, why he's still with you, robs you of self-belief, success, and peace. It strips away your ability to feel peace at this very moment. And it stops you receiving properly. It's very difficult to receive a date with a man who is privately jetting you out to his private island when you doubt yourself because you are not approving of yourself. Instead you'll think he is showering you with all this attention for ulterior motives. You won't believe it's because of you, because you doubt you. So you doubt somebody's good intentions for you too.

Are you doubting something right now? It strips you bare and makes you feel cold on the warmest of days. Many years ago I attended the engagement party of my ex and his new fiancé. It was a lavish "do" set on the water to sumptuous food, dreamy sunset lighting, and twinkling lights. It was a warm, beautiful night. His fiancé approached me and said hello. And then stood back and fixed me with a very hollow stare.

"You know Marina, he's never loved me the way he loved you." I was stunned. I told her, "But he never *asked me* to marry him. And here I am, at your engagement party, pregnant to another man that I'm probably going to end up marrying. I'm never going to go back to Tim. He's all yours." "Yes," she said, "But I wish he loved me like *I know* he still loves you!" I was so shocked. At her *own engagement party,* she still doubted the love he had for her and *he* had asked *her* to marry him! We had broken up years ago and neither one of us held a candle for the other.

This was her nasty little habit of self-doubt that reared up at what should have been the least doubtful time in her life! Her doubt didn't just strip her of peace in that moment; it propelled her to do something that I bet she still regrets to this day. In order to assuage her doubt, she then dirty danced with Tim's work colleague. And how can I put it? She fondled his bum and then kissed him passionately whilst still on the dance floor. My ex was gob smacked! What was she doing? Why was she doing this?

D_O_U_B_T

I had to spell it out for him. I gave the relationship 6 months. I knew doubt would eat it all up.

Doubt can make the most sane woman insane. This woman was a beautiful successful woman in business; regularly earning a 5-figure month, back in the 1990's!

Wanna know what happened to Mr. Sure and Mrs. Doubt?

They married in a lavish Californian ceremony and the TV camera's rolled; it was a high profile wedding... it was glamorous and romantic. They lasted longer than 6 months, 5 years in fact, until her doubt killed the very thing she loved the most: him. It was too much for them both and so Mr. Sure became Mr. Doubt and divorced Mrs. Doubt.

4. NOBODY WANTS TO THINK THEY'VE BOUGHT THE WRONG PRODUCT

Picture this: You spy the perfect party dress for that party at the weekend and you try it on – *ooooh it's perfect!* There's no doubt in your mind. It graces your curves and makes you feel like an absolute Goddess. You waltz over to the counter to pay, flushed with your good find and the girl behind the counter gazes lazily at you, "Good luck with this, we've had five returns already on it." "What for?" you ask, shocked. "The zips don't hold and slide down when you're wearing it. If it happens to you, don't be surprised, they're not very well made. I mean what can you expect for the price?" And just like that, you slide out of sureness about your dress and into doubtedy doubt.

Now picture this. Your eyes meet across the crowded room. Oh he's gorgeous you think and smile. Next thing you know, he's offered to buy you a drink and, 6 weeks in, he is having the best time of his life with you. He's even told his mum he thinks he might have met "the one". He wants you to meet his mum. He wants you to meet his friends. He is so proud of you and wants to show you off to the world. He thinks the world of you and can't believe his luck. You've held it in until this point. How you feel about your thighs that is, how you've never felt as pretty as your sister... your nasty little habit of doubting yourself has been held in by the first flush of love, you don't have the heart to tell him. And then the inventible happens. He wants to make love to you with the lights ON. God no, the last thing you want is for him to see you in a different light, the cold one of your bedroom that is. So you make some excuse and light some candles instead, ensuring you bend your knees a little, so your thighs don't "splat out" on the bed à la modelling shoot. A few days later you go shopping for some jeans with him and ask him the question most men dread the most, "Does my bum look big in this?"

Two things happen to a man upon hearing this: 1. Utter distress. He knows that whatever he says will get him into trouble. 2. His attraction to you dies a little. See, nobody wants to think they've bought the wrong product.

He knows there is no right way to answer this. It's a trap. A man trap. A Mrs. Doubt A type trap. Because the woman (aka you) has already already made up her mind see? She has already decided to doubt how she looks in these jeans. And he knows this. So he only has two options as he sees it all the while thinking, "Shit, how do I get out of this?"

Scenario 1: He says, "No darling, your bum doesn't look big in it. You look beautiful, really lovely in them." "God!" She says, "I know you're just saying that to make me feel better. Thanks for the vote of confidence, but you don't have to pretend. I know what I look like, fucking fat that's what!"

Scenario 2: He says, "Yeah, they do make your bum look a bit big. How about you try on that other pair?" "Charming!" She says, "And I thought you were supposed to love me as I am! So, you think I'm fat do you?? Well now I know why those other women left you – fucking idiot!"

Either way, he can't win. Either way, he feels he's bought the wrong product. Now let's go back to you in that party dress. Yes, you've decided to buy it anyway. You're talking to some friends of yours and all the while about 30% of you is taken up with swinging your arm around and religiously checking the back of your dress. You are doubting your dress, so it takes away from the situation. You cannot be sure anymore. You cannot enjoy what you bought.

Let's go back to this man – he starts to doubt his decision. It's not a conscious thought, "Oh. Did I choose the right girlfriend?" It's more a feeling: if she is doubting herself and the way she looks so much, maybe I can do better. Maybe, she's not good enough for me. Maybe she is a bit too frumpy, fat round the edges, boring, lumpy, not sexy anymore... maybe I'm with the wrong woman. No man wants to feel he has bought the wrong product. No man wants to feel he picked the wrong woman. And yet, if you doubt your beauty, your talent, and your ability to be a good mum enough of the time, who is he not to believe you anymore... and do you know why?

5. BECAUSE YOU SET THE TONE OF YOUR RELATIONSHIP, NOT HIM!

Yes, this is a little known fact. It's one that most men know and some men who want to keep you down don't want you to know. And it's this; you set the tone of your relationship with him: not him, not anybody else, but YOU, sweet, gorgeous you. Think back to your childhood, when your mum was up and happy: do you remember that happily filtering through to the rest of the family? Things got done in the home, you were listened to, you were loved, and there was laughter in the house. Do you remember what happened when your mum was down? What was the atmosphere in the house? Did it go downhill? Do you remember what happened if your dad went up or down? (I'm not talking about violent, or domineering men here.) Was he just ignored? Can you remember at all? Most of my clients can't because that's just it. *Nothing happened.* When he was down, no one else went down with him. When he was up, well that's nice, welcome back. Most of my clients can remember exactly what mood their mum was in for most of the time. She was in sharp focus because women set the tone of the relationship and family life. What about you? How Goddess friendly is your life? Here is how to tell if you are setting the tone right now or not:

The Goddess Gauge:

1. Are you less inclined to meditate now that you're with him? Whereupon before you never missed a yoga class, now you *just do less* for your divine spirit.

2. Do you watch TV at night because he switches it on and that's just what you do? Before you met him you watched a bit, but not half as much as you do now.

3. Have you stopped keeping an endless supply of Goddess delicacies in your fridge? You know, posh dark chocolate, that organic *straight from the farm* yogurt, smoked salmon, and those marinated olives

that you so love? Have you stopped buying them because *he's not into them? So you do the "we" shop instead?*

4. Look at your house: has it stopped being Goddess friendly? Visibly and invisibly? Is there a vibe that's warm, sweet, and super comfy with soft throws everywhere? Soft rugs? Gentle lighting? Soft wafting smells from candles, oil burners, and flowers? A beautiful feminine energy that says welcome, warmth, and you're safe? Is it ambient, loving, do you feel free to be super girly here? Is your bathroom fit for a goddess? Does your lounge reflect you? Does your bedroom reflect you? Where do you apply your makeup, (if you wear it) is it in a nice space? Is your wardrobe enough for you? Is there a room in your house just for you, a sanctuary where you can meditate, find peace, and just be?

5. Do you dress differently? Because he likes short skirts, do you wear them more, even on cold days?

6. When he asks you, "What do you want to do Friday night?" Do you often answer with, "I don't know, what do you want to do?" And then settle for whatever he says, which doesn't exactly rock your world.

7. Do you pride yourself on knowing the right time to ask him something?

8. Do you go out with your friends less than once a week?

9. Do you anticipate his needs before he even knows them, so he has an easier time of it?

10. Who comes first in your household? Is it you first, then the kids, then him? Or is it the kids first, then him, then your job, your dog, the state of the house, the state of the garden, the car, football, the kids' sports, bills, keeping up with friends, then you? Who gets to play on Saturday mornings?

11. On weekday mornings, does he set the tone of the morning with his needs? Leaving early because it's the only time to get to the gym/ get some work done, with no interruptions? Are you then left with

getting the kids ready for their day, then cleaning up the kitchen as best you can... so fitting your breakfast in on the run, and doing what you need to do after everyone else has done theirs first? And this doesn't just happen 1 day out of 5. This happens 5 days out of 5 or at least 3 days out of 5. Yes, you take the hit because you can. Because you're meant to. Because your mum did it, or whatever you're telling yourself. The end result is: *he is setting the tone, not you.*

12. Do you tell him what turns you on in bed, like can you touch me more lightly here, would you kiss me hard now... or do you just hope he knows, and settle quietly for somewhere in between?

13. Does sex seem more like a chore than a delight? Is the thought of closing your eyes in your comfy bed so much more appealing than sex after a long day?

Did you get one yes? Or all yes's? It's ok whatever you got; this is just a snapshot of how Goddess friendly your life has been up until now. It doesn't mean it's how it's going to be in the future. If you just felt a little inspired, that's your intuition talking to you. What would your Goddess heart love to see in your life? What if you took a baby step in that direction this week?

Your result only means one super-duper delicious thing for you and your lover right now. It means your relationship is on its way up because *there is room for you to set the tone.* And if there is room for you to set the tone? Then there is room for you to create a love affair for life with him! And because you set the tone and not him, you're not reliant upon him. Women are very powerful and can make a relationship go this way, or that. Deep down most women I talk to feel this intuitively, but don't act upon their deep knowing. In the film "My Big Fat Greek Wedding", the mother, Maria, says: "The man is the head (of the house), but the woman is the neck. And she can turn the head any way she wants."

6. THE RELATIONSHIP YOU HAVE WITH YOURSELF

Scarlett is a 29-year-old administrator. She works full time, just like *Ross*, her boyfriend of 5 years. He gets paid more than she does and they live together. They split the rent, groceries, and bills in half. *Ross* doesn't understand why *Scarlett* is always broke at the end of the month. He often says to her, "Why do you spend so much on clothes and shoes?" She gets cross at him, but has started hiding the receipts out of shame. Who's setting the tone for this relationship? Answer = *Ross*. Is it working for either of them? No.

Or what of 42-year-old *Sasha*, an incredibly successful Marketing Director who is working 12-hour days and cannot think of anything else, but having a child with her partner? Her partner on the other hand doesn't want children because he likes their independence and executive lifestyle. *Sasha's* been in limbo for 10 years and thinks it might be too late. Who has set the tone for a decade here? Answer = Him. Is it working for either of them? No because *Sasha's* unhappiness is seeping into their lives, whether they're on a yacht, or having sex. He feels it. She feels it. All the time.

And *Karen*, a stay-at-home mum of four? She's tired and has eaten so much chocolate to cope she is now a size 16, while her husband is lithe, lean, and a little bit distant. He cycles to work and regularly goes on work trips, where he stays in nice hotels. *Karen* tries to make home life as nice and as quiet for her husband as possible as she worries about losing him. She gets up and does the night duty with the kids, so he can sleep and be fresh for work. She creates a lovely warm atmosphere at home. Who is setting the tone for this relationship? Answer = her husband. Is it working for either of them? No.

*These gorgeous women are not setting
the tone in their relationships, and
so the men in their life suffer.*

And before I go on any further: Goddess, you don't just set the tone for you and him; you set the tone for every relationship and every single situation you find yourself in. How? *It's all in the way you treat yourself.* The way you're treating yourself *right now as you read this* is setting the tone for how people at work are treating you, for how he responds to you at home tonight, and yes, to how much money you make and yes, how your children talk to you, too.

As I said before, it has everything to do with you and nothing to do with him.

How are you treating yourself right now? On a scale of 1–10, 1 being not very well and 10 being extremely well, where do you sit on it right now?

Tell me the number out loud.

OK, this is your sweet starting point. Let's take *Scarlett's* relationship with herself. The relationship she has with money is that if money was a man, it wouldn't stay by her side for long. She even says this to her friends at work "No, I can't go shopping with you this weekend. I can't be trusted!" She's laughing like a drain, but as soon as she has it, she spends it. So she didn't feel empowered during their "who paid for what" conversation and just went with everything *Ross* said because she trusted him more. She gave him authority over how her money is spent. She chose to let him set the tone with the money and thus their lifestyle in the relationship.

Darling *Sasha* has become so disappointed with not starting a family that she has already given up. But, there is a tiny part of her wishing that something in the outside world will happen to make children a reality. I call this the Making Do Fantasy. She is making do and fantasising that something outside of her will rescue her. She has been doing this for 10 years. She has forgotten that she can set the tone right now, but she is stuck in her Making Do Fantasy where "one day" it will happen.

Karen's relationship with her worthiness is very fragile. She feels that unless she keeps a quiet tidy home, her husband might not want to come back. She worries a lot that he's only with her for the children, so tries to be the "perfect wife" holding her feelings of loneliness in while she makes the kids school lunches. She won't let him in for fear he might see her damaged. She watched the Stepford Wives film but didn't find it funny. She has chosen to let him set the tone for not just their relationship, but also how much she does for the children. She's exhausted. She's forgotten her power.

Have you forgotten yours, Goddess?

But it's so rich and decadent!

The relationship you have with yourself will set the tone:

Because the level of love you have for yourself is exactly the same level of love you will allow in from him.

Remember the *does my bum look big* story? She didn't love her bum, so when he said, "You look beautiful," she couldn't let him in. She didn't believe him.

You know how you wouldn't dare forget to buy a birthday present for certain friends, but for other friends it's OK for you to be late? Well, this has nothing to do with how much love you have for them right? It has everything to do with how much love they have for themselves. It's like an unwritten, unseen gas, which we'll call self-love gas. You can't see it, you can't smell it, but boy is it there and boy do you react to it! That's why there are some people you treat a lot better than others.

Right now, make a quick list of five of the closest people to you. Who do you not worry too much about if you forget their birthday? Who do you really care about? You can see *who* in your sphere has high self-love for themselves.

And doesn't it feel really good to care about them? If their self-love level is high, then it raises yours.

So if the relationship you have with yourself is one where you put yourself last (because you're always giving to others first) you'll find that you won't receive much from your friends. Most of them will say, "Sorry I'm late" before each catch up with you.

If the relationship you have with yourself is one where you don't like yourself very much, you'll find your friends will not call you, or ask you out as much as they do with your other friends.

Do Goddess, answer this question in one simple sentence: what's the relationship with yourself, right NOW? If you could put a word to it, what would it be? If you can't answer this, all you have to do is look around you. How is everyone treating you right now? There's the word you've been looking for because *that is* the way you've been treating yourself.

If you're complaining because your friends don't listen to you as much as you do to them, then that is what you do to yourself. You are not listening to your deepest need.

What is your deepest need right now? Now, go act on it.

So, if you're not entirely happy in your relationship, I am going to look you deeply in the eyes and say very softly and gently to you: Goddess, you set the tone for this, so we are going to start with you.

Do you want to know the four steps I give to my clients for them to set the tone with their men, with their ex men, with all men everywhere, so YOU get DIAMONDS from him, instead of the usual?

The world is set up for men to look after women, so we are able to nurture either a project, or the next generation. Short-term we women can do it all, but long term it is just exhausting. (Just ask a single mum.)

Nobody wins if women have to look after children *and* men. Children, women, and men are short changed. To go against that, the natural order short changes us. All of us.

Men looking after us must deliciously occur at almost every interaction with him. Otherwise it won't feel right. *Because it's not meant to*. It actually won't feel right for him either. It *is* the natural order of things.

A big part of every healthy man's life's purpose is to look after women, so women can look after the next generation. And if he's gay? You'll still see that some part of his life is about honouring the feminine, whether it's adding to women by listening to your problems or in clothing, beauty, architecture, or design as example, whether in his personal life or work life, he will feel good when he actively helps you.

But, what happens to a man when you take part of his life purpose away with your, "No. I can handle it thanks," answer to his question of "Do you want me to call him instead?" He dies a little inside. He won't know it at the time, but he'll feel it, and so will you. A gentle hardness begins to spread throughout your relationship and little by little the light goes out. So, stop trying to save him from doing *"it"*.

... He begins to forget. And for some men, they've lost their confidence in making you happy. Maybe they've given and given to a woman who never appreciated him. Maybe he's tried to give to you in the past but you've blocked him from doing so – so he's bang out of practice.

So Goddess... whether the man in your sphere is keen to make you happy, or you have one that has broken down along the way. I dare you to try it! Start with setting the tone on day 1 and try saying yes each time he offers to do something for you. Try it and see what happens.

Let him in a little. You will both soften and start to open up to each other again.

I was sitting on the couch with Paul, my husband, and we were talking about this, so I asked him: What should a woman expect from a man?

A note from Paul

"A woman should expect to be and feel: Loved, cared for, safe, understood, worshipped, treated like a Goddess, feel fantastic, and be fully in her power with him; she should expect to be happy, excited, encouraged, challenged, supported, adored, and of course BE herself!

One of the things I love about Marina is that I don't have to be a mind reader to know what she wants. Because she communicates what she wants and how she wants it; I easily know how to make her happy. Loving Marina is as easy as breathing. (And not just because she knows what she wants!)

Ultimately, what I think it all boils down to, when you strip away all the fluff, is that a woman should know what she wants and expect to be happy, and happy to her core! She could be with a well-meaning, wealthy, caring... fill-in-the-blank... man, but if he doesn't know how to make her happy, what difference does it make if he does X, says Y, or is Z? It's all pointless."

– Paul Leonard

Men actually love to produce for us; they love to make us happy. If a man is not worshipping your heart and YOU, he has missed his true calling. He is missing the most masculine of all his traits; *making you happy*.

It is a privilege for any man to get close enough to you – to *know how* to make you happy... and to *actually do it* and make you happy? He's living his sexy life's purpose oh là là and... he has come home to himself.

It also means he's found the freedom he longs for. His freedom isn't bound up in finally never having to work again; that won't fill him up as he fantasises it will. His freedom comes when he acts on how he was made. He was made to magnificently make you happy, so the next generation will be. Your safety and happiness are paramount to him because he was made this way.

Now at this point when I'm talking about this sort of stuff, a woman normally rolls her eyes and says, "Yeah I'm sure men do love to make us women happy *as you say*, but you haven't met my David yet, have you?" And you know what? I haven't met her bald headed bear of a husband! But, I have met plenty of women who don't know how to inspire the great man that he is. And you don't have to do anything, but set the tone of you receiving with him. That's it. You don't need an "up do" and you don't need a plunging neckline to inspire a man. Just him being *able* to make you happy is enough. And so I know that this woman *hasn't learnt* how to inspire the legend in him *yet,* or David would want to make her happy. Every day. And be thinking about ways to when he wasn't around her.

Today is a normal working Thursday and I just popped out to take a blustery walk down the beach. Do you know what I came home to? Two packs of natural hair dye with a membership card on top, one pack of chilli seaweed, a small box of chocolates, a loaf of spelt bread, and the mail. All sitting on the kitchen bench. *What?* My husband had dropped into the house quickly to surprise me.

What you don't know is that I'd been searching for that damn hair dye for over a week, and that not only had he found it, he'd gotten me a special membership card too. WOW. Did I ask him to do this? No. But does he know how happy he makes me? Yes. So I rang him. "Thank yooou!!"

Think that I'm living a life you can't possibly relate to?

I was at a dreamy summer party a few years ago. The men and women who were laughing and chatting over clinking champagne glasses as the sun went down were considered highly successful. Some were in TV and some millionaires; successful, rich, the city their oyster... OK, OK, so I wasn't at a *normal* party that even I could relate to, but bear with me...

So, I started chatting with one of the men. I knew he wasn't happy in his marriage from the way his wife would embarrassingly yell at him in public; it normally drew sniggers from all around them. So I started planting a few seeds for him to do when he got home. I really wanted to help him. He was inspired as well as unsure, but he said, "OK, I'll give it a go, but I expect she won't care." And I said to him, "Does your wife realise that you actually want to make her happy?" And he looked at me shocked and said, "No." As we continued talking, I suddenly became aware that several men had drawn closer around us, around 15 actually when I looked around and I thought, *you know what? This is invaluable research for me and my clients.*

So I stood up and started asking them lots of questions like, "Right, so out of all of you guys, whose wife actually knows that you want to make her happy?" They gathered closer and you know what they murmured, almost to themselves? "No, she doesn't know that." And I said, "So who here wants to make their wives happy? Who wants to give them everything that she wants?" And they all looked at me and said, "Yes. Yes" in unison, it was quite a moment.

I wish you could have been there with me because you would have seen the confusion in their eyes, where they wanted to make her happy and were so disappointed and undermined that they hadn't been able to yet. Not truly. I then had 15 unofficial clients huddled around me with my husband looking on smirking, knowing what I was up to, as I set about helping them to create the kind of marriage they wanted. A marriage where they make their wives happy and a marriage where she knows HOW to receive it. Afterwards my husband asked, "Do those men know how lucky they were to be at this party with you?"

And you know what? All the men I've ever met – the ones that women are in love with *and the ones that women complain about* – they ALL want to make us H.A.P.P.Y. It's in their DNA. It's just that some are better than others because some have been enlightened by you and others not... yet.

This is really about you teaching the man you are with, whether he's somebody you work with, or it's your dad or your brother... it matters not a jot – it just matters that you set the tone for your relationship with him. You appreciating what you receive from him and letting that cycle grow your relationship into one that nourishes you both. This is you living beautifully to your feminine form, which in turn means he can live to his brilliant masculine form. What a relief!

HOW TO TURN ON YOUR MAN

Want to know how to turn on your man? It's not by doing something for him, actually. It's by being turned *on* (to what you want) while in his presence. *And appreciating him, when he gives it to you.* That's it. Truly.

Let's think about it logically: If that man by your side is meant to *produce happiness for you* then it makes sense that *you're meant to reciprocate* by appreciating *every last drop of him*. Doing things for people that don't appreciate you makes you stop pretty quick doesn't it? Is any man going to want to go all out and make you happy, if you poker face it? Nopety nope! He's only human and he has feelings too, just like you do.

So your desire + asking him + appreciating him + receiving without blocking, like the Goddess you are = You turning him ON.

So your desire + your silence + complaining + doing it yourself because it's quicker = You turning him OFF and another woman turning him ON.

And you know how you turn him ON? Not by giving him anything in particular, but by giving him your desire and appreciating him when he gives it to you. Watch that man of yours turn back towards you with more energy than he's had for you in a long time, before your lack of receiving began squashing it.

So appreciation is the key for turning on both your engines!

Turn your appreciation ON:

- Show your appreciation for what he does for you. "Thank you" "I so appreciate you" "Great! I appreciate it." From taking out the bins to making you tea to sweeping you off your feet with a luxury holiday for two, thank him at least twice today. And rinse and repeat all week. Notice – what happens to your week?

- Inspire Technique: Inspire him into being his highest possibility, when he hasn't done something lovely for you. E.g. "That's not like you to swear in front of the kids," and "Oh wow, how unlike you, you're usually so good at this!" "You know how good you are at..." This turns him straight into turn on (for you.) He will rise to the occasion (yes!) Or he'll droop to your lowest irritated communication with him. Are you expecting him to make you happy right now, or are you expecting him to disappoint you? You hold the keys to this part of your relationship. Are you turning it ON or off?

↶ And what happens when you're chugging along quite nicely on the Appreciation Train and you get off on the wrong stop because you've been triggered by something? So you get off at Naggy Hill or Accusatory Mountain? It's OK; you'll get another chance, just do a 180 and hop back onto the Appreciation Train, so you travel in style non-stop straight to Turn On Town.

Let's get back to you setting the tone. As you can see from the party story, *even the most successful man* needs *you* to set the tone of *you receiving*. Otherwise whatever he produces for you will just bounce clean off you. So:

1. Remind yourself that you are *the only Goddess* in this relationship, so it can *only be you* who sets the womanly tone.
2. Remember you need to *know what you want*.
3. Communicate it to him, for him to produce it for you.
4. Then it's up to you to receive it easily. Men produce, we receive.

In unhappy relationships it's the other way around, women know what they want, communicate it to him, *who may then* produce it for her, or not. But she'll produce it anyway because it's quicker and more reliable.

Which one will strip you of your life force? Which one will make you really happy?

Shall we tone your relationship? I call it toning because you are toning it in both the emotional sense and the beautiful sense!

Let's begin. On a scale of 1–10: how much have you set the tone with him this week? Let yourself hear the answer, honestly. Would you like to deliciously increase this number, easily? Yes?

OK, pick something that you're not entirely happy with. Take this and run it through the Four Step Toning Process below:

HERE'S HOW YOU SET THE TONE:

What do I want?

How do I want it?

Ask him for what I want. (Align; Ask; Appreciate.)

Show him it's made me happy (thank him happily) or smile with teeth.

Simple, but oh so powerful! Because when you set the tone, you teach him how to treat you. And if you don't exquisitely tell him what you want? Then he's setting the tone by default. *Because you don't have the guts to share your desire with him.* He cannot read your mind. He isn't right now peering over your shoulder reading this book with you nodding in appreciation is he? He isn't going to know what your sad sullen face means on Saturday morning. He'll know you're not happy but he won't know it's because he hasn't organised a night out for you two. You might want to remind yourself of The 3 Amigos (page 79).

So, let's play with this tone setting thing this week. Let's try it with a stranger, with someone you love and with someone you work with.

STRANGER

What do I want? Good service from my waiter.

How do I want it? I want a coffee just the way I like it.

Ask him for what I want – Using The 3 Amigos:

Align – Hi there, I've heard you guys make really good coffee.

Ask – So would you personally make sure that my mocha is really thick and creamy, served in a cup not a glass and has an outrageous amount of chocolate sprinkled on top? I would so LOVE that!

Him – Sure we can do that for you no problem.

Appreciate – Thank you!

Show him it's made you happy, and don't be afraid to show him a huge smile when he says yes.

SOMEONE YOU LOVE

What do I want? I want us to spend more time together.

How do I want it? I want him to organise a special night for us.

Ask him for what I want – Using The 3 Amigos:

Align – Jonathon, you know how you like to surprise me?

Ask – I would love it if you would book us the kind of night that I have to get really dressed up for!

Him – Sure – if that's what you want – I can do that.

Appreciate – Oh fantastic, thank you!

Show him you are excited and kiss him as you leave the room...

Remember; turn your disappointment into getting what you want. Often the other person doesn't know how to make you happy in exactly the way you're yearning for. Can you put how you've been feeling aside and just ask them? Give this a try, I promise you will create the kind of relationship that is age proof when you are brave enough to ask in a way that makes you and he feel good. You both deserve to get what you want!

SOMEONE YOU WORK WITH

What do I want? I want my colleague to include me on the project, too.

How do I want it? I want to go with her on the client visit.

Ask her for what I want – Using The 3 Amigos:

Align – Barbara, I know you've been planning to go to this client visit alone.

Ask – I would really like to come with you; can I get an introduction from you?

Her – OK.

Appreciate – Thank you so much!

Show her – I'll be there at 2:00pm. Thank you for saying yes!

7-Day Toning Workout – let's try this for a week and see what happens to your relationship/s when you set the tone rather than others setting the tone for your pleasure. Do you find you have more pleasure in your week, just how you like it? I'd love to hear! Have you sprinkled lots of universal sweeties behind you as you walk, so the universe can follow you and give you what you want?

TURN YOUR LIGHT ON

Your light is b-e-a-u-t-i-f-u-l.

It's emanating from you right now. Can you feel it?

And your light has the power to simply turn your day *on or off*.

Your success on or off.

Him on or off.

Your life on or off.

Do a quick check in with yourself this minute; is your light switched on or off? Is it turned up or down? Um... who are you giving your light away to right now?

Your job?

That woman?

Him?

Your boss?

That situation?

The way you look today?

The state of your sex life?

The man you can't get?

That pay rise? The one you never get?

The one you admire? You could never be as good as her...

The male attention she gets, but never you?

Your crappy clothes?

The people in your industry who are doing *it* better than you?

The atmosphere at work?

Their judgement of you?

Him ignoring you?

Your stomach?

Are you shrinking your light to fit another? Are you shrinking your big fat desires to fit in with the practical constraints of your everyday life?

How does this hurt you *gorgeous woman?*

Imagine I'm handing you a magic wand right now. When you wave it, your dreams for yourself come true. What are they? What would that do for you and those around you if you got the success you deserve this year? What would be the best part about it?

So, what's stopping or slowing you down from being here already? Is it you? Is it them?

We are all born with the same amount of pure brilliant light. We have the same level of absolute *brilliance* at something; and we are all born with the same ability to love deeply and be loved deeply.

The difference between those that shine brightly, like those you admire, and those that do not, is because the shiners decided at some point *not to give their light away.*

... Not to give their light to somebody, or something that happened. And right now, today, they are choosing not to give their light away to a person that has their light switched off. They chose not to shrink their light to fit another, no matter whom they are talking to, no matter how bad the situation seems, regardless of what the other person is internally criticising them for.

This is real light. Your light switched ON, *no matter what.*

No matter how low in energy they are.

And what is light really? Is it the absence of dark? No, your light is your essence; both light and dark, both to be loved and celebrated. It's your "youness" shining out for all to see. And it's specific and glorious to you and no one else.

See, I told you. You are special!

You *know* when your light is fully switched ON; it's much easier for you to turn a "no" into a "yes" because *you know* as you drive out in the morning that the world is your oyster. And it matters not where you are, be it in the kitchen unloading groceries, or dancing with the love of your life under the stars tonight, your light lifts you to live your best life.

Your turning your light ON means the world gets lucky – as me and the rest of the world gets to benefit from your greatest talents; it means we don't miss out this lifetime. And we cheer when we see you at your highest, because secretly, your light gives us permission to shine our light too.

But do you ever find yourself too busy and mechanical to shine your light some days?

If you held a barometer in your hand, where it measured the level of light you *permit yourself to emit* on a daily basis, would your light be fully ON, ON, ON? Or halfway depending on whom you speak to? If it's that miserable woman in accounts, do you turn your light off because she brings you down? *It's often hard to keep your light fully on around certain depressing people like her. So really what's the point?* And what if you find that being a mum overwhelms you? And being around *him* sucks your light away? And your job takes more than it gives? How can you shine your light brightly, when you've got all this stuff dimming it?

A great deal of every day is spent navigating situations and talking to people. We women are gloriously sensitive, which is needed to nurture the next generation, a project, someone, etc. Our sensitivity is one of our best feminine traits, but during conversations and situations it also lends itself to the – *it must be me* – side-effect of sensitivity. You're more likely to take things personally. And if you take everything personally? You will go up and down like a yoyo and give your light away; like a date cancelling on you, a client cancelling on you, a friend not inviting you to her party, your boss telling you you've been passed over for promotion, and your kid shouting that they hate you!

And you know what else dulls your light quicker than reaching for chocolate, only to find that some other chocolate termite finished it? That at some point when you were younger, you deftly decided, "You know what? *What makes me, ME, isn't as good as I first thought,"* because, "I'm not good at math; no one really likes me at school; men leave me; I don't have many people that truly *see me* in my life; I'm not where I thought I'd be by now. Um, if I'm honest my light has dimmed a bit over the passing years with disappointment and just life, really."

"My essence isn't shining as bright as when I was little because these things have taken away from it. Sure, when I get that man/house/pay rise/pain in my back sorted I'll feel happier, but I know my light isn't going to become as shiny bright as a 6 years olds again. I mean how can it when we're haemorrhaging money; I'm invisible at work, and nobody seems to genuinely care about me? I feel like I'm a bad mother at night because I passionately detest the bath/bed routine. I am my own worst enemy and I can't shake off the past".

How can I shine when I have all these things bothering me?

Goddess, you SHINE by not taking everything that does or doesn't happen to you, *personally.*

Your light switches on strongly when you stop placing a meaning on yourself each time something happens.

What do you make it mean about you when someone lets you down?

What do you make it mean about you when someone says no to you?

We women can slip so suddenly into becoming that thing that's happened to us, like we must be worthless because he left us. We must not be good enough because... That's why I used to walk on the beach most mornings to remind myself that I was not what was happening to me. (And I had to remind myself most mornings.)

If you didn't give your light away with each thing that happened to you, would you see each situation as it is?

A divine learning experience, camouflaged as a sticky situation. Remember: the world is always conspiring to turn you on.

Do you really want to spend the rest of your life switching your light on and off like a car indicator each time something goes your way or not? Because it's not her or them that switches your light off, it's not the situation that turned your light off: *it's you.*

It's you that decided you weren't very good because of what happened. *They* might be saying it, but it's only you that has access to that switch –

no one else, so it's only you that can turn it on. Properly. For good!

So if it's only you that has turned your light off, if it's only you that decided to turn the essence of you down...

... Then that kind of lets *them* off the hook doesn't it? It means you can love them and let them love you hugely or hate you with spitey venom – for it has no power over you – you're free. They have no power over you anymore.

I once had a client, *Sharon*, who had a boss that made putting her down an Olympic sport. Daily. He was the gold medallist. And she didn't know why because she was doing such an amazing job at work! Everyone said so. Except for him. The gold medallist was a millionaire and had a life she could only dream of. But unknown to her, he was secretly in awe at just how many customers she bought to his company, which made him embarrassed because he could *never do what she did in the lovely easy way she did it*. He made her success mean that he wasn't good enough. You know what he did? He came to me for coaching and man did he switch on his light. Woopla! Now, when he steps up to the podium to accept gold, it's for non-light squashing reasons. He is level with *Sharon*, neither outshone nor insecure. And that is how a real company becomes really rich. By letting each member of staff shine their light and rewarding them for it, rather than squashing it and keeping them down.

Decide to switch your light ON. You deserve it. You will always win when your light is turned on. You may want to turn it down at various times in your life; for example, to protect yourself in a dangerous situation, but your light is *YOU*. And, you turn the world on when you turn your light on, including him!

IMMUNITY NECKLACE

I'm a big fan of the TV show "Survivor" where they give an immunity necklace to someone who won a challenge. This immunity necklace stops your light being snuffed out. So it got me thinking; could I give you a powerful necklace that would make you immune to the diminished light in another? So you didn't get affected by their dense, unhappy energy during a conversation?

Question: On the light scale of 1–10, how much of your light do you allow yourself to shine in each interaction with the 5 closest people to you? Pick a number. What about if you're talking to someone whose light switched off long ago?

Do you shrink your light to fit them?

I'm walking over to you now and I'm placing the immunity necklace around you, à la Jeff Probst, and it's this: Stay in your own stream of love, laughter, and happiness. If people around you are grumpy or downright nasty, don't ever drop down to where they are because they've dropped out of their own stream and have weakened themselves. Yes, you can cry, shout, and scream for your own life because you are a delicious woman after all! But do not drop to their diminished light stream; you can only help them when you are GLOWING in your own light. Stay in your stream by laughing and treading softly, by talking in a way that gives you pleasure, and by remembering to come back to delicious you when you've gone too far into someone else's stream that is darker than yours. Doesn't that feel more sumptuous to your heart anyway?

So I dare you to SHINE your light rather than SHRINK to fit others today. Don't turn off your light for anyone – it doesn't suit you Goddess!

Let's self-heal:

What's syphoning your light away? What makes it dim? Make a list. Why? Look at each thing on your list, what are you making each situation to mean about you?

Example:

I'm left with all the dishes in the sink after everyone's gone to work/school. *I make this to mean about me* – that if I was a successful businesswoman we would *all know,* that I wouldn't have time for this, and the others would pitch in every morning. But, because they don't and because I just let them leave, it's that unsaid thing that completely affirms my failings as a business owner.

You might be surprised at what is syphoning your light on your list. I know I was the first time I looked at mine. Maybe you jump a little with each sharp trill of your phone? Or, you feel anxious in your stomach as your e-mails download? Or even, just thinking about *that person*, that constant situation *with him*, that pain in your body? Notice what or who you give your light away to. *Clarity is the ability in that moment to turn your light back up.* Ask yourself: at what age did I decide to dim my light? Let yourself hear the answer and trust the first number that comes to you. Why? What was happening around you at that time? It's time for you to reclaim your light! It's yours, it always was.

So let's reclaim your light. Go look in the mirror: what do you look like when your light is shining brightly? How can you tell? What would it do for you and those close to you if you switched your light back ON with him? In your marriage? Relationship? Health? Career? Would you dress differently? Mirror, "I am the light." Do that until you know unequivocally that you are.

Make a list of 3 people you admire. What is it about them that you admire? (It's always their delicious light that you're attracted to, which you haven't fully ROCKED within yourself yet!) So try this. Here's an example to get you in the groove:

E.g. A famous actress:

Her luminous quality

Her beauty

Her success

Go to process C "I wish I was more..." (on page 143) and run these traits through, so you turn your light ON! You're freer than you think to rock your light wherever you are.

FALL IN LOVE WITH YOUR DARK SIDE

You're just like a HOT pink flower! You too need the sun and the rain to flourish. The sun reflects your light side and the rain reflects your dark side to you. And make no mistake, you gotta LOVE both because you're made to! Without sunlight you cannot show your beautiful self to the world; and, without rain oh no... you Dry-out and become brittle, until you... SNAP!

Ahhh... Goddess, it is time for you to fall in love with the rain inside of you and to really own your brilliant shining light. You are nothing without one and everything with the other. The psychotherapist and psychiatrist, Carl Jung once said, "It is better to be whole than good." My grandfather, who knew Carl Jung, was closely associated with him. Hans Jacoby, an analytical psychologist, renowned graphologist, and author of many books knew back then in the 1930s that this was true. My grandmother Marianne Jacoby, (who also knew Jung) was an eminent Jungian psychotherapist in the 1940s, '50s, '60s, '70s, '80s, '90s and '00s and founding member of the British Association of Psychology; she spent her whole working life guiding people like you and me to come back to their whole selves. Falling in love with yourself just the way you are will make you that HOT pink flower *and then some*. And hating bits of you is to rip your petals off, one by one, *shredding you* into tiny pieces.

Really, what is there to hate about you? You were made perfect, I promise you. And before those voices inside your head that say "Yeah but what about my..." I'm gonna scream "WAIT!"

Breathe. Stay with me here. Every flower needs her rain and sun to truly flourish and grow, just like you.

You are made up of lots of sunshiny parts: like your happy-go-lucky self, your kindness, your fun self, your charisma, your genius, your beauty, intuition, and so on. All the things *you love* that you are, plus all the things that you'd love to be more of. This is your light. And you're also made up of the rainy parts of you: such as your procrastination, your anger, laziness, the bitchy you, your nastiness, the pathetic, ugly, stupid and depressive you. Basically, those parts you don't like people to see, that you're ashamed of, or that you feel bad about. This is the dark part of you that you judge and spend a lot of time hiding from the world.

Constricting little girls to constricting little lives

For most little girls, we grew up with the story of being a good girl and good girls were taught that it was better to only be the sweet sunny part and not the troublesome dark rainy part of ourselves.

Remember? *"Be a good girl Sally* and run along..." "Oh, isn't she sweet?" "Have you been a *good girl* today?" As we got older, we cried less and less and hid our fears more and more. We were taught, "To use our words" rather than shout when we were angry. Anger unsettled the adults around us, so we learned that we shouldn't do that too much. We realised that being the dark part of ourselves seemed to upset people, they didn't like us as much, so we learnt to hide them. When we did let out our anger, it was judged by others as ugly. When we did cry a lot, we got called a cry-baby, so we stopped. When we showed too much fear, we got laughed at.

Pretty soon we realised which feelings were deemed ugly and which were not. As we grew up, we decided it was better and safer to show our sunny selves to the world and become our rainy selves at home when no one was looking. But, because we knew they were ugly, we treated them as ugly now and berated ourselves for feeling that way. We would eat crap at night and do other deviously creative stuff that no one knew about to push down our rainy feelings, so *even we* would not feel them. Because in the old ethos we grew up with THEY WERE NOT ALLOWED in the amounts we wanted to let them out in. So we held our breath, and we held them in.

And when we made new relationships with boys who then became men, we decided that instead of showing our ugly feelings to them; we would hold them in, in case he left us. Because we kind of left ourselves too when we let them out. Because they were sooo ugly. And the shiny people in the magazines certainly didn't have them. And the rock stars taped to our walls didn't show them. And if that pop star saw us blobbing out on the couch, he would go "euwww" at us. And if my lover saw what I did when I got my period, I think he'd judge me. I think he'd love me a bit less, worship me a bit less. I don't think he could handle me when I'm a hormonal mess, sitting in pain on the toilet or if I'm crying about something on my bed. And if I showed this rainy part of me at work to my boss, I wouldn't be the favoured one anymore.

But see, when you hate something, you give it power. When you love something, it transforms into the most beautiful thing.

What if you *could* love your poker hot anger? Would it protect you more? Would your 16-year-old self have been able to say "No" with conviction to *Kenny* when he asked if he could touch you there?

What if instead of feeling bad that we are down and depressed today, we LOVE it? Because it's our barometer for when we need to stop and receive what we really needed?

If you loved every bad feeling you have right now and felt right about feeling it, wouldn't it be a relief? *Darling, it is the difference between flourishing sometimes and all of the time.*

It's you loving YOU when you simply cannot stop crying. So, instead of blubbing, "Sorry, I'm c-c-crying so much I'm getting your shirt all w-wet" and holding yourself back *just enough (pretty crying like they do in films)*; instead, you grab onto that man, you let him be your rock and roar yourself crying, you howl your lungs out like a banshee. So he really feels you. So you really feel you.

Would you feel better after ugly crying loudly? *Hell yeah.* Let him see all of you and start loving your rain, which can only bring him closer to you. Isn't that what we all want? Hiding our feelings isolates us. The more you let your feelings out, the more used to it you will become. And then? It becomes good to cry. Good to say no. Exquisite to express how you feel.

Take *Sarah*, a 35-year-old business owner. She likes to be her sunny side at work, which is her pro-active, dynamic, gregarious and successful self.

She flicks her long wavy blonde hair with the confidence of a gleaming professional *because that's what she is.* She hates showing her rainy side, which seeps out of her once she sets foot through the door after a hard days' work; she drops her bags down on the floor, she is tired, snappy, cold, and withdrawn. She says to her partner that she's given the best of herself to her day and that's why it comes out. But has she?

Let's see: Because *Sarah* only allows herself to be her sunny side at work, she brushes off any rainy feelings, so she doesn't take the cues that she needs to take breaks when she needs to; she says "Yes, of course" to them when she wants to say no; she worries about upsetting people *all the time,* so she often says, "Oh, that's alright," when really she wants to say, "No, this is not fucking alright with me." But she doesn't have the ovaries to do this see? Her days are sunshiny and her nights are rainy. And because she doesn't like herself when she's low, tired and flat *she eats.* By 8:00pm, she's in front of the box with an array of munchies by her side. *Well I've earned it,* she thinks, looking forward to blotting out the uncomfortable feelings inside with sweets and a sit-com.

What if *Sarah* loved her rainy side? Would she be able to say *no* with delicious gusto to that high maintenance client? Would she show her co-workers her vulnerability, so they could be more aware of her feelings? If she loved her rain – could she, or would she *be it* more during the day, to lovingly protect herself? So she wouldn't break agreements with herself? Is it possible that when she loves her rain she is free to use it for her good?

And what about you and him? How does this exactly work?

Juliette and *Elvis* had been married for 18 years. He loved the fact that Juliette wasn't like the other wives he heard about in his office. She was like a beacon of light compared to them. She'd made a real home for him and their three children while running a small business. She looked after herself and he was still really attracted to her, he *still* couldn't believe she'd chosen him. *Him!* Compared to her angelic sunshine, he often felt like the grumpy rainmaker. Irritable, igniting arguments with his children when he got home. *Juliette* would always calm the whole lot of them down, she *really* was their sunshine and that's what he calls her, "My darling sunshine." *Juliette* meanwhile loved her husband, but often felt freer as soon as he left the house in the morning; parenting and running the household was much simpler when he was away. She didn't like how strict he was with the kids and she hated the way he often berated himself for not being a good enough man for her, and she had to be careful in the way she talked to other men because he would often get jealous.

They came to me for relationship coaching and I saw that they were two sides of the same coin.

She was the sunny side on the left and he was the rainy side on the right. She needed to also be the rainy side on the right, so that creating boundaries with her children felt good. If she avoids setting boundaries by making excuses for them, *nothing changes*. And we ask, *"Why does she gloss over the bad behaviour from her children?"* The answer is of course *because she can't be with her rainy pain; she'd rather gloss over it* for a short-term "sunnier life".

> When you feel your pain fully and are honest with yourself, you will always make the right decision.

Elvis meanwhile needed to do the opposite: he needed to infuse himself with his own sunshine. Yes, he was good enough, she'd been with him for 18 years, wasn't that proof enough? He needed to place more importance on being his sunny side and then they can use both sides of themselves when needed, which takes away the pressure that is so often put on one parent to be the disciplinarian, or to be the one who smooths things out all the time. And just like money, being both sides of a coin is way more valuable to those you love, than just being one. So the question is: are you brave enough to try something new? We're going to talk some more now, but head over to page 177 for process T – "Diamonds are a girl's best friend", if you want to fall in love with your dark side now.

WILL BAD THINGS HAPPEN TO ME IF I'M NEGATIVE?

A special note to those of you who have been taught it's good to be positive and bad to be negative. We judge ourselves so harshly when we feel negative. So much so that we feel guilty and worry that something bad might happen to us if we continue being negative. I call it LWG: AKA Light Workers Guilt.

Did you know: it's actually your judgment of your negative side that is actually the problem? Not, your actual negative side? So while your girlfriend is apologising to you, *the inside of your head might look like this:* "I can't believe she did this, what a bitch! She knows how I feel about this!" The outside of you though sounds like this: "It's okaaaay. I *know you* didn't mean it!" So you trying to be positive and nice to your girlfriend; and hating yourself for thinking bitchy thoughts *means you must be selfish and thoughtless towards yourself.* And not stand up for yourself. And not show her that you have feelings, too. As if you don't matter.

So by trying to be positive, you're being super negative anyway – to YOU! Like a lot of light workers I know, *Moira* a 58-year-old business analyst wonders why life isn't kinder to her. *It's because she stopped being kind to herself years ago.*

Another woman I know called *Danielle* often refers to herself as a "really positive person". She is strict with herself and tells herself off internally when she starts to feel negative. "Stop it stupid, now you're just going to attract more crap!" When she can't think positive, she just withdraws from everything.

Can you see that the meanness is just directed inwards with positive people?

Goddess, your negativity is within you for *the whole ride,* it's never going to leave you. So, you may as well make friends with it.

After all, if *you* trying to be *positive* had worked by now, you wouldn't still be feeling negative, would you? Even in this moment?

You'd never feel it again.

So the answer? Make friends with each negative part of you, so each part of you can finally add to you. You're now free to use each part of you with grace: Like your LOUD anger when you powerfully warn a 14-year-old boy to back off and STOP bullying a boy for being fat. *You stop the bully in his tracks. The world is cheering you.* Or when walking down a darkened alley and you need to put your, *"Don't fuck with me face"* on for protection.

Make friends with your negative side, you were made with every negative trait so that you may put it to good use. Love it and you can. Nothing bad ever happened from feeling your negativity fully in one sitting. But do expect to make the right decision for yourself. Not allowing yourself to feel how crap you really do feel will only delay your happiness. And so it gets harder and harder to feel "positive."

Let me explain: staying anything for very long – including making yourself stay positive when frankly you're not feeling it – isn't good for any of us.

Because you negate your truth when you're positive all the time.

You don't hear how you really feel, so you can't really act on it. There are millions of "positive women" everywhere putting a *positive spin* on everything all the time and for the millionth time; they are stuck again. You were given your negative feelings for a reason and so the more you feel those negative feelings, *the less they stick around* – because they don't need to see? *You've heard them.*

You want to find yourself sliding between feelings easily: like happy, sad, crappy and then happy again, just like you did as a kid. That's still you and as long as you don't talk yourself out of feeling negative, you'll put it to good use. Make friends with your dark side so it has no power over you anymore.

Do yourself a favour and come back to being natural again. All of you is made to be loved, because all of you has a purpose and this darling, is real self-love.

SO YOU'RE HAVING A BAD DAY...

... Good! Because we're going to celebrate the crap out of it!

... And if you're reading these words right now thinking, "Nope, *I'm good thanks.*" Can you remember a time when you weren't? Might have been yesterday? Can you? Yes? Good! Because you're going to learn about real self-healing here. *The type that will transform you and your future.*

I'm not talking about the type of healing where you see someone once a week and talk it out, so you get clear on what your issues are and learn to "be" with it. No. I'm talking about deep transformation inside you, the type of healing that once you've done it, there is no need for positive affirmations every morning in front of the mirror, or talking yourself into being positive.

You. Just. Are.

(Healed already)

You were made to. So, off we go: let's heal your sticky.

What do I mean by the sticky?

I mean the sticky stuff that is sticking to you – look at you – it's the stuff that's hurting you right now, like that thorn in your side that's stopping you from being 100% happy, putting a cloud over your day today, *over your life.* It's as if you're sitting in a bath of sludge, and no matter what you do to get out of it with "positive thinking," it remains stuck to you. It isn't washing off, is it? You are stuck with the sticky!

So, no matter where you go: why you could be in a glorious room full of shiny happy people, but you have gloop all over you invisibly sticking to your nice new dress. It doesn't matter where you go today, you're going to be thinking about it, or you're going to try *not thinking* about it.

If you're in the sticky, it's just going to come with you, a little like a toxic friend because it's stuck to you see? I never understand those people who "like to keep busy," when they are in pain because they haven't realised yet that they can heal their pain 100%, so they try to ignore it instead, only to bring it into every situation and conversation. Oh it's there all right, *everyone can feel it.*

Have you ever had a conversation with someone and walked away and felt heavy, or not quite right? Even though the person was smiling? It's because *you* are feeling their sticky stuff creep in between you - as they tell you how good it all is. I remember bumping into an old friend of mine. As he told me *how great it was all going in his shop*, and how busy it was getting, all I could hear was his pain. My body reacted first and I was suddenly tired. Without realising what I was doing, I looked down to see my hand already over his squeezing it and I heard myself say, "What's really going on?" His eyes immediately filled with tears and, he said, "I have throat cancer again. They just told me this morning, it's come back," and his voice cracked.

This is his sticky, it was stuck to every happy word he told me and yes I am pleased to say he totally healed himself from it.

So, let's get real. Let's dive in together. If you've procrastinated over doing anything about this, I invite you to stop delaying the healing (by telling yourself it's going to be alright or whatever you do or say to stop feeling it). It's there. It's here. It's in you and it's in me. My mentor had a great saying that I love to use with my clients. She said, "Stop putting ice cream on top of poo!"

If I give you ice cream while your knee is bleeding, your knee is still bleeding. If I give you a proper homeopathic cream to put onto your knee to properly help it heal plus a plaster, then you are healing and you can enjoy your ice cream. It's very difficult to look up and be inspired by life when your body and heart down there are hurting. To plaster over your hurt with positive affirmations, laughter, pleasure, sex, and a good night out is wonderful and so needed. It works for a while until your sticky rears its ugly head again and just comes right on back. Because it's still there, *it never went away*, you just plastered over it with nice stuff.

> Feel the ugly feelings; they'll get you much closer to healing than pretending they don't exist.

If you're in pain right now, the kindest action for you is to be brave and travel to the core of it. And it doesn't have to be scary. *Although it might be.* Although what's scariest is carrying it around with you for a minute longer...

How interested are you in your happiness? Interested enough to go there with me, even if it scares your pants off? Because it's exciting to know that you can self-heal anything!

Turning your ability to self-heal *on*, will stop you wasting your energy for a good portion of your day and give you the genuine healing you crave plus the confidence to navigate your own life's ups and downs. Which also means you're going to get to your desires quicker...

Now, I've done enough talking about this: I know, I know! Oh, but just one more thing before I forget: just know you can heal anything 100%, so why would you deny yourself the right to heal, by denying it right now? *You're worthy of healing this.*

Let's get back to you:

If you're in the midst of a bad day and it's following you around right now – shrouding you in a grey cloud, so each conversation and each situation you have today feels heavy, start by congratulating yourself right now. Deeply, from within. Go on, congratulate yourself. *Right now.*

Because it means you are on your way up. So, well done you! (More about this on the next page, stay with me here.) For now, breathe in, and then breathe out the day you've had so far. It's OK, you're in it and you're in it with me. Together you and I are going to heal you. Actually I am having a particularly bad day today, so you are not alone; I am right with you!

BEFORE YOU SELF-HEAL, GET CLEAR:

1. So, what's upsetting you right now? Name it. Say it out loud to yourself. "I am upset with... because..." Give yourself space to say it out loud now. *All of it.* The tiny shitty bits and the big shitty bits. You might have eaten that chocolate/done that thing again... when you said you wouldn't. Have you let yourself down again? Has someone upset you? Have they not given you what you want? Are they saying nasty things behind your back? Is a situation really getting you down? Has someone close to you died or are they not very well?

2. Now write this out in a few sentences. This is really important: don't just think it, it goes no-where, but back into you when you only think it. And do you really want to be carrying it around with you like a clumsy shopping bag, dragging you down like that? (You're way too beautiful to be carrying heaviness.)

3. *Feel it. What's the feeling?*

4. *Bring these feelings into the next couple of pages till we self-heal.*

I'm going to show you what having a bad day could look like when you decide to self-heal, so you only flourish: Because having a bad day can be one of the best things to happen to you; from where I sit, I might be having a bad day, but actually because I know what to do, it's becoming a very powerful day for me. And I have to tell you, today of all days I feel as if I've had my heart ripped out. I feel really, really sad.

So to do this, I have to feel what I feel. I'm not going to talk myself out of it with, "It's OK, it'll get better" and I don't want you to either. Never EVER be afraid to feel your darkest deepest pain. Give yourself permission to fully feel *all* of it right now, in ALL its SLUDGY GLORY!

Because it's here that some of your best decisions *will be made*. When you are honest with how you feel, you *can only* make the right decision for you.

And it's OK; whatever is or isn't happening to you right now, you are not alone. Even if you feel you are. Breathe that in. You are not very far from healing this 100% even if you feel there is no hope.

Because...

... *You are made to heal*. Did you know that? You might know this from the cut you had on your knee when you were little. Is it still on your knee? Nope, it's gone; there's a faded scar now, but you healed from it, didn't you? Your body is made to heal and so is your soul.

Yes, breathe that in: There is *nothing that cannot be healed* within you.

That is my belief and your belief deep down. I have seen women who have healed themselves of illness and women who have healed themselves from the most violent abuse to their heart. I have seen bankrupt women go on to double their income each year.

I have seen other women not heal from illness, nor a broken heart, nor from bankruptcy. What is the difference?

It is not what happened to them, it is *how* they dealt with it.

There is *nothing* in *you* that cannot be healed, unless you don't want it to be so.

Would you like it to be so?

Then, what is your choice?

To heal? Woooo! Congratulations!!! If you choose to *not* heal, because of_____, then it's best to skip this chapter. You'll come back when you are ready to face yourself and heal the sticky. You deserve to, darling, and I hope you do.

And if you choose to heal your sticky today?

꿈 The painful dynamic of *this situation* – GONE. Emptied out. You've transformed your patterns of behaviour, painful dynamics, hurt, and emotional blocks. The highest good has happened to you so you are flourishing again in this situation. Accept nothing less than a complete and deep 100% healing.

- Side effects of you healing 100%?
- PEACE.
- To be free again and to receive everything you want. *Because there is nothing in your way anymore.*
- Your light is turned back ON.
- You find yourself glowing with happiness again.
- You look younger today and your skin has that kind of sexy sheen that makes you look like you've just been on holiday.
- He, she, or they are treating you like a Goddess again because your relationship with yourself and others has healed.
- Hey your MOJO is back!
- So you've learnt to resolve conflict quicker and can use it to create deeper emotional security within.
- Knowledge that you've turned your ability to self-heal ON has embedded solid confidence in you.
- You've become twice the woman you were because now you know how to navigate your life successfully.
- You get to create a life that turns you on. You know, the one that makes you really happy and it's stopped being that elusive feeling for you.

TURN ON YOUR SELF-HEALING

First Course Self-Healing – First thing we always do is...

1. **Celebrate your brilliance** because this sticky = you must be on your way up, even if you don't feel it right now! How clever are you to have invited this situation to you? Stickiness means you are *so ready* to have a better life than before. *Yes, really!*

2. **Wrap your arms** around you; your self-love will keep you warmest on this coldest of days. Be gentle with yourself. This *is* what self-love feels like. Don't beat yourself up. It's happened.

3. **Decide that you are in the right place now. Say out loud,** "My feelings are right and I am right to feel this way" (no matter how weird you feel, don't make your feelings wrong, that's just a double whammy you don't need). Your feelings will feel big and overwhelming at this point; this is always what it feels like in the beginning; like the sticky might just stick forever to you and you'll never get out of it. You will.

4. **Decide to heal.** Out loud affirm to yourself: "I am healing this right now."

And we're going to begin by creating a healing room inside of you. This only needs to be done once and it forms the basis of your self-healing that you will find yourself using again and again:

HOW TO USE YOUR HEALING ROOM

You were made to heal. I've created a free audio for you to listen to so you can create your healing room inside you now. It's at marinaj.net (remember to use your special code TYOGoddess to access it!) Press play on the audio now. Let's visualise and brilliantly create a healing room inside of you, where you can go any time of day or night to heal yourself beautifully. You are a Goddess and you deserve a beautiful way to heal YOU always.

When you're ready, gently close your eyes and breathe 10 breaths slowly into your belly, so you get really relaxed. Then, see, sense, or imagine this room (it matters not whether you see, sense or imagine at this deep level; *how* your wisdom comes to you is always how it needs to come, trust it) so make your healing room exactly as you want it, particular to you and no one else. Have in here anything that will heal you. My healing room has large crystals hanging down with the sun pouring through them. It is where I go to heal, and I make it so that it's a place of pure bliss for me. I love coming here.

Take your time and make yours really special, just for you! You can go all designer or all spiritual; it might be a mass of swirly colour's or just you in a blank canvas. You might have a pink chaise longue in there; a golden throne encrusted with huge jewels, or choose to sit on a big ball of light. There are no rules, just what feels heavenly to you. Go ahead and create your own healing room complete with healing seat and table – any which way you wish. If you see it and it gives you pleasure, then its right for you.

If you're more a feeling person than a visual one, create a safe feeling space inside of you, one that is like a blank canvas for you to go heal in anytime you want.

You are safe here to be you and it's here that you come to create your life exactly as you want it. Take a moment to look around you: what does it all look like? What feeling have you created here?

OK, gently come up and out of your healing room and open your eyes; *however you saw it or felt it is perfect for you.*

HEALING ROOM

To heal, we need to have a conversation with you at a very deep level and who do we talk to? All the different parts of you! It's the easiest way for you to hear yourself. So when you're in your healing room, know that all the different parts of you are in the waiting room at the back, waiting to be loved by you. Some of them you want to meet, some of them you don't. But each is needed. Remember, each and every part of you is just a friend you haven't made yet.

Are you ready to fall in love with these friends? And so, all of you? I know that each part of you: like the scared part, the jealous part, the idiot part, the not good enough part, the part of you that feels so very ashamed for what you are doing, and all the sunshiny parts of you, like your complete and utter beauty, your massive talent, and your 'Queen like worthiness' all need to be met, accepted, and loved. *That in actual fact,* instead of hurting or scaring you, they'll become your friends, *all of them.*

The way in which you heal is very important. We're going to go deep, you and me. All the following techniques are exquisite and really work if you follow them to the letter.

You need a process from the opposite page because:

Something has happened externally to you.

We are going to use everything painful that has happened to you, or is happening to you now to heal beautiful you 100%. So come to your healing room exactly as you are, scared, worried, exhausted by it all, bloody angry, or...??

Or

You just know an internal shift is needed.

The second way of healing is because you simply want more for yourself, so it's not triggered by anything in particular; this is your internal self-love talking!

MENU

MAIN COURSE SELF-HEALING: WHAT WILL IT BE TODAY?

Choose from A–T: Which healing process do you need?

1. Healing Room Healing (From Page 142)

A – I am hurt by you because...

B – Why does this keep happening to me?

C – Wish I was more... (e.g. confident, intuitive...).

D – I just want to go to my healing room and see what pops up.

E – You're bugging me! The Love Bug Technique.

F – Turn on the shower of sequins.

2. Flourishing when you're fucked off! (From Page 149)

G – Get your anger out NOW!

H – Go fuck yourself! Arguments.

I – Un-sticking your sticky situation.

J – Quick un-stick!

K – Quick un-stick for you and him.

3. Extras (From Page 156)

L – What am I secretly ashamed of?

M – Be inspired by my best Goddess me!

N – Become the best friend I ever had.

O – Turn-on process.

P – Short turn-on process.

Q – Belief be-friender.

R – Down in the dumps?

S – Self-sabotage.

T – Diamonds are a girl's best friend.

Once you've chosen the process you most need, then you're ready to begin. Flick to that page and remember before each healing you do, gently close your eyes and breathe 10 breaths slowly into your belly, so you are fully relaxed. During the healing, you can go as deep as you want and know that however you see, sense or imagine this part of you is perfect for you. They are a genuine part of you so it doesn't matter if you don't see them, if you've asked to meet a part of you, they will show up and you'll just know they are there. If you don't hear your answer, it's OK, know that asking the question is enough for the healing to begin. Remember, they're going to become a good friend to you. After you've completed the healing gently come out, squeeze your fingers and toes and firmly feel that you are back in the room:

1. HEALING ROOM HEALING

A – I AM HURT BY YOU BECAUSE... (Write down how they've hurt you.)

1. So, I feel... (write down, then close eyes to feel fully).
2. Healing Room – meet the feeling. It's a part of you – who is it?
3. They need to be listened to; ask them, "Why are you here?"
4. How are you actually trying to guide and help me?
5. What's my next step? Why? How will this help me?
6. Commit to beginning this act of self-love in the next 24 hours.
7. Thank your new friend, choose to understand, like, or love them.

B – WHY DOES THIS KEEP HAPPENING TO ME?

1. In real life you are treating me like...
2. Healing Room, meet the part of you who treats you the same way.
3. What does she do to you?
4. Why, what does she believe is true?

5. Is she treating you like a Goddess?

6. Have you been treating her like a Goddess? Time to make friends.

7. Ask her, "How are you trying to help me?"

8. What does she need from you to be at peace with you?

9. Pledge to do this as an act of self-love in the next 24 hours.

10. How will you know that you're doing it, or have done it?

11. Thank your new friend, choose to understand, like, or love them?

C – WISH I WAS MORE... (e.g. confident, intuitive...)

1. Healing Room, who do you need to meet to help you with this?

2. What do they want you to know?

3. What's my next step? Why? How will this help me?

4. Commit to beginning this act of self-love in the next 24 hours.

5. Thank your new friend, choose to understand, like, or love them?

D – I JUST WANT TO GO TO MY HEALING ROOM AND SEE WHAT POPS UP

1. Healing Room, meet part of you who most needs to be healed. We will call her *current you.*

2. Ask her, how much goodness is she currently willing to let into this part of your life on a scale of 1–10?

3. Invite *successful you* in this area of your life to come.

4. Let *successful you* show *current you* how letting in 10/10 goodies into this area of your life will benefit *current you.*

5. Let a Q & A take place, where *successful you* talks *current you* into letting in a higher level of goodness.

6. Will *current you* raise to 8, 9, 10/10? Keep going until it rises.

7. Finish at the highest level of success you are comfortable with.

8. Write down whatever your heart tells you to.

Healing Room Healing D – For example:

Imagine you are sitting in your healing seat. What would you like to heal today? Bring forth a particular situation that's been bothering you, or a belief you want to heal. Now I want you to imagine there is a waiting room next to your healing room and this room contains the next part of you, the you that you most need to heal. We'll call her *current you*. Let's bring her out and see/sense, or imagine her coming out from the waiting room and into a seat opposite you at your table. Who is she? For example, is she the part of you in charge of your career? Your success with men? Your success with women? Is she your gatekeeper to receiving? Is she your block on receiving more money, more happiness? Is she your confidence, your power, or your motivation? It could be any part of you, trust what comes up for you, it's always right! Seat her opposite left. This is the part of you currently in charge of this area of your life. Does she look like she's having a good time? Mostly, she won't be. Ask her how much goodness she is currently allowing into this part of your life on a scale of 1–10?

Now please invite *successful you* who is already successful in this area of your life to sit to your right and tell *current you* why it would benefit her to let in a full 10/10 of success. Why would it benefit her to let more goodies in, what would she get? Then let a conversation naturally take place, where the two parts of you talk it out until *successful you* convinces *current you* to let in as much goodness as she dares to. What number is she willing to go to? An 8, 9, or 10? See her open up and expand to receive more. Thank her for being Team (insert your name here) and Yaaaay! Your subconscious has caught up with your conscious mind. You are all on the same team now. Hug yourself and gently open your eyes. Write down whatever your heart tells you to.

E – YOU'RE BUGGING ME! THE LOVE BUG TECHNIQUE

I called it this because when someone bugs you, you're going to turn it into L.O.V.E. This technique allows you to THRIVE every single time there is conflict. Because every time there is conflict, every time *they* exhibit behaviour that *hurts you, upsets you, annoys you, or squashes you*; I want you to immediately say to yourself:

"I give myself permission to fall in love with that part of me too"

Because this is an opportunity to LOVE that part of me that I find so abhorrent in them. And that's how I want you to think! I want you to rub your hands in glee – every conflict; every upset means more of you to LOVE. This is YOU evolving. (And this is real self-love.) Even the bits you think you're gonna hate!

Goddess, the more of YOU that you can genuinely LIKE today, the more of YOU, you can love; the less people need to show up in your life displaying these traits *because you've healed your resistance to them within yourself.* So, no internal resistance means the outside world will no longer need to show you the part of YOU that you need to love because you've done it! Baby, you've evolved.

And once you've done The LOVE Bug Technique? If a person comes into your orbit super angry with you? They'll have no power over you anymore. You're at peace with that emotion of anger in you because you understand it; you love it because it helps you in certain situations. So you will have the same level of compassion for them as you do with yourself. It doesn't mean you condone what they do, but you will be able to stand tall in their presence, stay in your power during a conversation, and state clearly whatever you wish. Now you can use this process inside your healing room, or do it consciously with your eyes open. You are free! So choose a person who hurts you:

1. What annoys and bugs you about them? (Pick one trait.)
2. Where is that in me? Do I like being this, or do I judge myself for being this?

3. If this trait were a person walking into the room right now, what would she look and be like? How can she be a friend to you?

4. In what area of your life can you use this trait to help you?

5. How can you use this trait as an act of self-love in the next 24 hours?

6. Permission to L.O.V.E. my new friend because she helps me.

7. You've caught the L.O.V.E. BUG! Spread it around!

Oooooo, you've just filled yourself up with more acceptance and love. Congratulations Goddess! Rinse and repeat with all the other things that annoy you about them for more and more LOVE. Notice what you feel inside; does it feel as if your chest has expanded? Many of my clients report this and it's as if the body reacts immediately. If you don't feel anything it doesn't matter, it will work whether you feel it or not. Now you'll be able to support yourself in the moment and you'll also see through their pain and have compassion for them. *Because when somebody does this to you? It means they're in pain.*

Fancy an example of how this stuff works?

Well, let's say you work in an office where the payroll staff are bitchy and complain a lot. The Moaning Minnies! They invite you to join them on their way out to lunch most days, but you decline to go and choose to eat lunch at your desk (just so as to avoid them).

1. What annoys you about them? Bitchy.

2. Where is that in me? Are you doing this to yourself or another? I'll walk past a woman and think, "You definitely don't have the legs for that skirt!" I hate that I say it, but I can't help it! I'm such a bitch sometimes!

3. The bitchy part of me would look all slanty eyed and super bitchy. She'd be one of those superior looking women who are quick to air your faults. Bitchy Cow, that's her name. God, I hate her. OK, big breath, *I know she can become a friend when I see the help she also gives me...*

4. Hmm... she helps me in all areas of my life in that she allows me to say exactly what I think; especially when the person in front of me isn't hearing me. Like the French maître de at the restaurant last night, who wouldn't apologise to my pregnant friend about the raw fish she served her because, "It eez disgusting to serve it any other way."

5. As we left, my Bitchy Cow blurted this out in a large boomy voice in front of the whole Saturday night crowd, *"I'm sure your customers would be disgusted if they heard what you've just told us!"* One quick ushering away and a huge discount and apology later, we'd helped this spiky maître de finally give the good service she'd meant to. Thank you bitchy cow, love you!

6. Now I've realised that this is a part of me and that I love her and because she has become a friend to me, something in me is changed. The Moaning Minnies in the payroll department don't upset me anymore because I just see them as women who haven't figured out how to heal their problems yet in a way that makes them feel good – or how to be happy. I feel a lovely gentle compassion for them and funnily enough they are softer towards me, something in them has changed, too. There is no longer this undercurrent between us, they have no power over me, so I now find myself doing what I want to do, which is – skipping out to lunch on my own, or meeting up with friends. I'm very, very able to say out loud in a fabulously loud booming voice, "No, thanks!"

When you love and enjoy every part of you, you are free to use them when needed and won't fight them on their way out of you.

F – TURN ON THE SHOWER OF SEQUINS!

Now, I thought you might like a little shower of sequins to wash off the darkness if people have passed judgement on you, have been nasty, or bitchy towards you *and you've been affected by it*. It's a little extra love from me to you. Here is your gorgeous new mindset:

1. What did they do to you?

2. How did they make you feel?

3. Their treatment of you: did it add to you, or take away?

4. Would a truly happy person act in this way towards you?

5. So, they're in pain. *This is them in pain.*

6. Why did you attract this to you? *Because you need to make peace with the part of you who treats you the same way.*

7. Go back to your answer from No. 1. In what way have you been treating yourself in the same way? How did you already make yourself feel smaller, unworthy, rejected, abandoned, and ashamed before you even came into this situation? How were you already not in your power? Can you see that you were already weakening yourself with your own thoughts about yourself at some point? Can you see that you were already putting yourself down? Was it just before the situation? During? After? How were you already judging yourself, being nasty, or bitchy towards yourself? What did you say? Take a breath...

8. Somewhere you were already doing this to yourself. If you can't see *how* right now, it's OK. Just know that it is there, ready to heal.

9. It's shown up in your life for you to see that you set this judgemental, nasty, bitchy precedent and they were vibrating low enough to follow your lead and treat you the same way.

10. Now is your time to thank them for showing you your own judgemental, nasty, bitchy way of dealing with yourself. Thank them for being brave enough to show you because if you treated yourself beautifully, then what happened would not have rattled you. It would have had no power over you then, or now. You'd see it for what it was, which is – that they'd slipped off their happy horse.

11. Time to heal it, go inside and make friends with the judgemental, nasty, bitchy side of you. Go to your healing room and choose process E, LOVE BUG TECHNIQUE.

12. Remember: when people are bitchy towards you, they are just as bitchy towards themselves. When people are nasty towards you, they are just as nasty towards themselves. And when people judge you, they pass just as much harsh judgement on themselves. It's them that suffers the most. They've disconnected themselves from source. They've just fallen off their happy horse. Leave their harshness behind and remember – YOU'RE BEAUTIFUL. *It's them that are teaching you to NOT treat yourself as they've just treated you.* They've just given you a very generous present bless them. They are trying to *up* your standards for you. Do it. Otherwise their world doesn't change and neither does yours.

2. FLOURISHING WHEN YOU'RE FUCKED OFF!

G – GET YOUR ANGER OUT NOW!

What do you do with your raw, ugly, anger? Your incandescent rage? What's irritating you pussycat? Wanna meditate it out? Are you trying not to feel it, so you swallow it down, down, down and assure yourself and everyone else that you've *"let it go?"* Ah, yes those ridiculous words at a time like this... "let it go." Because that's what enlightened people do, isn't it? You don't want to be carrying around all those negative feelings around with you. And knowing you, you'll probably end up manifesting something quite horrible for yourself anyway, so quick, quick, let the ugly thing go and then you're done with it. But are you? You might be thinking you are, but how is your body feeling? Check in with it. I'm betting you can still feel you're angry, but the difference *now* is that you've decided *that feeling angry isn't right, so you choose not to.* And yet... *it's still in you.* See, it doesn't matter how much yoga and meditation you do, if you have felt angry in the past, or are feeling angry now, I have three words for you:

GET IT OUT.

(Actually! It's four!)

NOW!

What do you do when all you want to do is yell and scream? GET IT OUT.

What do you do when you don't even think you're angry, but instead feel tired, depressed, lack lustre with a MOJO rating of –1. GET IT OUT.

What do you do when you feel angry at the world, yourself, him, or them? GET IT OUT.

Anger is a thick, heavy emotion. To not let it out means it blankets your insides with heaviness. And it stays in you. And darling, if it stays in you, it has a nasty habit of coming out at the wrong time *at the wrong person,* "F**K YOU! You yell whilst driving." Great, and cathartic though that was; *you know it's still in you.*

How do you know if it's in you?

If you haven't allowed yourself to express your anger *fully* in the last 7 days, then you're carrying it Goddess, *oh yes you are tra lá lá lá lá.* Irritated with that slow person who couldn't walk any slower if they tried? Wanna yell at the unhelpful help desk? Always annoyed at the same things your children forget to do, though you try to hide it? Do you find yourself brittle and snappy with him? Like a brandy snap only waaay less sweet and waay louder when you SNAP?! You might be saying to yourself *"Well this would make anyone angry"* and you're right. All of us carry anger. And if you're reading this right now thinking, "Well I don't, I just cruise along," then Goddess, I'm going to assert that it's in you all right. Even if this paragraph is making you irritated, then bingo it's in you! Found it!

Here's the thing about your anger: when you GET IT OUT, you unleash your POWER and this is where it gets really cool. Imagine you're walking down an old cobbled street in Spain, seeing those big mamma's shouting at their not so little sons anymore whilst putting their washing out? Think they have a problem with getting their anger out? Would you want to mess with one of them? Thought not. They are in their power. And you are about to be. We are far too quiet, *swallowing down what that awful woman just said to us*, where does that anger go, I ask you? In you and it stays in you. And if it's invited to stay long term, it also has the power to add illness long term. Goddess, it has no place in you anymore. No amount of yoga or meditation is going to get it out of you. You cannot meditate your anger away; you can only cover it up. Ready to get it out?

Good! You deserve to feel lighter and empowered *NOW*.

Here are your three anger choices; choose the one that fits you like a glove:

#1 Lion Pose. We're going to do Lion Pose together because we need to ROAR it out of you. This is an ancient yoga posture and it's fabulous for getting out your anger, your shame, and anything else that's in your way of having the BEST day today. Be in a room on your own, out of earshot. Wherever you're sitting, sit up straight and close your eyes. Breathe deeply; gather your anger and anything else that's in your way of having your best day into a little ball and put it into your stomach (like tiredness).

In a moment, you're going to say bye bye to this energy as you ROAR this old, dusty energy out of you. But just before we ROAR, there are two rules you must follow: 1. Is that you ROAR from your belly (not your throat, so you don't scratch it) we do this by breathing into the belly first and 2. That you are as loud as you dare!

Ready?

Hold this old energy in a tight little ball in your belly. It has no place in you anymore. Take a deep breath in through your nose, stick your tongue out fully, eyes gazing up to the sky, hands placed on your thighs, push your chest out and ROAR it out! Close your eyes again, pull whatever else needs to get out into a tight little ball in your stomach, and repeat two more times. Feel that extra space in you? Now, there is more space in you for the good stuff to come rushing in! ROAR!

#2 Anger Liberation. Tape up a wedge of magazines, take a wooden rolling pin and put on some gloves to protect your hands. (Trust me on this one, you do not want pillow like blisters). Place the magazines on your bed. Put on some LOUD music that pisses you off as you slam the wooden rolling pin onto the magazines: bash, bash bash and arghhhhh! Scream, shout, and bang that wedge until you have GOT IT OUT. Repeat daily until your anger is fully gone. Only you know when that is. And if at first you feel a bit self-conscious, embarrassed, and well, *silly*? Fake it till you make it honey! Out of no-where your real anger will come out and your real power will rush in to take its place.

#3 Humming Bee Breath. (Also known as Bhramari Breath) This is brilliant for getting your anger and fear out. It's also been proven to lower blood pressure.[3] I use it before I go to sleep at night if I've got a busy head. I sit in my parked car before an important meeting and 'hum'. (Windows up – don't care if you stare – *cause this really works!*) You'll feel decidedly still, centred, and peaceful afterwards: So, sit tall, place your finger on the flap of each ear so you block any sound. Close your eyes and take a deep breath and 'hum' until there is no breath left in you. Repeat 10 times, then keep your fingers in your ears, and see if you can feel your heart pumping blood through your body. Place your hands in your lap and sit quietly for a few moments. Feel the silence that surrounds you. It's been there the whole time.

H – GO FUCK YOURSELF! ARGUMENTS.

What happens to you when you argue with him? Do you get all hissy and explosive like Pompeii? Or do you give him the silent treatment because *he still doesn't bloody understand?* Whatever argument style you use,

---

3   The result indicated that slow pace Bhramari pranayama for 5 minutes induced parasympathetic dominance on cardiovascular system. Department of Physiology, Nepal Medical College, Jorpati, Kathmandu, Nepal.
Nepal Medical College journal : NMCJ 09/2010; 12(3):154-7.
Source: PubMed

---

there's one thing always happens to us women: We close up. Yup. Where once our petals were open to receive from him, they've now closed up. And what happens if you've been arguing with him since the turn of the century and he still doesn't listen to you, so nothing actually gets resolved? You remain closed to him. Closed to receiving fully from him so you don't get hurt again.

You might have just argued with him today. Or maybe you can recall an argument you had with him, a loved one, or someone at work that still hurts? This process will detox you, so that you can receive from him, the way you were made to.

P.S. This also works if you've argued with a woman, or it's more about a situation rather than a person; either way, just turn the *he* into *she* or into *the situation* below!

I want you to take a deep breath in and take the stance that both of you are right. There is room for both of you to be right. Can you look to his side of the argument and see how he was right for him?

WE ARE GOING TO DO THE "I AM RIGHT, HE IS RIGHT" PROCESS TOGETHER

1. On a sheet of paper, write at the top what you've been arguing about or making do with. On the left hand side, write, "I am right because…" Make some space underneath this and write, "He is right because…" Make some space underneath this and write, "I receive the gift, which is…"

2. OK, why are you right? Why are you right to feel the way you feel about it all? And so, why is he right to feel the way he does? Why is he right for him that he did what he did?

3. What gift is this giving you? This might be really easy, or it might be a case of, "Geez, I have no idea!"

When my first husband walked away from my baby girl and me, I lost financial support, our home, and was left with no external security.

At the time he said, "I'm actually doing the right thing by you." Now at the time, the government agency that collects money on behalf of single parents said otherwise. My family, my friends, and even their husbands were disgusted with him and said otherwise, and so did I. I was fragile and in shock. How could he do this to me?

You could have had 100 people in a room and 99 of them would have agreed with me that he is wrong. He would have been the only one to say he is right. I had the next 18 years ahead of me to prepare for, alone.

But, if I had kept that feeling that he is wrong and I am right, then it would have kept me stuck and heavy with grief for years. I wouldn't have gotten what I wanted so quickly if I'd stayed stuck there. And so I remember deciding consciously to make him right as a way of untangling from the situation, so I could open again and receive from the world. So, I decided that *he was right for him* to walk away, and here is the clincher: How *can* this be right for me? Well, what is the gift of him leaving? What did I get because of it? A me that is twice the woman I was! I chose to use what happened to me as the biggest springboard I'd ever known! The gifts are countless. One of which is my coaching. Pretty much anything and everything that could have happened to me in those years did, so if you tell me about your life nothing about it will scare me, nothing. I also know the pendulum will swing hugely into you being really happy when you heal, just like it did for me. I'm so grateful he turned away from me. So, so grateful! What gift did you get?

I – UN-STICKING YOUR STICKY SITUATION

There is a situation sticking itself to me and I can't get it off!

1. What are *they* doing to you? Why are you upset? Write it out.

2. Go back to what you have written in step 1 and substitute where you have written *they, my, them* to "I" or "me".

3. Close your eyes, ask yourself, "In which part of my life, am I doing this to myself, or another?"

4. What do you wish *they* would just do?

5. Go back over step 4 and substitute *they* for "I". So, what is this situation teaching me? Write it out.

6. What part of you is this trying to turn on?

7. Out loud say, "I forgive you now because this gift is far greater than the pain you caused me. Thank you."

Congratulations!!!! You have just used your sticky to become more magnificent!

J – QUICK UN-STICK!

(Takes 1 minute and is portable, you can un-stick yourself whilst you are walking.)

1. What's happening in your outside world to upset you?

2. Where are you doing this to yourself, or another?

3. HUG yourself as you receive this present from them.

4. Thank them!

Once you've learned the lesson, it no longer needs to appear; so the stick is gone and you've unstuck yourself. Oh, you're fabulous!

K – QUICK UN-STICK FOR YOU AND HIM

Example:

1. Look at him and you. What upsets you the most? What annoys you? What do you wish he would stop doing? Start doing? Do more of? And so on. Write a little ditty for you right now *on you and him*, e.g. is it his flagrant disregard for your needs? Can he just skip out whenever he wants: to the gym, to a boy's night out, to his business retreats, with scant regard for what you and the kids are needing? And yet when it's your turn to leave the nest, you don't get the same love, forethought and care back?

2. Well, is it possible that how he hurts you is how you hurt you? E.g. your flagrant disregard for your own needs?

3. HUG yourself as you receive this life-changing gift from him because you're choosing to *raise your standards*. Your own relationship with yourself is demanding that you respect yourself. Choose to, because this is the gift. If you don't learn it now, he will continue to need to show it to you. You don't want this! So, what are you going to change about your mornings?

4. Thank him. Without this, you would still be trundling along with that same level of mediocre respect for yourself and Goddess, you so deserve this next level, it becomes you!

3. EXTRAS

L – WHAT AM I SECRETLY ASHAMED OF?

Every woman carries inside her something she wishes she didn't do. So, she hides it and thinks no one else is like her.

There is money shame = "I have $23 left in the bank until I get paid."

There is parental shame = "I shout at my son, but in public I am the perfect mummy."

There is body shame = "I am addicted to eating a tub of ice cream in one sitting after I work out, every bloody time!"

You are not alone!

Every single person in the world can remember a time as a kid when their parents, or a guardian, asked them to stop doing something. Maybe nicely or angrily. Can you recall a time when the same thing happened to you?

I can. I was 12 years old and went to fetch the milk that had been delivered to the door by our milkman (remember that golden age?) As I breezed past my parents, defiantly holding one glass milk bottle by its very top only – as well as gamely swinging the other above my head like it was the flag of Britain. My dad snapped, "Don't do that, carry them properly!" "It's fine," I smiled and thought, *parents can be soooo uncool, can't they?* Just as both milk bottles spectacularly shot right out of my hands, smashing like big glass drama queens all over our brand new carpet. (Green.) Gawd, milk and glass everywhere! And just like their parents before them, and parents around the world, they told me off big time hoping to curb any future shenanigans.

I remember that incident like it was yesterday. Can you remember one, two, or maybe a whole bloody truckload? What happens next as a child? You take the person's anger, or their nice way of saying, "No, don't do that," and somewhere in you, you feel a bit of shame, *or a lot of shame.* You internalise it. You believe it. Your parents must be right, right?

And in most cases, they are. However, to little people being gorgeously self-centred beings, as they are supposed to be at that age, they take that message and make it to mean something *about them* rather than the *action* that they've just done. They take that pain and put it inside them, and it becomes their norm for walking around the world in. And we just bring that little pocket of shame with us into adulthood. Difference is, now I know I'm not going to swing milk bottles and steal my sister's Sunset Malibu Barbie any time soon. (Unless drunk.) So, where would I like to put my shame now?

Hmmmm. For most adults, the sticky in life they are stuck with is where you will find their shame. For instance, mine used to be money shame. I would be successful in every area of life, except money. The same way I felt about my lack of money was the same way I felt after those milk bottles broke: Guilty, stupid, and wanting to run away from it all. And you know what? Everybody that you know, people who are famous, people that you hate, and those that you admire all harbour secret shame. And it's either stuff they've done in the past, or stuff they're doing now.

Meet *Arielle*, a successful film producer. When I began coaching her, she told me that when she was growing up, her dad would tell her off, *like any dad.* Except it wasn't any old person, it was her very *own dad.* So when he told her off she felt *every single* emotion attached to it. *How bad* he felt, his shock and *his disgust.* She felt it all.

When he told Arielle off, she began to believe that she must be a really bad person and bad people don't deserve good things. This is Arielle's secret shame. It put her into desire Dry-out at the tender age of 12. The only time she would allow herself to desire was when it was super-duper urgent. Otherwise, she lived in the Dry-out zone where she didn't desire anything much in her normal normal waking life. She just "went with the flow". How many of you reading this prefer to *go with the flow* rather than go with your life force and follow your important desires? It showed up most noticeably in Arielle's finances, which were always up and down; born from her deepest pain that she doesn't deserve unless she's at a knife's edge*. Once Arielle firmly transformed her shame into forgiving herself, she realised she deserved to have her finances in great shape. She has hired a lovely financial advisor, who now helps her grow her money. Yes, now she knows she is always worth receiving.

*This is quite common in the women I meet. Could this be you too? Tell-tale signs are that you only feel the full force of your desire when you really, really neeeeeed it. But when you don't, your desire and life force nose dive, until the next time. Up down, up down... huh.

SECRET SHAME CIRCLE

Which part of your life makes you feel ashamed and embarrassed? Is it stuff you've done in the past, or stuff you are doing now? Is it something you are doing to yourself, or to another? Have you stolen something? Pretended to get something on insurance when it was in your house the whole time? Do you mainline sugar like a pro? Do you feel acute shame that you are divorced? Short of money? Do you pretend to be something that you're not? Can't stop spending? Are you utterly horrible to someone? Are you ashamed that you haven't done more with your talents? That your husband is an alcoholic/embarrasses you in public/

doesn't desire you anymore/has a job that is beneath you? Are you pulling the wool over someone's eyes and lying to them? Write it down on a sheet of paper. All of it. What makes you keep this a secret? *Fear of judgment,* from either yourself or someone you love. *They will think less of you.* Whatever it is that you've written on the page, it's either something that you've told no one about, or you hide it regularly. And so it's a double whammy isn't it? You're hurting *and* you're feeling ashamed about it.

I want you to imagine we are all sitting in a circle with candles burning brightly in the middle. I'm here, you are here and so are *Claire, Debbie* and *Shoshanna*. Our secret shame circle is where you are safe to let out *your secret.* Sounds like hippy stuff, but go with it. See, sense, or imagine it, this works brilliantly when you are alone with me talking to you like this. So share your secret with us. Out loud. With all the specific details. If you have more than one, keep talking until you've got it all out. It's really important to say it out loud. It begins the process of you realising that we, as humans, are all the same and we all share the same guilt and shame around remarkably similar things. They may look different on the outside, but the inner feeling is always the same: embarrassment, shame, fear, guilt. Go ahead and free yourself. You deserve it. And if you feel you don't? Well you really need this secret shame circle and I built it for you. Go on, say it to us now: what's your secret shame? What do you do? "I..." I'm going to ask you some questions, go ahead and answer them out loud to the circle:

1. How long have you been doing this for?
2. Are you doing this in front of people?
3. How does this impact your relationships?
4. We are all going to say thank you to you now, thank you for being brave enough to share it. And thank you for listening to the others, too. Know that you are not alone.

Goddess Claire, what's your secret shame?

I sneak chocolate and have a hidden stash of it behind the piano, where I hide it from my husband, who thinks I'm trying to lose weight... Well, of course I am, but I love nothing more than to eat a whole family block of chocolate because I need it. About three times a week. (And I love it!) There I said it. I feel ashamed because I know it's not good for my body and I also feel ashamed because I can't control it and because I'm hiding it from him. I don't feel so ashamed that I eat it, because I need the sugar hit, so I can keep pushing through to the next thing I need to do, or if someone hasn't been nice to me. I can't just stop at three pieces! And you know what? I think he's hiding his secret stash from me too, so we're both eating secretly in the same house!

1. How long have you been doing this for?

    I've been doing this since I started my business.

2. Are you doing this in front of people?

    No, I do this on my own in the car, or between clients at home as I don't want my children to see my bad example. And the biggest shame? I work in the health industry. So my clients are people who come to me to get healthy!

3. How does this impact your relationships?

    On the days I mainline sugar I feel kind of grungy and overtired; so by the time I climb into bed, I often turn away from my husband, so we don't get close and have sex. This happens on average about three times a week. I don't feel sexy if I've been eating crap. So lots of missed opportunities because I feel bloated and want to pass out in bed.

4. Thank you, Goddess *Claire!*

Goddess Debbie, what's your secret shame?

Ah, mine is a past shame. When the kids where naughty I would smack them and my hands would leave red hand marks on their legs. I felt very ashamed when I did do this; I would just crack when I couldn't take it anymore and wallop! Then they would cry, I would feel hot in the face and then later on when no one else was around I would cry for me and I would cry for them. I've never been able to reconcile it and I feel so ashamed and guilty.

1. How long have you carried this secret shame?

   30 years.

2. Are you doing this in front of people?

   Nobody else witnessed it.

3. How does this impact your relationships?

   It's like I feel evil inside still because of that. It only happened a handful of times, but it's so against everything I believe in, and yet I couldn't help it. Like Goddess Claire, I couldn't control it.

4. Thank you, Goddess *Debbie.*

Goddess Shoshanna, what's your secret shame?

I'm carrying a lot more debt than I'm comfortable with to finance the growth of my business. It's all on credit and my business hasn't caught up yet, so it's kind of a crippling feeling. I feel terribly ashamed and heavy carrying this big debt. My family have no idea, and neither do my clients. I'm driving around in my Audi sports car giving off this vibe to everyone that I am so successful. If my clients found out, none of them would hire me.

1. And how long have you been carrying the debt for?

   Four years. $192,000 all on different credit cards.

2. Are you doing this in front of people?

   Oh my God no, my mother would have a heart attack!

3. How does this impact your relationships?

   It's made me drift away from everybody really because I can't share this; no one knows.

4. Thank you, Goddess *Shoshanna*.

It is our secret shame that becomes like a fantastic sling shot inside us deflecting everything good we deserve. It blocks us from easily receiving money, the right kind of love, and from living the way we are wired to. It is our secret shame that secretly tells us that we are bad, that we are not good enough, that we are not smart. *Who are we* to be rich, successful, and beautiful? It's not actually that thing you did or didn't do, it's actually *how you feel* about what you did or didn't do that stops you from receiving, and leaves you feeling heavy, ashamed, and guilty. And so secretly you harbour this, hoping nobody finds out...

But, for everything you're ashamed of, I can guarantee you there are lots of people in the world doing the same thing. And some of them won't feel in the least bit ashamed. Perhaps they should. Perhaps they shouldn't. I'll let you be the judge of that. Because really, who is right? Perhaps smacking your child was the better evil because in that moment, the only other option was throwing her into oncoming traffic.

There is no judgment here because the biggest judger is YOU!

We are going to do a re-frame. I want you to write down a really negative explanation for your secret shame. The worst you can think of. For example, you might say I smacked my child because I'm a horrible woman, who is an evil mother beneath the smiles. Or, I'm such a bad businesswoman because I haven't managed to earn the money back yet and time is running out. I'm such a loser, or I'm such a greedy ugly woman who is fucking fat.

Imagine hearing the worst judgment about yourself and write it out.

Now I want you to write a positive re-frame – an empowering explanation so it feels good to you. I smacked my child, which saved us both from something much more serious happening. My aspirations are so huge in business, and I'm so very brave to take this risk and follow my heart. It's what I'd mentor my clients to do if they believed in themselves and their business, as much as me. I've gone all out and I inspire myself; there is no turning back now! I eat so much sugar because I'm actually a very sweet person living in a life that is sour to me. It's cold and hard, and I need to make up the gap until I create a life that has real sweetenss in it.

Now hear these words: you are worth forgiving, for whatever you've done or not done. You are worth it. Why?

Because if you hadn't lost a part of you back then (like your self-love) you know you would have done better.

What part of you was lost to you? Was it your self-respect? Your self-love? Your kindness? Your self-worth? Your concentration? Was it yourself that was lost?

It's OK; you are worth forgiving because your capacity for good is so much more than the sum of what you did, or didn't do. The only way to get to your good fully is to fully forgive yourself. Firstly, it's very hard to be your best you for the world if you are ashamed and guilty. Secondly, how much light can you let in when you feel like this? So then how much good can you do in the world? *Exactly.* It's time.

Now, we are going to forgive ourselves and in doing so, you are going to break the chains that have kept you shackled to your shame. In the process below, you will see these chains: they might look like chains or kind of like gloopy chords. They won't be bright and happy looking, that's for sure. Let's do it. Close your eyes and go back to the age you were when you began this secret shame. You might have been 13 years old, or you might have been 44 years old. Go back and see yourself just at the point you are about to "do it." What feeling is emanating from this *secret shame you,* at the beginning of it all? What do you wish you'd known then that you do now? Go ahead and share your hard earned wisdom with *your secret shame you.* Share how much this secret shame has hurt you since its beginning. Don't hold back, *say everything.* Now, ask your secret shame younger you to tell you why they did it? What did they believe to be true about themselves? What has your secret shame actually given you? It's given you a huge gift: what is it? It might be strength, or the ability to bounce back. You might not know what it is, but I want you to decide to receive it. Let go of your shame.

Repeat out loud, "I happily receive this gift. I thank this situation for what it is teaching me. I now decide to stop doing this to myself or to another." See, sense, or imagine you now at that age and see the chains that are keeping you stuck in this old pattern of shame or guilt hanging between *you now* and *you then*. When you're ready, cut the chains because you are done. You are done with hiding. You are done with the shame. Yes, break those chains of shame. See those chains crumble into nothing. Gone. Send love to your younger self: wash her in pink and wash you in pink. As you breathe her into your body, she is healed and say out loud, "I'm sorry. I forgive you and I bless you."

I want you to imagine that the other three Goddess are saying in unison: You are forgiven. Three times. To you.
You are forgiven.
You are forgiven.
You are forgiven.

Breathe that in; you are now left with the gift. I want you to forgive those three Goddesses too, say it out loud three times for them:

You are forgiven.
You are forgiven.
You are forgiven.

You are so worthy of so much love for you. Whatever there is, there is no shame, go out there with your head held up.

Any time you feel shame, hug and love yourself, literally wrap your arms around yourself. All of you is worth loving and forgiving, especially when you feel like this.

Stand in front of the mirror and look into your eyes and say the words, "I forgive myself," three times and feel yourself soften. Then do it again and again, until you are fully open to you, until you know you have genuinely forgiven yourself. Make full eye contact and know that you are worth this for the whole rest of your life, no matter what you have or haven't done.

M – BE INSPIRED BY MY BEST GODDESS ME!

I want you to imagine you're all cosy in your healing seat in your healing room and you really want to meet your *Best Goddess You*. Why? Because your *best you* is always available to you. Take a few moments as you watch her come towards you and take form. This is you as the *Goddess you were born to be*. This is you at your highest potential. What is she like? How does she look? How does she stand? What's the energy around her? Make eye contact with her and check in, "Are you my best self?" Then ask her, "What's possible for me? (Ask for details.) When she's finished, really feel the energy coming off her – *know that this is you*, you at your highest! Feel her energy; this is your energy. If you can't see her, focus on her energy. What kind of energy would your best you have? Connect to that. Then, gently inhale her into your whole body and you are going to begin becoming your best you. How would you like to start? Pick one thing and do it within the next 24 hours.

N – BECOME THE BEST FRIEND I EVER HAD

Every feeling you've ever had is your friend. A feeling you hate to feel is just a friend you haven't made yet. You will. And when you do? You'll be able to use any feeling to bring you back to self-love. Follow the thread and you'll get there. Abandon the thread for a distraction like TV, over eating, *fill in the blank* and you'll remain enemies. You'll run from your feelings and blot them out, or you'll fight them forever, saying for example, "I have huge anxiety." Hatred of feeling this way will mean you'll fight it and try to push it down. Plus, your fear of this mounting feeling in your gut will make you even more massively fearful. – Arghh!

If you don't make friends with your anxiety?

Guess what?

You're on a collision course. Ignore your true friends in real life for long, and what happens? They get angry with you! Or upset with you. Or they'll ring you incessantly for attention, so it's all about them. And if you keep ignoring them? They'll stop being your friend because *YOU walked away* from that friendship.

And that's the same with your feelings: ignore them and they can't be a friend to you. They'll just be too big, too scary, and too clumsy; you'll see them as your enemy to a happy fulfilled life. You'll be too scared to cry hugely and let the tears roll, in case you crack and never come back from it. You'll ignore your anger for years and then you'll let rip at the wrong person. "God, I'm so sorry. I never meant to say that to you, it came out all wrong."

Make friends with your anger and *you cannot use it unwisely.* Make friends with your tears and you won't carry too many of them in your heart for very long. I remember when our beloved cat, Snowball, died suddenly. He was just divine can I tell you? Like a little snow tiger. There we were, my daughter and I balling our eyes out in the massage clinic. Inconsolable. Our beloved masseuse said: "You know when someone dies, it's such a good excuse to cry for everything else in your life too, isn't it?" Um, no. These tears are just for Snowball, I've already cried for everything else, so I could just cry for him and let it move through me. My daughter thought it was a strange comment. Like all children, unless they're told not to cry, she cries, and doesn't make it to mean anything about her. It's just crying. Like laughing is just laughing. It just needs to move through you.

Your feelings are always there to bring you back to self-love. If you don't feel your feelings as soon as they come up within you, but decide instead to *"let it go"*, you miss out on truly making friends with yourself at a very deep level. For example, when proudly "taking the higher road" to *let what he said go* (without telling him how bloody hurt you are) you disconnect from source, from you, from your heart, and from the person in question. "I've let it go, there really isn't any point in talking to him about it." Yes there is; the point is: Your hurt teaches him how to love softly this lifetime. This world is always turning *to turn wonderful you on,* but disconnect from this and the learning is lost. So it will have to knock on your door again, at a later date. Do you really want this situation knocking on your door again tonight? Thought not.

And when you make friends with each and every feeling? Fear becomes a friend that steers you clear of danger. Feeling negative allows you to *not put* a positive spin on everything, so you truly connect to your deepest need.

Then you can be with another's worry and not let it topple you; then you can be with your son's negativity, your daughter's crying, and it cannot frighten you, or get you down. Because you can be with your own deep feelings. When you can be with you, you can be with another. Try it.

A feeling has a thread, called a turn on thread. Every feeling is properly designed just for you, so that if you follow its thread, it will turn you ON. If you abandon it in search of something to fill in its place, you will never turn ON. You will be turned off, instead. Think about how you feel after you've over-eaten and sat on the couch watching mindless TV? How do you feel afterwards? *Mindless and switched off?*

So... this is the Turn ON Process. It's safer to be turned ON than turned OFF because you cannot hurt yourself. You cannot reach for something else like food, drugs, alcohol, work, and the constant need for validation or whatever it is you to do to escape from feeling. *Because it won't feel good anymore to do.* You will feel what it actually is, that you are doing to you. You will be able to love yourself at the beginning of this, not just at the end of your escape, eating that *whole* bag of crisps. You can turn yourself on with each painful experience, each fear, and each worry, so you become twice the woman you are. After you complete this process? You will easily receive your love for you and support from others without feeling ashamed of your feelings, or self-conscious. Just worthy of love. Want this? Close your eyes...

O – TURN-ON PROCESS

1. Be brave enough to feel the feeling for 10 breaths.

2. What's the feeling? Why?

3. Being honest and not abandoning how I feel means I will always make the right decisions for me.

4. "My feelings are right for me and their feelings (if someone else is involved) are right for them."

5. When I make friends with this feeling, it cannot hurt me, only help me.

6. This feeling is always leading me to self-love. Connect to your divine intuition. What act of kindness is it leading me to do for myself? Is it the act of transformation, strength, self-love, or do I need to receive? Write this down. "It's forcing me to nourish my soul when others aren't." (For example...)

7. This is the specific gift of this specific feeling. Thank you, feeling!

8. This feeling is now a friend to me. The next time I feel it, I know the gift.

9. Allow a new desire to be born.

10. Take my self-love action from step 6. What will tell me I am doing it? When am I going to do it?

This feeling has just turned my self-love on. Thank you!

Turn yourself UP. This is you turning up your divine intuition and turning your volume up, which are one and the same. The universe wants more of you because it wants the volume turned up on its masterpiece, aka – YOU.

P – SHORT TURN-ON PROCESS (to remember during the day is...)

1. Feel.

2. What self-love is it leading me to?

3. Hug myself and that feeling. Hurrah!

Every feeling and every belief is your friend. If you make friends and peace with a belief such as "I'm not good enough," it can become a friend to you rather than the enemy. Every belief will add to you when you make friends with it. What if every negative belief you ever had was a friend in disguise? A friend who wants to see you succeed... which is only possible after you accept and love them for the job they do? How can you make friends? *When it arrives with a present.* When you forgive and accept. Close your eyes...

Q – BELIEF BE-FRIENDER

1. Meet the belief. Imagine it a friend you haven't made yet. They've come to you to make peace. Do you like them, or hate them right now?

2. *This belief leads me to self-love when I be-friend it because it carries a gift for me.* Connect to your divine intuition. What has this belief allowed you to receive? How has it helped you in your life to get you where you are now? What is its gift to you?

3. What does your new friend need from you from now on? Why?

4. Tell your friend if you choose to understand, like, or love it? Why?

5. Celebrate your new relationship with this part of you by doing something different for yourself this day or this week. A healing act of self-love.

6. Allow a new desire to be born.

7. Take your self-love action from step 5.

Want an example of how this works?

Let's say you want to meet the part of you that represents the "not good enough" part of you. You never feel good enough at work and you hate it. What has feeling not good enough allowed you to receive? Answer = A determination to become more than good enough. You put everything into that presentation last month. Feeling not good enough fuels me to do my absolute best, I really try hard and it's helped me secure a really good job. My new friend (not good enough) needs me to love feeling her because every time I do: it's just my sign to GO FOR IT! So this week I'm going to accept this feeling and let it lead me to greatness in my life. I desire to love this feeling within by the end of this week.

R – DOWN IN THE DUMPS?

What do you do when you find yourself falling into the dark pit of utter despair, unworthiness, and self-sabotage? It happens to the best of us and somewhere along the way we've been taught inadvertently to "stay positive". This actually stops our natural healing from taking place; we've actually been designed to self-heal and feeling negative is the beginning of this healing process.

Climb out of your pit quicker by allowing yourself to follow the six steps, which we all naturally go through, but stop ourselves from doing. Why do you stop yourself? See if you can spot yourself here:

When I fall into a pit, I stop myself from fully going there because:

1. I am bad and don't deserve any niceties including getting out of the pit quicker.
2. I will manifest something bad if I am negative.
3. Who has the time to do this? I must get on.
4. I am scared of going "there." What if my feelings are too big for me?

We judge ourselves harshly for wanting to do something that is so natural. Yet, children do this all the time because they allow themselves to feel the depths of their feelings; so they aren't down there for very long. It's just us adults, who judge ourselves so harshly for being in one of the below six steps, like guilt for feeling negative and guilt for doing something nice for ourselves. Yet you are wired to go through these six steps and they are entirely natural to you.

Repeat after me:

"Just like a rose, I am beauty, softness, and love. Just like a rose, I have thorns. I love them because their gift is to protect me, so I'd not ever cut them off and pretend they are not mine. Without my thorns to protect me, I cannot open fully. Without my dark side, I cannot open fully into the power that I am. I love and accept every part of me that I have ever hidden or felt ashamed of. This is real love. *And this is real self-love.* So: I deserve all the sweet niceties of love, happiness, success, and money. All things that I desire are not conditional, so they flow easily to and from me."

Become a master climber:
1. Fully feel "it".
2. Sludge it.
3. Decide to heal.
4. Detox.
5. Desire.
6. Self-love.

1. Yes, fully feel "it", because feeling negative is the beginning of the healing process. Let yourself stand in the pit and feel all of your feelings, while you cry them out, write them out, and say them out loud. Brownie points for being Mrs. N. Negative. Allow yourself to admit to yourself how bad things have got.

2. Sludge it – everyone has sludge days – everyone! And that means you too, you and me, me and you. This is the second stage of being in the hole – know it for what it is. It's natural. It's when you can't

be bothered to *do anything*. Give yourself permission to sludge, call a girlfriend and cry, buy a tub of ice cream, eat whatever you want whenever you want and make a meal of it – peanuts, crisps, raisins and chocolate make an exceptional sludge lunch. Watch crappy daytime TV; scrape your hair up into a greasy bun, dress sludgy (putting on the same socks from yesterday and the same top are sludge GOLD). Do not clean. Do not cook. Do not answer that phone to the needy "me me" friend. Do not compromise on your sludge time; this will only make it last longer. Case in Point: *Athena* kept falling into her sadness pit because her ex-boyfriend had left her and her two children. She decided to sludge it, instead of positive think her way out. She didn't wash her hair for a week, she didn't wash up for a week (all dishes were piled in the bath), she didn't vacuum for a week and strewn around her couch, like a lazy slack arse student, were empty pizza boxes and Chinese take away boxes. Yep, she was really sludging it. And a funny thing happened. When she let herself consciously sludge, she bloody enjoyed it! The first time it went for a week and she came fully out of it and flew. Didn't have to think positive – *just was!* The second time she sludged it, she went till Wednesday, by which time she was truthfully ready for step 3, deciding to heal. The third time, she was most disappointed and actually rang me. "I just set aside time to sludge today and I only felt like doing it for 30 minutes – and damn it, I am already ready to heal, what's going on? I was really looking forward to it!" Ahh yes, when we allow ourselves to genuinely do the first and second stage of healing with gusto, we will come out of it quicker and quicker. Think of it as a wonderful side effect to you living the way you are wired to. The more you feel "it", the less time "it" needs to hang around because "it's" been listened to. So, sludge to the best of your best ability; *whatever you've got on today*, there is always a way to sludge when you are determined!

3. Decide to heal. A simple and profound decision that you make with yourself. Yes, you are worthy, no matter what you have or have not done. Re-read the chapter "Decide" for more on this.

4. Detox: pick a process from this book to self-heal. Choose the one you most need and carve out 10 minutes today to do it. Do it. Do it!

5. Let the pit you've just been in create new desire within. Often your desire will be for the opposite of what you've just been through – good! Desire it hugely. Stretch your legs more on this by reading the chapter on desire.

6. Self-love it! Do something, anything right now to get your nitric oxide up. Laugh till you pee, dance NOW, sway those hips as you walk, sing out loudly and badly, self-pleasure in the middle of the day, meditate by staring at a candle, do yoga to funky music; yes, self-love it within the next 30 minutes of step 5.

Yes, you deserve this. Use this process each time you feel yourself falling into your own personal pit of despair. Do each step fully and only step out of that step when you are truly ready. You'll find that the more you use it, the less time you'll need in step 2, the sludging step. And that's the step we normally avoid, yet find ourselves in and hate ourselves for it. Funny things us humans, we thrive the closer we live to our natural way of being! Let yourself go all the way with all six steps. The only way is through.

S – SELF-SABOTAGE:

This is quite a long process, but it's so worth it. Don't worry if you feel blocked at any time, just sit for longer with each question and the answer will come to you. It's helpful to write your answers out as you go along.

Freeing yourself from self-sabotage: Why do you day after day stop yourself from doing what you want? Because really, what you want in life is to:

- get well
- get healthy
- stop hurting yourself.

It's like an internal fight. You say you want to get fit and here you are muttering to yourself at 6:00am that there is no way on God's earth that you're getting up for that run now...

Sure, *you're good at running* – but mostly in the opposite direction (of what you want.)

What sort of person would do that to themselves?

Tell me in your own words.

Somebody who doesn't care about herself very much?

Somebody who doesn't like herself very much?

Someone who is angry and wants to hurt herself very much?

Close your eyes: when did you decide to start doing this (self-sabotage) to yourself? Let the age that you started doing this come to you.

Why? What was happening around you at that time?

What do you remember most about that time? Re-live it just for a moment.

What feeling where you trying to escape to? Why?

So you did this, which at the time gave you *that good feeling* you were after.

But for how long? How long did *this good feeling* last for?

(I.e. for as long as you smoked, for as long as you were eating, and maybe for an hour after?)

And then what feeling would you be left with afterwards? Regret? Shame? What happens to you, normally?

So, would you like to find a more pleasurable way to get to this good feeling instead? In a way that enriches your life with no aftertaste?

Because you deserve it you know, you've suffered long enough.

So stay with me here. This good feeling that you've been trying to get to...

Can you see that the very thing you're after produces opposite results not long after?

Darling woman, why do you only deserve just a small amount of happiness followed by shame, guilt, unhappiness, and regret filling up your body? Is it because you're bad? Not good enough? Stupid? Scared of your power? Just say it. Saying it is to halve its power.

Can you feel the most recent time you sabotaged
yourself in this way?
I want you to imagine that your self-saboteur is standing next
to you urging you to sabotage yourself, again.
You'll probably hate her at this point.
But what good feeling is she actually trying to get you
to feel again, quickly?

Can you see she's trying to help you? But, because you haven't fully followed the thread of this self-sabotage, you just get stuck in the cycle of it. You never reach the end, which is self-love. She really needs you to listen to her. She is actually trying to help you. Listen:

Ask her, "What's hurting you?" Can you hear the hurt?

What does she want you to learn to do? Ask her to finish this sentence: "Every time I feel my self-saboteur, it's my sign that I need..."

- to escape from harshness as I am a gentle person
- to create a kinder life for myself
- real support
- to become present
- to tell myself that I'm going to be alright
- to really take care of myself
- to get help
- to be hugged
- to spiritually re-align myself
- to learn to truly support myself through this
- my real needs met
- to change who I hang around with
- freedom
- to accept and love myself just the way I am
- to be kind to myself.

So in following the real thread of your self-saboteur back to self-love, what does she want you to put into place each day?

Hear it and write it down. This is your self-love action.

When you feel your self-saboteur, listen to her. She's your sign that you're aching to implement self-love again, *before you do anything else*. Really thank her because she's your sign for deep self-love. So, your self-saboteur can now become a friend to you. Because you're *LISTENING* to her. And when you choose to? She'll have no power over you anymore.

T – DIAMONDS ARE A GIRL'S BEST FRIEND

This is the Turning your Coal into Diamonds Process: And I LOVE it. I adapted it from the wonderful work that Debbie Ford, author, coach and incredible being, did. Use this process when you want to shift a relationship dynamic that is hurting you.

This process polishes the coal in your life into diamonds. If you have a situation with someone, or a feeling within yourself that threatens to topple you which has gone on for too long, that saps you of energy, of your very essence, then this is for you!

Ahh, this is your self-love growing... if you can love what you find so abhorrent in another, and can make friends with this same part in you? You have diamonds! Diamonds, I tell you! After all *we are everything* and to say "I am that too" means you become deliciously whole, humble, and free. Free from reacting to this person. Free of that awful feeling you keep getting. Free to break this dynamic once and for all.

Want to know how this works? Let's the take the word "control freak." If I were to call you that during an argument, how would you feel about it? Happy?

When you can say, "Yes, I am a 'control freak' and I LOVE this part of me!" Guess what? You become free to use it in your life for the right reasons: To protect yourself and to create high standards for yourself. If you hate to be a "control freak," then you won't own "it" as a trait of yours, so you'll try not to be "it." But, you can only hide a part of you for so long and then your "control freak," (which we will never get rid of) will come out sideways when you least expect it, *and it will come out wrong.*

What if *Pam,* a 41-year-old woman, who prides herself on just "going with the flow" were to own the fact that she herself was a control freak? Would she then be able to use it with pride in her doctor's office to make sure she got the very best care? Would she then use it in her business more often, particularly around a member of staff whom she suspected was stealing? If she freely allowed herself to be a control freak, it would always come out at the right time because that's her *really going with her natural flow.* And then it wouldn't come out sideways at her husband at the end of her day. Because by allowing herself to be a control freak during the day, her day would nourish her; so leaving her happier by the end of it. (And not feeling like if another thing didn't go her way, she was going to explode.)

So, what's to stop you smiling in front of the mirror right now and owning control freak?

Write down the benefits of being a control freak. Let's do this example together because it's something most of us, unless we're uber successful business people who love our controlling nature, have not rocked yet.

Benefits of being a control freak:

My standards raise for myself.

My business runs like clockwork.

I won't shout at my husband when he gets home.

What are yours?

Then let's you and me go in front of the mirror, start smiling and say over and over "I am a control freak" until we remember we like it, until we remember it's good to be it, until the lightness spreads throughout our bodies, and we think we could fall in love with it. No, wait a minute, we already *are* falling in love with it. It's ultimate freedom because we are free to use our control freakiness in a way that will benefit us and those around us, *rather than it hurting us and those around us.* So, "control freak" becomes your best friend on the way to self-love. And make no mistake, this is self-love. This is you loving every part. Just as you are made to. Hurrah MS CONTROL FREAK!

OK. Let's go get you a pile of dazzling diamonds! Take a piece of paper and draw a line quickly down the middle:

Your coal is what you cannot be with, either within you or with another. Write the word coal in the left column. Then write the phrase "And your gift to me is" at the top of the right.

Back to the left hand column, write a list of everything you cannot be with, within yourself. So you might write "I am ugly," or "I am very beautiful," or "I am needy," or "I am not good enough," or "I am successful." If you're yelling internally *no I'm not that!* Then you know this is the one for you. And write what annoys you about another person in your life, like "foul tempered, critical, selfish, lucky, rich," all in a big list down the left side. If it's long, don't worry, I had 60 when I started!

Now, get ready to fall in love with each part of you listed in the left hand column, because yes it is a part of you. Remember, it will have *no power* over you anymore when you make friends with it. It will have no power to make you act a certain way or think a certain way, instead you take that power back to use it for the right reasons! Hurrah! The dynamic is broken and you're BACK baby!

Now, in the right hand column, can you write what this coal gives you? Sometimes you will *know* what the gift is and sometimes you might have to sit with it for a bit. There is a beautiful gift in every single part of you; usually, the gifts are of freedom, of keeping you safe, of coming back into your power, of providing you with protection, or of being your barometer for when you need to stop and look after yourself. Who do you admire that exhibits these parts? Madonna, Pink, Lady Gaga – they all rock their dark sides beautifully and we love them for it. Now go love yours too.

Turn to face yourself in the mirror, yes there you are. God you're fabulous! OK back to it...

... Now make un-wavering eye contact in the mirror and tell yourself over and over that you are this coal until you can understand, like, or love this part of you. It might take a minute. It might take an hour. It's worth it for a lifetime of freedom. "I am a failure. I am a failure. I am a failure." Tears might roll down your face, you might feel angry, or feel nothing. Keep going until you feel a lightness spread through your body, until you are genuinely glad to call yourself a failure. When there is no fear of failure, then great bravery can form in you. When you make friends with failure, you'll use it as a learning tool for future success. Sometimes you might not know what the gift is. That's OK. Each part of you is a friend, remember that.

And until you do it, this trait that you hate or can't accept will always have power over you. If it is a trait *in that person*, they'll have power over you when they're being that trait because you will react. Like when you see someone driving an ostentatiously rich flashy car and you roll your eyes, "Lucky bastards." Hmm... if you can't comfortably be with ostentatiously rich, you will begrudge them and lower your energy and vibration in the process, hurting you.

If you can't be with your critical mother-in-law because she drives you mad, own "critical" and see what happens in your next encounter with her. I'm betting she won't affect you. It doesn't mean you excuse her behaviour or want to be with her for longer than 20 minutes in a room, but it does mean you are free in that moment to look straight into her heart, straight past her ego, and have compassion for her. *Because if she's being ultra-critical; she is in pain.* And you can relate to her at a much deeper level, not reacting to her ego and just to her heart. Even if she doesn't connect to you, you are free of that power play, and then you are free to rock critical within.

Goddess, where is it good to be madly critical? *Oh in so many places,* like what about when weighing up the pros and cons of buying a house? Sure, this is the right place because being critical might just save you from buying a big mistake!

What about the biggies? The things *we really don't want to be?* My clients often find that as they call themselves a "bitch" over and over, or "fake", which is their worst fear, that at first, they don't want to do it. I mean let's face it, who has ever wanted to call themselves their worst fear straight into a mirror? Then she might cry, or get really, really angry, until finally she starts to feel a lightness in her chest or head... and it feels kinda good to be a bitch, it feels kinda brilliant to be a... big fat *fucking bitch* actually. Yahoooooo!!!

It's very freeing. Because truly, what's not to love about you? You were made to be absolutely perfect, absolutely divine, and absolutely, positively GORGEOUS! What's not to love about you being a big fat fucking bitch? Yes, I said it twice and if it annoys you, then go ahead and add it to your coal list. Because I LOVE being a big fat fucking bitch;

she's one of the best things about me. Without being her, I wouldn't feel strong enough to stand up for my rights, and neither would you.

And you know what? For those of you who don't want to say something negative to yourself in the mirror, I'm going to assert that you say or do these things to you anyway! You're already doing this to you, (I look old. God, I'm such an idiot!) So you may as well come clean in front of yourself in the mirror in order to genuinely let this toxic dynamic within, go.

Anna is that everyday woman you pass in the street who looks nice. She hates the thought that she could be evil deep down and tries to be very nice to cover it up. She often has a whole other conversation going on in her head when talking to someone like you and it's not a nice one. Also she hates that her boyfriend doesn't lift a finger around the house. So, in her coal list she has "evil" and "lazy arse".

She faces the mirror and says over and over to herself I am evil, I am evil until she can understand that sometimes she can be and sometimes she will need to be in the future and that's OK. Or, until she likes it or loves it.

I love my evil; it gives me a wicked sense of humour and will make me jump you when you walk down our hallway at home. It will hone in on my clients weakness and draw it out unmercifully to heal it. My evil isn't necessarily a despots' evil; I may not be that extreme. Because what I choose to do with it is up to me. But evil is evil. And I need this part of me.

What's not to love about all of ourselves? We are given *each part* of ourselves to be useful, if we ever need it. If we don't accept this part of ourselves, then guess what? It will come out twistier than a coiled up snake because we'll try to hide it out of shame.

SHOOT 'EM UP, COWBOY!

For example, we were shooting a video for Marina J at home years ago when I heard loud arguing between two men next door. It sounded like cowboys fighting in a bar. Only it wasn't a bar. It was my dainty tree lined street. I halted filming and went outside to *nicely* ask the builders to keep their voices down, so we could film. We began to film again and then... the yelling began again. Pow – Pow – Pow! I asked even more sweetly a second time hoping that would do it. But only moments later their yelling filled our room and we had to stop again. For the third time, I went over and I said in my powerful bitchy voice, and using my *don't mess with me evil stare* that they needed to stop NOW. "Filming was scheduled until 2:00pm, until then NO Shouting." They meekly agreed and when I opened my front door to head over to thank them for being quiet, a bunch of flowers was on my doorstep with a note. Do you think this would have happened if I'd been deeply embarrassed to be angry with them? I would not have been in my power and it would have come out all twisted and wrong.

So, what if you're *still* thinking that you like the idea of all of this, but you *still* don't want to say something negative to myself in the mirror?

Goddess, nothing you can say will bring on negativity. It's your fear of it that will. And if you don't want to do this? You're already fearing this part of you. Don't. It's just a friend you haven't gotten to know. It's just a friend you haven't made yet. Be brave. You may not call yourself a bitch out loud, but I'm betting you sure can be bitchy to yourself, or to others. So you may as well come clean in front of yourself in the mirror, so that you can genuinely let this go.

You have such power to heal your life. Go mirror and go wear those diamonds because you deserve them and you deserve to love all of you.

OK, so we're at the end of the chapter... Congratulations!!! You've just learned how to turn on your self-healing and you can heal any time you want because you are the QUEEN of your inner world at this very moment, and always.

Chapter 6

Turn On Your SELF-LOVE Action

• • • • • • • • • • • • • • •

This is the "s" in the 3 Ds ethos, the fourth and final part: Self-love: What's NOT to LOVE about you?

I see you.

And I don't care what you've done just now that's been crappy towards yourself or another.

I don't care if you are not good enough, pretty enough, or think you don't deserve *it*. Because of whatever you have or haven't done.

In the nicest possible way, I also *don't care* if you've been laughing like a drain and you're feeling fucking fantastic!

Because either way I do know this: *Because of the very virtue that you were born,* you are 100% worthy of love. Your love, for you. Completely and utterly. Your love for your very essence, and your youness. Your light, your dark; all of YOU.

Just as you are right at this moment.

What's not to love about you?

Nothing.

OK, so what's to love about you?

Everything. Yum. True love. When you decide to love yourself utterly, utterly – and it really is just a decision, all your cells in your body rejoice. See, you knew as a baby you were completely and utterly lovable. You didn't judge your anger, your jealousy, and the way you look. You accepted and loved yourself when you cried, till you were blue and squishy in the face; when you crapped your pants and when you made others laugh. You knew you were beautiful and what did you get back? Adoration from everyone – even strangers!

Can you imagine a world where everyone truly loves themselves; just as they are? How would people treat *you*, if they loved themselves? What would that world be like? Would there be less emphasis on pain and more on pleasure? Would there be less illness? Could a war actually eventuate under these circumstances? Would self-harm occur? Could a person love a cigarette, more than their wellbeing?

Could a person *love a person* more than their own wellbeing, daily? Most women that I've met have been brought up by their families and schools to "think of others before themselves." I call this external love and its great – but external love without internal love is dangerous because it hurts us. It hurts our health and our wellbeing and our future. Only having external love hurts those we love too; they worry about us, they can't trust us to do right by ourselves, and when we don't, they often end up having to look after us, so in the end, we all lose.

The saying could have gone, "think of others as you do yourself." Somewhere along the way, the message of what love is got mixed up. We decided that focussing our love externally was more important; we think nothing of spending a lot of time getting *just the right birthday present* for a friend, but when we need the bathroom? We hold it in. It can wait, there are far more pressing matters to attend to. Almost every woman I have ever talked to does this before they grow their internal self-love. But until then, we think focussing on our internal love is selfish. And of course it is, but – it's the best kind of selfish! Love the selfish! Spreading love throughout your entire body and life, so that you can spread it into the world? Your love really does make the world go round.

Which kind of love do you find easier to do? External love or internal love? I invite you to keep your level of external love high and increase your self-love to match it, read on for the how.

Your relationship with yourself is never more transparent that when we are talking about self-love. Because it's an inside job. It's never about what he's done or what he's said. *Because he couldn't do it to you, if you weren't already doing it to yourself.* Permission for him was granted the moment you started doing it to yourself. So, the relationship you have with yourself on the inside is the most precious one, its gold. It's way more important than the relationship you have with the love of your life, with your children, and with your customers. And as I said earlier, there are always two relationships at play in every relationship: the one you're having with them and the one you're having with yourself. The one you've having with yourself sets the tone of each relationship.

Why?

The way the world treats you is always the way you are treating yourself. Think the world has forgotten about you and your talents? YOU have forgotten about YOU! It doesn't happen by accident that suddenly nobody see's your gifts anymore, because you set the trend 6 months ago, by not speaking up proudly about your upcoming workshop. Because you didn't want to appear *"brazen"*. You set the trend 2 weeks ago of ignoring your back pain and trudging into work today only to be nominated *as the person* to work over Christmas. It's too much – you can't take it... but you started it. The world is always showing you how you are treating you and the world is always showing you your precise level of self-love. And this is a good thing!

So take a look outside gorgeous and tell me what you see? Do you see your friends putting you first? Does everyone respect your talents, your heart, and your time? Do you see the men around you racing towards you to make you happy? If your answer is a resounding no or a 20%

yes... where are you saying yes to yourself 20% of the time? And make no mistake: the world is always responding to your deepest belief about yourself, so don't be fooled that you look like a yummy mummy, if your deepest belief about yourself is that who you really are isn't important, and that you are invisible, and only worthy of attention during a conversation *because you help someone*. Then, the outside world won't see you when you are hurting, they will just see what you do for them.

You've seen *Marianna* before, she's a forty something living in luxury with her four children and *über* successful husband, she is on more charity committee's and parent committee's than you have rooms in your house. She drives a flashy black four wheel drive and is always throwing some party for some cause. You don't know her very well, but you do know that she stands out. Big time. With her big voice and big life you see what she does for people. But, do you actually see her with the same sensitivity you see a friend with? No. You just see what she does for others because you are responding to her deepest belief about herself that she *herself* is invisible.

So, if you don't want people to ignore you today, get up right now and go to the bathroom and stop holding it in! Have that bath you've been promising yourself and pick up the phone albeit gingerly, but say no for tonight. If you are hurt by the world, stop hurting yourself this very minute. The world can only be a kinder place when we are kinder to our hearts. Stop waiting for someone to come and rescue you, it isn't ever going to happen. No one is coming for you right now – look out your window – is that Prince Charming coming down your driveway? No, it's the mailman.

Are you going to treat yourself like the Goddess you are? Because then you teach *them* how to treat you and there is no greater life lived than one spent in utter love, for the self and for others in equal devotion.

What defines your self-love is how much action you take in the name of it. How much are you going to allow yourself to receive today? For it's not a luxury. Self-love is a necessity for a life filled with love and happiness. You cannot have it if you cannot receive it from yourself to yourself. What person does that make you if you block receiving it?

A big fat fake.

Because you fill others' lives with love and are OK with receiving less. Nobody wins long-term, even if it seems that they do at the time.

I can love you.

Won't you?

People are always subconsciously responding to you, spend this morning adding to yourself with a green juice at sunrise and delectably notice how the outside world will respond to this vibration. Skip breakfast and watch the world skip you.

It always starts with you. Ignoring you didn't start with Carly or Catherine, it started with you ignoring you. People just follow suit. This world just follows the stubborn precedent you set years ago.

You might remember a particular time in your life when you treated yourself really well? When you had high standards for yourself and if you look back, do you see that the world responded to you differently? I came back from a yoga retreat a few years ago and I walked around all week and noticed that even strangers had picked up on my new self-love with several drivers letting me in first time, which almost never happens in the city. Then I forgot about it a bit and some of my old patterns came back; like when I took a pair of shoes back to a shop and the sales assistant kept going off in different directions, taking sizes for customers instead of serving me properly. And then I remembered ahhhhh it was me sending her the unconscious memo "ignore me, I'm not worth it." It wasn't her that began this dynamic, it was me!

So I now use the outside world as my gauge. If someone has disrespected me, the first thing I think is, *Oh, I've slipped. The outside world is showing me I've slipped. I must be doing that to me, but where I am doing this to myself or another? Where am I disrespecting myself? And I get to take myself to the next level of self-respect. Thank you disrespectful person for making me respect myself more.*

Do a little experiment today: use the next hour for your enjoyment. Don't be rushed, do exactly what you want to do, when you want to do it, without worry. Have everything just so. And notice what happens in that hour for you and for anybody else that approaches you.

Jo, a beautiful professional woman in her mid-30's didn't ask anyone for what she was yearning for; a big hug, love, and closeness. She had gotten stuck being Ms. Independent somewhere along the way and it was here that she was completely comfortable, yet intensely lonely. Her friends knew her as bright, happy, *Josie Jo* – the *Jo* that always cheered them up. And *Jo*? She didn't realise that there was room for her to take up space and ask for what she wanted. And that it would be easier to do than what she had been doing. She'd struggled all her life with feeling worthy enough to just ask for what she needed from people – always worrying she'd be a burden. She dropped this note after doing her blisswork:

"Oh I brung it! LOL. I texted six girlfriends YES SIX! More than I could fit on one hand!! I requested that they shower me with love, compliments, and beautiful blessings. Whispering 'sweet nothings' were also welcome.

I put it to the test last night with my friends and I have to say that this morning that painful hole in my heart is filled with beautiful words and feelings and LOVE!! :-)

SOOOOO this morning, I took aside a manager who is visiting from the states and asked him for a job! (Better than the one I was settling for yesterday) and told him to hire me cause I am so awesome!! I just spent the last hour telling him how amazing I am. His comment was, "Is there anything you can't do or haven't done?!"

So before I knew it, he came to provide me with the job description etc. And his assistant was already emailing me stuff pppfff I AM IN DEMAAAND! My favourite affirmation is dancing to the sound of the violins 'Life Loves Me.' And I love me xx"

It simply is the most important relationship you will ever have.

You are never alone when you love yourself. *Because you have you by your side.*

See nobody knows how you feel minute to minute, second to second. Only you. So, who knows *how* you need to be loved any better than you? No one.

So even if you're surrounded by love or you've been disappointed in the way *they've* loved you, shown up for you or done right by you; *Bedazzle yourself with self-love.* And this is the cool thing about self-love; you can set it to the exact level of bedazzlement you deserve. Did you know that? You can set it to exactly how you like it. Like...

Take yourself out to a café and *have it all exactly as you like it.* Order two desserts with a green juice for lunch. Take yourself shopping with nobody telling you how long you should be. Go exactly where you want. Know what it's going to do for you? Something very gorgeous happens when you love yourself in the exact way, shape and level that you need, want, desire, right now. You'll GLOW. You'll stop resenting others and revel in making yourself really truly happy.

Goddess, no matter how many delicious people you have around you, or however many you don't – there is always going to be about one-third of you that can only be supercharged, filled, loved up by YOU – GORGEOUS YOU! Did you know that? Really truly?

That one-third of you can only be filled with what you want to eat, with how you want to walk, with that dance you need to do right now, with your hair blow dried just so, with the exact way you want to listen to yourself, cherish yourself and love and celebrate yourself! Your way!

It's big glorious stuff like the choices you make today for your health, future, and life and it's tiny sweet stuff like wearing that sticky pink lip gloss because it's just cuteness personified.

And loving yourself actually feels really, really good... so that means that there is a very special one-third of you that's wanting *you to seduce it with your love.*

Always.

How much you love yourself will determine what sort of day you will have.

And on difficult days?

Your self-love becomes your warm jacket on the coldest of days.

If you're feeling kind of off-kilter today, wrap yourself up in a soft blanket of self-love until you feel better.

Whatever is going on for you right now, your jacket of self-love will insulate you – it will take the edges off a sharp day. It will fill you up when you are left empty and becomes the difference between you falling down with a problem, or becoming twice the woman because of it.

For example, I find that the level of self-love a client has for herself dictates how deeply she is able commit to her blisswork. The more she loves herself the more time she will naturally give back to herself. When you follow through on a priority that will add to you, you know your self-love is in graceful motion.

What is self-love?

Self-love is you being kind to yourself.

This is my definition of self-love. And if you love yourself fully and utterly, it turns outwards to others immediately: If you are kind to yourself, it is impossible to be unkind to another because it will hurt you too much.

I once had a client who hated that she yelled at her kids, she yelled at her husband, hell she even yelled at her sister when she came to stay.

She was a self-confessed *bona fide* yeller. She'd gone to see a specialist who'd given her strategies to stop yelling at her kids. But she couldn't. She was totally and utterly sucked dry by her life and was at the end of her tether. Yelling was the only thing she had left. She wasn't *just* a yeller of course. She was a stunningly talented woman who hadn't learnt how to be kind to herself... *yet*.

She came to me in tears because she couldn't stop yelling and couldn't do the strategies, so on top of everything else she was feeling like a failure too. A lovely self-hate sandwich if ever there was one. Mmmm. Softly, I told her that these strategies *can only truly work* when you have enough self-love to do them. Roll on 6 months into my coaching program and she wowed herself and her family. Her self-love had grown so intensely, that she found she couldn't shout at them anymore because it didn't feel right. It *hurt her* too much to shout at them, so she stopped. The bona fide yeller became the bone fide mother.

I want you to cherish yourself and be in awe of your very essence and your "youness". I want you to fall in love with everything bad you have just done to yourself and everything good you have done for everyone else. Because it always leads you back to self-love, if you let it. I want you to fall in love with your hair that has a mind of its own, your crooked nose, and externally the exact way your life looks now. Your youness, which is everything that makes you, you. I want you to fall in love with the good, the bad, and the ugly in you and in your life.

Why?

Because you are too beautiful not to.

When you leave being good to yourself till the very end of the day, because you put others first all day long and give them the best of your love, (which is towards everyone else, but you) Goddess, that's your teeny tiny level of self-love talking. And when you practice teeny, tiny levels you begin to resent doing for those you love. Poison emanates from you instead of pure love and the cells in your body receive your poison moving through them and out into the world. And that is the start of some types of *illness; being angry with yourself as well as all types of hating yourself, being angry at him and the world, and so on. When you practice generous lashings of self-love, it will feel selfish *because it is;* but during that same day, you also become the most unselfish person you know. Because you have more to give. It's very hard to ask someone who is dried out and empty to give to you. But it's very easy when that someone loves herself and lo and behold; it becomes a divine pleasure to help you! And she will help you a lot! And the world a lot.

*Let's talk about illness, particularly cancer. I'm not talking about the type of cancer wonderful people get by being in the same place as toxic waste for example. I am talking about the kind of cancer wonderful people get that isn't from something outside of them attacking them, but from something inside. So, why would our bodies attack us? Is it possible that our bodies just follow our mind?

According to the Journal of Psychosomatic Research, "Extreme suppression of anger was the most commonly identified characteristic of 160 breast cancer patients." (1) In other research: "Extremely low anger scores have been noted in numerous studies of patients with cancer. Such low scores suggest suppression, repression, or restraint of anger. There is evidence to show that suppressed anger can be a precursor to the development of cancer, and also a factor in its progression after diagnosis." (2) In an article (3) about the oldest documented woman that ever lived, Jeane Calment, the most interesting thing in this article is that a woman that lived 122 years smoked cigarettes for 100 years without any ill effect. Why didn't smoking lead her to an early grave? I would say, "Because thought is more important than lifestyle."[4]

I was listening to the Sydney radio show with Kyle and Jackie O this morning. A girl phoned in, said her mother has breast cancer, and that

---

4   (1) Journal of Psychosomatic Research Volume 19, Issue 2, April 1975, Pages 147–153
    (2) Cancer Nurs. 2000 Oct;23(5):344–9.
    (3) Retrieved April 28, 2014, from http://anson.ucdavis.edu/~wang/calment.html

her mother is not worried for herself and for what might happen to her. At this point, the girl's voice cracked; her mum is worried for the reactions and effect on her children and family. Kyle said, "Why does it always happen to the good ones?" You know what I yelled at the radio? "Because they are only good to others, never to themselves – so their body just follows their lead!"

When you put others first, to the detriment of yourself, it sets a precedent in your body. When you hold your anger in, your feelings in, your deepest darkest wants and needs in, your body sees this as an attack. Your body follows you and what you do and say. For example, when you attack yourself by saying yes to another and so a mean no to you, your body just follows your lead. Some people call this Breast Cancer. I call this a misunderstanding of love in that person. Somewhere along the line that person has believed it better and more worthy to serve and love someone else first. Repeatedly. At their own expense. Day after day, year after year. They take pride in external love; resulting in becoming entrenched in helping others, not from their extra, *but when they have nothing left to give.* Others become more important than them. Their needs become repeatedly bigger than yours.

Why would your body attack itself?

It wouldn't, it can't, unless the climate has already been set in you to attack. And nobody else is setting that, but you. You might have learnt it from someone else, but nobody is holding a gun to your head right now saying "Don't you dare love yourself today!"

So, the level of self-love you have right now in your body is really important. It will dictate how much love you let in from everyone and everything. Scary, but fabulous at the same time don't you think? Because you can love yourself, right now. So no matter where you find yourself: having to look after sick kids, or your older parents, no matter how stuck you think you are in having to help others you're not.

And you know what it's going to take?

You being the absolute Goddess of implementation. Let me explain:

Your self-love is either growing or dying in you. It cannot do both.

To grow it you need to take a daily dose of self-love every day. To kill it off, you need to love something or someone at the expense of yourself, repeatedly.

So, the No.1 contributor to your Dry-out = poor discipline to implement self-love.

So, what to do?

You have to implement self-love for it to *be* self-love. Without action self-love becomes self guilt, you know you should do it, but...

Imagine two groups of women. The first group have slithered down the butt crack of life, but really action their self-love. The second group have slid down there too, and are making cups of tea with group 1, but *don't* take action on their self-love. Who will fare better? Who would you bet on to be creating a life that turned them on? Group 1 or group 2? Your self-love can only take place if you do it. I encourage you to self-love yourself silly and then do it a lot! *Starting now.*

Shall we make the decision right now? To fall in love with ourselves? So we can take action for ourselves in the name of love? "I decide to LOVE myself." Say this to yourself and HUG yourself. It's going to take bravery on your part to forge your own path. Wanna receive a dollop of your own self-love now?

Blow a kiss to all that you are and all that you are not, you are perfect just the way you are. X

It's time to fall in love with the good, the bad and the ugly in you. When you ever so surely fall in love with yourself, you'll find that *they* will too. This is going to take some deep practice to love yourself just as you are.

Not when you lose weight, not when you get that client, not when you live the life of your dreams, but right now as you read this very page.

What's in your way of you choosing to love yourself now?
Let's do a detox.

Write down all things you don't like about yourself. Really get it out. I'll start you off with some classics from clients of mine over the years:

I don't like my:

- squashy tummy (it spills out over everything)
- spotty skin (I'm 35 and still suffer from acne!)
- inability to earn proper money like my friends
- social awkwardness (I find chatting to the mums at school hard)
- shyness (I feel really tense when I am invited anywhere)
- girlishness around my boyfriends (why can't I be more womanly?)
- over-eating at night
- child-bearing hips
- procrastination (I still haven't done my tax for last year)
- reaction to my children when they interrupt me
- addiction to trash mags
- kitchen (it's disorganised)
- eyesight (it's fading).

OK, so you get the idea, write it about everything including all the little self-hates too. Now write what you do like about yourself. Here are some to spur you on:

- I like my laugh.
- I like my confident nature.
- I like that I am kind.

- I like that I always put a brave face on when I am dog tired.
- I like that I am a good driver.
- I like my eyes.
- I like my unshakeable belief in myself and my talents.
- I like my aptitude at work.
- I like that I am always polite.
- I like that I...

Which list is longer? Do you like yourself more or dislike yourself more? For most of my clients, when we really get down to it they actually don't like or approve of themselves very much. I like them very much, but it doesn't matter see? It doesn't matter how much I like you if you don't like yourself. Because it just falls on deaf ears. It has nowhere to go if there is no space for it to live inside of you. I want there to be rooms and rooms inside of you to move boxes of self-love into because loving yourself is the difference between an OK marriage where she rolls her eyes at him, complains about him to her friends, versus the kind of marriage that nourishes every inch of your being. The type of marriage that fills you up with so much love, you think you might burst and you get teary at the thought of never being with him again. The kind of marriage that is your love affair for life.

You cannot have a love affair for life with him if you haven't begun a torrid love affair with yourself, FIRST. He may gaze across the shopping trolley at you in the supermarket and mouth "You're beautiful," but if you don't believe him because you're wearing your red corduroy "period" jeans, his love for you can go nowhere, but into the air around you and possibly into the bananas behind you. And believe me, the bananas know they are beautiful! Your beloved's love for you cannot go into you and so it cannot infuse your marriage with life force. Instead it goes around it.

Similarly, if you are on your way to a party and are looking fabulous with freshly blow dried hair and that super tight super *ooh là là* dress on and he mouths "You're beautiful" and again you don't believe him because all you think is, *thank you, but it's not really me see, it's the hair and pushed up boobs talking*. It's the *same thing* as before, you don't really love yourself just as you are, so you can never let him. And Goddess, he so wants in. He knows he has a Goddess by his side, but do you?

I remember my sister saying to me after my wedding, "Marina, you should have seen the way Paul was looking at you." The way he looks at me feels natural (now) because I have risen to see myself in the same light. I didn't used to and I remember the first time he really looked at me, I mean really *looked at me*. He saw all of me with that one appraising gaze and I felt a prickly hot embarrassment sweep over me. I couldn't help smiling goofily as I looked away. I couldn't meet his gaze. I thought, "What *is he* looking at?" but at the same time I really, really liked it and would look back at him shyly. It was what I had been searching for my whole life. *A man who really saw me.*

And then there are some days where I don't love myself quite as much, when I don't feel good enough and wish things had gone differently. On those days, Paul loves me so very deeply that I cannot help but be reminded to love and accept myself just the way I am. He loves me when I cannot. You may see me one day in the street sludging it, where I'm unable to shine, lunging around with crap hair and being all heavy and in pain with a bucketful of ugly feelings thrown in. I'd like to think that I will be able to heap as much self-love onto myself on those days and that I can love my imperfection as you can love yours.

> *Self-love is that soft warm blanket you wrap around yourself when you're cold from grief and pain.*

I want to make self-love the new fashion where yes you are the most delicious slave to it; and it becomes the new black classic. FOREVER.

Look around you, most women are not wearing it, in fact it's safe to say they've never even heard of it. Why? Because it's not been in vogue until now. Self-hate, *look at my fat thighs. Gawd, I hope she likes me*, calling other women "What a bitch!" at the drop of a hat, and seeing her flaws before you take in her beauty *are all in fashion right now*. "You stole my look bitch" seems to be really hot right now. But really, how does it make you feel to say it? Warm and sexy? Or cold and hard? Which dress would you rather wear? One that makes you feel warm and sexy or a cold and hard one? Which woman would a man rather be with? A warm and sexy one, or a cold and hard one?

Or what about when we hear about a famous celebrity who was cheated on by her husband, like Cindy Crawford a few years back? You know what I heard the most from women around me and magazine stories? "What chance do I have if even Cindy C gets cheated on?" Yet, are we hearing the same from our men about the actor Kristen Stewart cheating on Robert Pattinson? Are they saying, what chance do I have if even Robert Pattinson got cheated on? Can you even imagine that? Gossip male magazines saying that?

No, I thought not.

The current fashion is to watch painful films and TV that display far more self-hate than self-love. You only have to switch on the TV to see cop show after hospital show after news bulletin after... anyway, let me ask you this; what happens to a couple after they've been on the couch watching two hours of murder drama on TV? Do they really go to bed at 11:00pm and have the most outrageously sensual sex with each other? Does watching self-hate regularly really set you up for the hottest sex you've ever had that night?

But, what if you've both been indulging in the latest fashion of self-love; is it more possible to practice very HOT sex with your lover? O.O.O. YES.

So, go flaunt the latest line in self-love. So, however much you've liked or disliked yourself in the past, you've decided NOW to love yourself and that's all that matters – ready?

Let me explain: Your self-love can be turned on with the little choices like coming into the bedroom where you husband is waiting for you to climb in, feeling that your lips are a bit dry and going back into the bathroom to apply soft lip balm. Self-love is brushing your teeth in the sink without walking around with that damn thing buzzing in your mouth while picking dirty clothes off the floor. Self-love is taking time to decide what you want to wear in the mornings, so you walk out feeling beautiful and not leaving *you* till the last minute. Self-love is showing up on time for your appointments, so you get the most out of them. Self-love is saying no to that offer of lunch with a work mate when really they make you uncomfortable because they are so awkward and you can't actually be bothered. You may not be sure about what you do want, but you aren't going to say yes and fake it, which leaves her free to find a real friend.

And you can turn your self-love on with big things too: like deciding to divorce him, finally. Like saying yes to a work deal that makes you giddy with fear and rollercoaster with excitement. It's drawing a line in the sand and saying NO, I will not put myself through this anymore. Frankly, self-love can be uncomfortable and self-respect is one of the more difficult aspects of self-love because it's risky and we might lose that person, or make them angry. But when you decide to change what you do and love yourself instead? Your self-love becomes your powerful hero because it's HERE that you stop your addiction. It's HERE that you silence your hateful actions towards yourself and it's HERE that with every inch of your body you decide to be loved by a beautiful man. Big breath. *You're ready*. It's time.

Self-love is a lot of things, both big and small. When you first try on your self-love jacket, there will be certain places it might feel a bit too big for you because *it will* make you take up more room at home when you ask your children to help you more around the house. It will also feel too loud when you stand up for yourself and it will make you take up too much room in the supermarket when the assistant blithely tells you it's down that aisle, but instead you stop him and say, "Would you show me?" It's going to take bravery in the face of not being liked as much. Of moving away from tending to his needs first before your own. It's going to feel sometimes like you are the only one doing it and that others might think you're a bit prissy. But, for the trend setters among you, who want to blaze an outrageous trail of extreme self-love to get your love affair for life, to have an occupation that nourishes every fibre of your being, and pays you handsomely. Why not? Most people around you won't be blazing this trail... they'll be wearing last season's fashion for years to come and so enduring the same problems and pitfalls they had last time, over, and over. Ever met those people that say the same complaining things over and over? Yup. Their self-love has yet to kick in. Want to implement your self-love daily? Here is your discipline. It takes 10 minutes and I do this every day and I swear (like a truckie) by it!

IMPLEMENTING SELF-LOVE LIKE A GODDESS:

Self-love 1: Desire. Visualise. Sit close. Implement.

Self-love 2: Detox what's in my way from receiving my desires.

During my Day:

Self-love 3: When confronted with someone's brilliance or idiocy, I ask: Where is that in me? I might even be brave enough to rock that very same quality because if I've noticed it, I probably need it.

Self-love 4: Treat myself like a Goddess.

Self-love 5: So I can treat YOU like a Goddess!

Put on your pink self-love jacket today!

Have you ever been in a really good mood, had an interaction with somebody who seemed to disapprove of you, and then feel your good mood ebb away? I have; lots. Just the other day it happened. A small thing by all accounts, but it just goes to show you how insidious disapproval can be. I was singing out loud while doing some hand washing to "Primadonna Girl" by Marina and the Diamonds (isn't that the BEST name for a band?!) and we had friends of friends staying with us. There I was, elbow deep in hand washing, hair piled on my head having a boogie when the woman I barely knew bowls in, carrying a large bundle of washing and carrying a face that looked like she'd just been slapped with a wet fish. "Can I wash this now?" she snaps. "Yes, of course," I say. "After my washing has finished." (I was about halfway through.) She didn't smile once; in fact she looked positively furious that she, the guest, had to wait. She walked out without a word.

Good mood... ebbing away... I sighed and got on with my washing. Hang on a minute: what I have just taken on?

I'd just taken on her furious jacket – and was wearing that instead of my self-love jacket. OK, time for a turnaround.

THIS IS THE PINK SELF-LOVE JACKET PROCESS THAT IS JUST FOR YOU!

When someone says something to you that hurts you, here is what you do. Ask yourself:

1. Did she treat me like a GODDESS right now?

2. Give myself the OPPOSITE.

3. Thank me for being the glorious trendsetter I am as I put my pink SELF-LOVE jacket back on.

Ahhhh, that's better. There is enormous freedom for you if you don't do to yourself what they've just done to you. They've just fallen off their happy horse, that's all.

Here are some common scenarios:

Your partner walks into the room and gives you a perfunctory peck on the cheek, all whilst checking his phone as he leaves the room. Did he treat you as a Goddess right now? Nope. Did he treat himself to his highest possibility? Nope. He just missed out on really being with you. So, give yourself the opposite: real LOVE. Kiss yourself on the top of your hand like a queen would and say, "I LOVE you, (your name). My God you are just fabulous!" You can't not laugh. It will turn you around. Or hug yourself. *Yes, you are worth it.* What if you decided to do this every time somebody pissed you off? Now, there's a fabulous day waiting in the wings!

Your best friend only calls you when she needs to talk through a problem. Is she treating you like a Goddess, right now? Nope. Is she treating herself like a Goddess right now? Nope, because she isn't doing something that is making her AND you feel good. It's one sided. Again. Give yourself the opposite – take up space in the conversation with – "You know what Zoe? I'd really like to ask you something..." and if she doesn't like it? Then you know her self-love is down.

Let me explain.

As you know by now, every woman on this planet is a Goddess. If she doesn't treat you like a Goddess, then you know she isn't treating herself like a Goddess either. Because a Goddess *speaks* so that it feels good to her and to others. If she isn't being good to you, then she isn't being good to herself. Full stop. So the way she speaks to you tells you more about her than it does you. This will help you to stop taking things so personally when someone isn't very nice to you. If they cannot be nice to you, it's because they are in pain. I used to say this to my daughter when she was little. "Maya, when mummy shouts at you when normally she wouldn't, it's because I am in pain." She really got it when she was little and now if I'm uncharacteristically angry, she has taken to saying, "Mummy, are you alright?" She's taken herself out of the firing line. She's become very good at treating herself nicely; especially, when somebody else hasn't. It's her self-love jacket and she'll wear this safely throughout her life. *Yes, she's worth it.*

And you know if your friend isn't treating herself like a Goddess, it's because of her mindset or maybe she's tired, stressed, and feeling less than divine. Anyway, it doesn't really matter what is going on for her. If she isn't treating you like a Goddess, she definitely isn't treating herself like one. But, if she treated herself like a Goddess would she treat you better? Hell yeah! She would have surplus energy to give you and listen to you with. She would also know that listening to you makes more room in her to receive because the more she gives the more she receives.

So, if that woman staying with us treated herself like a Goddess, then she would have given me the same amount of respect as she gives herself and woken up earlier than midday to ensure we all got what we wanted.

If your partner treated himself better he would want to be present to you every day, so he doesn't miss a single thing.

And here's the thing: Relationships are meant to feel a bit yucky when neither party particularly loves themselves. You are meant to feel yucky, when the other person doesn't give you as much as you give them. You are meant to feel a bit taken advantage of. You are meant to feel as though they get what they want from you, but you don't get what you want from them. You are meant to feel this way.

> You are not meant to have a fabulous
> time of it, if you don't love and
> care for yourself.

Yes, the world is set up so it does feel uncomfortable when you do not love yourself. You are not meant to be rewarded for it – far from it! You will engage in relationships with people who also don't love themselves, the kind who treat you as badly as you treat yourself. Those who forget your birthday, who only talk about themselves, who only ring you when they've got a problem, who take more than they give, who have constant drama in their lives and need your help; until you get sick and tired of it, and decide. Remember everything starts with a decision. Your decision. You decide that you are going to stop giving them all the goodies at the expense of yourself and start giving back to yourself first. Guess what happens when you do? Others start following suit.

> ## "I've been in a relationship with myself for 49 years and that's the one I need to work on."
>
> *– Kim Cattrall as Samantha in the 2008 film,*
> *Sex and the City, naked, covered in Sushi,*
> *and pissed off from giving Smith her heart*
> *and not receiving enough back.*

---

7 LOVE Questions to bring me back to self-love:

1. How kind am I being to myself right now?

2. What if I didn't abandon myself today?

3. Is this adding or taking away from me?

4. Am I treating myself like a Goddess?

5. Am I reaching for my pleasure or my pain?

6. What self-love action is my heart really yearning for?

7. If I loved myself silly how would the next hour look?

LOVE is receiving someone to hug, hold, caress, and desire you. Love is somebody showering you with kindness, adoration, limitless support, and unconditional acceptance.

SELF-LOVE is receiving this from yourself. Self-love is receiving this from yourself on a day you feel bad. Self-love is you massaging your breasts and belly with warm nice smelling oil when your hormones are going wild and you feel teary, and angry, and in pain. Self-love is asking for your lover to massage your feet when he gets home today. And if he declines, you do it and enjoy it. Self-love is setting up that vibration of self-love, so that outside love has an easier time of following it.

SELF-LOVE is realising that you've slipped out of self-love; you've eaten crap again, or you just realised that somewhere along the line you stopped going to the gym – *when did that happen?* Self-love is a curious thing. It matters not what you just did or did not do. You can self-love it this very moment and turn this thing around! *Go run yourself a bath* even though you skipped that yoga class, *or play your favourite song right now and dance* even though you haven't meditated in ages.

What defines your self-love is how much action you take in the name of it, not how much *you think* you should do it.

It's Action Versus Thinking it.

Thinking self-love without Action = Overwhelm.

How can you care for yourself for the rest of the day Goddess? How about you do one of these after you put this book down?

Here are a smattering of ideas:

- ⚘ Never underestimate the power of sitting still for three minutes to melt away what isn't you.

- ⚘ Press pause, pour a cup of tea... and dream a little. It's good for you.

- ⚘ Draw yourself a bath during the day, throw in some rose petals, honey and rose oil, play some music and light some candles.

- ⚘ Stand up and imagine you are already living your dream: amuse yourself and act it out (remember my beach rehearsals.)

⚴ Buy yourself a bunch of flowers, or pick them from the garden, just because.

⚴ Give yourself an extra break today and thoroughly enjoy it!

Make little pit stops throughout your day for dollops of self-love. Remember – it doesn't matter what you just did, you have the power *now* to love yourself – *how cool is that?*

Surprise yourself!

---

1 Minute Ritual

My one-minute ritual for you to do anytime today...

✳ I HUG myself.

✳ I forgive myself for what I couldn't do.

✳ I CHEER myself for what I did do, "WOO!"

✳ I breathe in.

✳ I'm sorry body, mind and soul for hurting you knowingly, or unknowingly.

✳ I am ready for this next moment with open arms...

✳ ... Because I trust myself to love myself through it...

✳ ... To treat myself gently.

✳ I begin now...

Ahhh... Goddess, would you like more love coming back to you? And it's all in the way that you say it...

SPEAKING FOR PLEASURE!

Let me ask you something. How important are you to you? How important have you been to you? If you were really important to yourself, then would you make sure that everything you said felt delectably pleasurable to you? Can you imagine that?

What if every single thing that came out of your mouth today was pleasurable to you? What if you only spoke words that turn you on and him on? Would your energy rise each time you said something? What if you spoke, so it made you feel good and the other person feel good? Always?

What happens when you find yourself talking to a person who has heavier energy than you? Talking for your pleasure brilliantly insulates your light because it doesn't matter how dim their light is, you won't drop down to where they are.

This is what I call speaking for pleasure and it can turn any woman's life enticingly upside down.

See, we've become so used to talking *without pleasure*. When your husband comes home with the weekly shop and you ask flatly, "Where's the nuts?" you will more than certainly hear, "I got them" in the same toneless retort. It doesn't add to you, or him. It just adds more flatness to your day. Flat + Flat = FLAT. And long term, it kind of hurts what you've got between you, doesn't it?

But what if you spoke for your pleasure only?

Absolutely only using the tone and words that stroke you on their way out?

Before you utter even the tiniest word: take a breath and try it! What were you going to say? Now say it so it brings you pleasure to say. You've set the tone to receive a pleasurable response right back.

A client of mine, *Jackie* decided to try this. She worked in a colourless, staid office where most of the people who worked there didn't even make eye contact. It was sucking her dry. She tried it the first day with a guy named *Sal. Sal* was well known for being surly and a bit of a bully. He slammed a project file down on her desk and without looking back said, "By 5:00pm not a minute late." Not very pleasurable. Now who was setting the tone here? And was it working for either of them? Time to set the tone by speaking for your pleasure only. *Jackie* quickly called after him "Sure Sal, I might even get it in for 4:59pm." She made herself laugh. She got it in at 5:10pm and when she dropped the file on his desk, instead of being all awkward and apologetic, she looked him straight in the eyes and smiling with teeth, said, "There Sal, I'm 10 minutes late. What can I say? I wanted to do a good job for you."

He beamed at her, what could he say? Since that day, *Sal* has taken more notice of where Jackie is at and now asks if *she can* deliver a project in by a certain time. And he always makes a point of smiling at her when he asks... speaking for your pleasure sets the tone for everyone around you and feels really, really good!

And for extra cherries on top: what about saying, "No," with pleasure? When we say no in the name of self-love, we can often feel awkward during, but oh so relieved afterwards! What if you could express your newfound self-love during your pleasurable no's? So, instead of apologising to a friend that you can't make it and straining at the end with, "Is that OK?" to her; instead you say, "Zara, it's not going to work for me tonight, but thank you for asking. I love you," and all the while you're smiling, feeling pleasurable thoughts and feeling good. How much grace and ease can you add to your friendships?

OK, next up... drum roll please, I have a q-q-question...

W-W-WOULD YOU LIKE A HOT LOVE AFFAIR FOR LIFE WITH HIM?

Everything we've done up until now and everything we're going to do together will give you a hot love affair for life, but specifically I have a few things I want to add to you two love birds to pull it all together and have you skipping off into the sunset. And if you're not with a lover right now? Read on, you might just want this in your day, anyway...

Let your self-love set the tone for your relationships:

I know you're in the mood to have a hot love affair for life. But how does one do that when you're feeling fantastically fun and flirty and he's sitting on the couch moaning about the day he's had? How does a gal keep her mojo when he's picky, prickly, and shut off from you? In fact, how does one stay fabulously high and *Goddess like* when all around her is *not that?* The below technique can be used for you and him and you and everyone else. To be able to stay high and happy when all around you is not, is like Duran Duran all over again. Like the best thing ever.

To prep you so you're ready for this, hop to page 144 and do The LOVE Bug Technique in the DETOX chapter first and then come straight back to this page, so we can start.

OK! You're back. This works when he's either in the mood to be with you all hot love affairish, or is really not and currently channel flicking like a ninja:

The 5 commandments that keep you two HOT, no matter what!

1. Take your attention off what he is or isn't doing and bring it back into you. Remember it's always good where you are.

2. Resist the urge to ask him what he wants to do, or say, "Shall we...?"

3. Instead YOU set the tone! (Page 115)

4. Focus on what you want and ask! (Page 79)

5. Remember, if you were your lover, what would you want for you?

**You lead you both back to that love affair
by *you receiving your desires first.*
And you are the one that leads you both away from that
love affair when you *regularly focus* on *his desires first.***

How much pleasure *you* are willing to ask for correlates to *your* level of self-love, no matter how grumpy that man is on the couch. What can get in the way of a woman having high self-love? Not feeling pretty or beautiful enough to ask for what you want in your marriage or in life is a huge one. (Mr. Antisocial on the couch can be another one). Feeling undesirable is another. Not feeling special, gorgeous, worthy, important, lovable are others. If this still feels like it's in the way for you, go to Main Course Healing (page 141) and choose the right process for you to clear this now. Because the level of self-love you add in today is the same level of love you can let in from your husband, boyfriend, friends, children, and your co-workers. Goddess, YOU are so, so worth it!

If you don't fall in LOVE with you, then you miss out on creating the greatest love story with another. And men adore us with all of their being. It's us who forget. You. Are. DIVINE. Own it.

An ode to you...

READ THIS OUT LOUD TO YOURSELF TO FEEL DELICIOUS AGAIN:

"I am not what is happening to me right now. I am not my bank account, I am not how he is treating me, I am not the success of that project, I am not that thing I am worried about, I am not my skin or size of my belly right now.

I am not the success or failure of my life.

How could I be?

I am exquisite me. I am not any of that. I take the power I have been giving to *that situation, that person* and come back into my own loving energy field. It always feels good to be in me. I take a deep breath now into my belly (hold it in for a beat) and I breathe out fully from my mouth. (Do this two more times now as you read the rest.)

I have all the delectable power at my fingertips to feel how delicious I am NOW. I am free. The only person who can make me feel anything is me. Therefore, I choose to find myself perfect and delicious just as I am. I shine my light by smiling right now (with teeth!) Am I gorgeous? YES! Is there only one of these talents around? YES! Should I ask for what I want? YES! YES! YES!"

And the foundation for creating a hot love affair with him for the whole rest of your life is? Ta daaaaaaa! - carving out time to create a hot love affair with you! Having a hot love affair with him is to do with your own level of self-love.

How hot is your love and acceptance for you? Burning hot? Do you accept nothing less than the best for you?

Help him worship you Goddess...

1. Make a little heart list of how you want him to love you next. For example: I want him to find me in the house first when he gets home and kiss me full on the lips, properly before he sits at that damn computer.

2. After you've made your little heart list, go back and change each "him" or "you" word to "I" or "me". Shift the sentence around, so it makes sense. For example: So, I want to find myself properly loving myself before I do some work at home. Remember, when you put yourself first, he can follow. When you don't, he has no chance!

3. After you've made your heart list, write out your heart steps for the week. And write down what you want to ask him. So, it might look like this: "Hamish, I know when you come home from work you go straight to your computer, and for some reason... it's got me wanting to create a kissing ritual with you instead! I'd love you to come home, find me first and kiss me on the lips, hard. Want to try this tonight instead?"

Wow, you know you treasuring yourself and you asking him for what you want will move you faster in 7 days, than you wanting him to change! Truly. Utterly. Amazingly! Remember, it's all in the way you ask. Take baby steps and by the end of the first week: take notice. Are you both feeling the heat? Stay disciplined, I promise you, and your relationship will make you happier if you treasure yourself first.

Your level of love for you = His level of love for you.

If you're looking around and you're not happy with how he's loving you, love yourself more. Your self-love sets the invisible tone for how he treats you. He takes your internal cue. Remember you set the tone, not him.

Do you know what makes a relationship like yours really HOT?

THRIVING WHEN THERE IS CONFLICT.

This is a game changer: what would be possible for you and him if every time there was conflict, it brought you two closer together? How? I'll tell you.

1. What's the biggest thing you end up arguing about? What do they do that upsets you? It could be their attitude towards money, that they don't help you enough, or the way they speak to you. Let's say: it's the way they speak to you. (Remember, whenever someone is upsetting you it's because they are in pain). So, I want you to start recognising their signs. This will help both of you step out of this.

2. So, what tells you they are on their way to speaking to you rudely? How does their approach towards you change? Think back, and write down at least five bullet points that are visual, emotional, audible. For example:

↺ They do that thing with their forehead.

↺ It only happens when they're under pressure and questioning their ability to produce.

↺ They use my full name when asking for something.

↺ They only ever do this when we're out with friends.

↺ They start huffing and puffing in irritation at me.

3. What do they need at this point? Remember, they are in pain and need you to help them step out of it. For example:

↺ Physical touch is really important to them – so I'm going to grab their face, kiss it and say, "You can do better than this."

↺ Ask them what I can take off their plate.

↺ Make them laugh by making fun of the stupid stressful situation, so they can begin to relax.

Now, he is going to do the same for you! Sit down with him and ask him to go through 1–3. For example, if your biggest arguments stem from you feeling overwhelmed with the house and kids – what are your signs that you are on your way to becoming overwhelmed? Do you refuse his help? Do you start huffing and puffing? Is there a catch phrase you begin to throw about like "Why is it that no one in this household ever…" And what do you most need at this point, really? After you've both done this for each other, can you see how this will bring you two closer together? Damaging conflict only occurs when one of you is in pain, or you both are. Learning to recognise their signs is learning to love your partner in the way they most need and to help them step out of it.

Newness vs Hotness

Newness does NOT equate to hotness in your relationship with him. Ever. I remember when I first got together with my husband and my girlfriend *Kate* rang me one Friday night asking if I wanted to go to the flicks with her. "I'd love to" I said, "But Paul and I already have plans tonight." She scoffed, "Call me back in 5 years – you'll be dying to come out!" I remember rolling my eyes because she didn't get it. Then we both burst out laughing, me at her and her at me because she thought I was completely mad. Nine years on from the conversation, *Kate* is still leaving her husband at home and still can't understand why I would take mine out. And let me tell you something, her husband has the kind of looks, money, and kindness that really could make him the next Bruce Wayne.

What's newness? It's just stuff that's new. What's oldness? It's just stuff that's old. New and old. Old and new. It has nothing to do with love. It has nothing to do with how charged your moment is with him. When you peer at him from under your lashes and take in his own brand of hotness, the only thing he can think of is you.

> **Hotness in your relationship has everything to do with how**
> ***you* feel and nothing to do with *how long* you've shared a life**
> **together.**

When people crack jokes about marriage and sex, wait? *What sex?* It can only be said by people who have let something else dampen the hotness. And it isn't time. Its unresolved issues.

What can suck hotness from a relationship? It's when you and/or he are being continually sucked dry by routine and the running of your lives and the household. When you put routine and all else first and above your devout pleasure: you Dry-out.

Hot Love Affair Checklist:

✳ How close am I sitting to what I want? Deserve? Desire?

✳ Am I letting him produce them for me?

✳ Where am I blocking him?

✳ How much am I letting him produce for me?

✳ Who is setting the tone for the relationship him, or me?

✳ And is it working?

✳ Falling in love with all of me sets the tone for him to do the same.

✳ I ask for what I want with P.L.E.A.S.U.R.E.

✳ How am I appreciating this wonderful man?

✳ Am I mothering him with "we"?

✳ The LOVE Bug Technique increases the love between us.

✳ Thriving when there is conflict brings us closer.

✳ Read the sensuality and pleasure chapter.

✳ Talk to the hero in him, so he becomes his highest possibility.

✳ Turning on each part of me turns this relationship on.

✳ I am a Goddess; am I letting him treat me as one?

To turn your self-love on in an instant:

Start by stroking your thumb and say to it – I love you. Follow by stroking your arm and say to it, I love you – follow with the next part of your body and then the next and the next!

Receive your love for you over the next 7 days by creating a 7-day self-love plan. There's one for you at marinaj.net, just use the special code TYOGoddess and get in and start. And really enjoy this next week!

Chapter 7

Turn On Your Best Friend Within

· · · · · · · · · · · · · ·

Go ahead and wrap your arms around yourself. Feel that? This is YOU being a best friend to you in this moment. Kind, understanding, supportive, warm, and loving.

Your best friend is someone you go to when you're not feeling good and when you want to have a good time. She'll always listen to you, always want you to be happy, and unless she's squiggly gigglingly drunk – will always be *there for you* no matter what.

Are you this friend to yourself? Are you kind, understanding, supportive, warm and loving to yourself *all the time*? Are you completely and utterly creating a life that turns you on, or are you *in your own way*?

If I were your best friend, I'd want you feel so brilliant about yourself that you GO FOR IT in your life! I'd want you to go for it right NOW, not put yourself on the back burner. I'd want you to pick yourself up from your breakup, or from your disappointment this week with work; in fact, I'd want you to stand up to him, show him what he's missing, and I'd want you to want *MORE* for yourself. I'd want you to treat yourself nicely and not talk down to yourself. To fall in love with how you look and to do something about it, if you didn't. In short, I'd want you to be a best friend to you, *like I am to you.* Because you're lovely. You're so worth it, if you could just remember it every single day.

Yet when *I* want to do something, where I step out of where I am and into what turns me on, do I unleash myself fully and *go for it?* With everything I've got? Or do I hold myself back with some sort of story about *how it is, or how it will be?*

For instance, about how I'll never be really thin because I don't have model genes, so I'll give this morning's workout a miss, thanks, and lie in bed a bit longer. And what's the point in speaking up in meetings when nobody listens to me anyway? *You know how it is in this office.* Or put myself on a dating website? *You know what it's like out there.* Or book myself a life coach because I don't believe deep down *it can ever be different.* Story after story as to why we can't unleash ourselves fully and go for it, and all the while your soul is waiting for you to stop being that *toxic* friend to yourself. This is where, believing that you can't do it because of some story or excuse you tell yourself will suck the life right out of you. Day in and day out.

And when you do unleash yourself fully and go for it? You become that best friend to you, the toffee in your sticky toffee pudding and the cherry in your cherry cream pie.

I am convinced that living from a limited point of view about your life will age you over a long period of time. So what to do Goddess, if you are not feeling free about what is and isn't possible for you? Realise that you are the only one who can limit you:

> You are an unlimited being; to go against this is to go against nature, which is why it ages you.

There are no limits to you, not now, not ever! Be free *because you are.*

So I have a question for you: You're either being a toxic friend to yourself, or you're being your bestie. Which are you being to yourself right now? Are you wanting and doing the best for yourself? It's either one or the other. You can't be doing *both* at the same time. Trust the first answer that comes to you.

The story we tell ourselves as to why a situation is unmovable, *is our old story*. The story we tell ourselves as to why we deserve to move out of it? *Are the beginnngs of a gorgeous new one.*

Here's how to tell if you're stuck in your old story; you're either feeling free in a situation, or you're not. So bring a situation into your mind and ask yourself, have I been free to create exactly what I want here? No? There's your story, we're going to call it your old story because you've probably been living in it for a while, and haven't been a best friend to yourself in a while, either. If you stayed in this story, then how able are you to create the life of your dreams? If I bumped into you in ONE year, what would be the cumulative impact of your story after a whole year had passed of you being limited by it? How would you look to me?

Or, do you feel as free as a bird right now? If the answer is a yes, then congratulations! You've been a best friend to beautiful you and are telling yourself a story that empowers you.

Remember, it's never *what* happens to you,
it's always *how* you are with *it*.
And you can mightily empower yourself with your new story,
or ferociously disempower yourself with your old story
whenever you wish.

Let's say for example that you realise your story is that *I'm not good enough*. If you feel this inside, then chances are you're going to want to hide it out of shame because it's embarrassing. I mean no one wants to walk around not being good enough right? So, you're going to show *all them* out there; like your kids for example, that you are more than good enough thank you very much! Often at the expense of your kids, who can end up believing through the endless telling of this story that they'll *never be as good as you*. Do you see? In your story, your reactions are not based on fact. They are based on your need to show the world the opposite of how you feel. Exhausting isn't it? Does it make a child not good enough if they forget their school bag again? No, it just means they need a little more support in the mornings.

And how did your story start? Probably as a kid, like mine and everyone else's, where something happened and you made it to mean something about you. Because you had to reconcile why your mum was shouting at you. *It must be because you've done something wrong.* You were not old enough to realise yet, that people shout for all sorts of reasons, not all of them to do with you. But, because you're not old enough to realise about the big world yet, you come to the only logical conclusion that it must be you. And there's your story of "It's my fault" taking flight and making you responsible for other people's feelings, for the whole rest of your life, until it becomes so exhausting and boring that you decide you don't need it anymore. Goddess:

You can create anything when you're out of your old story.

So, would you like to know how a gorgeous woman like you steps out of the old story she tells herself where it's OK to compromise, it's normal to doubt that you can do it, and those phrases you throw at yourself during the day that delay receiving what you so desperately need? You know the ones I mean; for instance, the ones that make you a toxic friend to yourself, like when you tell yourself, "I haven't got time" "I will later," and, "What's the point, it won't work anyway." They sound innocuous, but they're all so powerful, they can stop a lifetime of success and your own beautiful self-love from ever beginning.

Like *Trudy*, a very clever dentist who subconsciously lived in a story that she wasn't good enough; and because she never felt good enough, she felt she had to give more than enough to just get through her day. She over gave to her patients, felt guilty if she said no, and felt inferior to everyone else, and because she ensured that she put everybody first, everybody had to put her last. They had to agree with her *see* to get on with her.

When you're in your story, guess what? You attract those that agree. So *Trudy's* story kept those around her selfish, sucking her time, her energy, and her goodwill. It wasn't their fault. *Trudy* was comfortable like that until she became so exhausted that she asked me for help. When she stepped out of her story, her income actually doubled, and she got flown first class to New York by a network of dentists. WOOO! And the people around her? They either shifted with her, so their relationships became deliciously equal, or they simply dropped out of her life; there was simply no attraction anymore on either side. This is the power of your story; it has the power to keep you stuck forever and the power to release you forever, so you live to your fullest potential.

> In my story, I treat myself like you treat me; out of my story I treat myself like a Goddess, especially when you are not.

You are free to step into a new story *that empowers you* when *you know* what your inhibiting old story is. You have to know what *it is* to be able to step out of it; otherwise, how do you know if you are in it or not?

You might be in it right now, and not even know. Operating from it. So, let's you and I put our heads together, and happily figure out what your old story is. I'm going to ask you some questions and I'd like you to close your eyes for each one and then write them down. Writing it down is much more powerful than just knowing it in your head. Come on; let's really unleash you, so you accelerate out of your old story at full throttle! You deserve to.

We're going to do this in three parts. We're going to start with the disempowering things your family used to say and do, discover what your current story is and then together we're going to create your new story. Yahoo!

And if this last paragraph made you roll your eyes, or moan that it's too hard and you'll skip this bit, then congratulations! Welcome to your story that tells you why you shouldn't bother with you. Can you feel that? It's the one that stops you from healing 100% and you're going to get really good at catching it.

BECOMING THE BEST FRIEND YOU EVER HAD: PART 1 – YOUR FAMILY'S STORY – WHAT WAS IT?

1. What were the sorts of things the people looking after you said to you when you were growing up that disempowered you and made you feel like you were not the queen of your destiny? For example: "You *behave* as if money grows on trees, well it doesn't!" "Your brother doesn't speak like that, *why* do you have to?" "Why can't you be *more* like your sister?" "You'll eat me out of house and home" "It's a dangerous world out there, you have to be careful" "If you're living under my roof you'll do as I say, no ifs, and, no buts young lady." "How dare you, *what's wrong with you?!*" "Well, *men* will be men!" (Cue sing songy voice). What did they say to you? Write out a short paragraph to remind yourself.

2. What did you take it to mean about you, when they said that? That you were...? Write it down. For example, that I'd never amount to anything, that I'd never be happily married, that I'd never be beautiful, rich, or lucky. That I'd never make it because I wasn't good enough. What did they infer to you by the way they lived? Was money hard to come by? Were men not to be trusted? Did your mother do it tough? Write them down and anything else that comes to mind.

3. Take yourself back to that time and remember when you were growing up. How did all these comments make you feel? Did they make you feel bad? Small? Stupid? Disempowered? Angry? Rebellious? Like you didn't belong? Not good enough? Wrong? Checked out? Completely unlovable? Less than? Unimportant?

Hurt? Scared? Untrusting? Write a list of how they made you feel.

4. If you were walking around with yourself when you were a little kid, what would you hear yourself thinking about the adults around you? What scared you? As a teenager, what did you used to worry about? How did you feel about yourself and the world you were in? What was the outcome of this? Did you try to please your parents? Rebel? What are some of the things you used to say to yourself? Write these all down. For example: Oh no, my mum is going to kill me! Why don't they listen to me? I'm stupid and dumb. I hope my dad doesn't shout at me when I get home. Notice here if you were able to be a good friend to yourself or not?

5. Describe in one or two simple sentences your family's story and write it down. For example: My family's story was one of not being good enough. Or, no matter what I did, I couldn't relax because there was always something more to strive for. Or, my family's story was one of 'poor me' because the outside world was terrible to us. *"They"* always got what they wanted, but we didn't, so we got smaller and life became harder. Or, my family's story was to win and be the best, *whatever the cost*. Or, because of my parents' successful careers, there wasn't really room for me. Or, everything was always my fault growing up.

I know you may not want to re-live the negative bits of when you were growing up, *it's not a feel good Kodak moment* but truthfully, we have to *so you get to know this*. Because *this* is the story you grew up with. This *is* what you were learning, consciously and subconsciously. It's what you bathed in when you got home from school. This is the story of your life, the ethos you learned, and lived by. And you probably told yourself quite a few times as a kid, "When I grow up, I'm never going to be like them!"

The funny thing is, by the time we leave home we've often forgotten that we're knee deep in our family story and so naturally, we bring it with us. We carry it along with us neatly tucked into our briefcase on our way to the first job we do, and unconsciously operate from it during our relationships. It's not until we become aware of it that we can step out of it.

Of course, it wasn't *all bad*; those that looked after you did lots of wonderful things for you, too. But, today we are just going to focus on yes, the very bad stuff because it's here that your subconscious story was formed. It's here that the stuff that stops you lives. This is the stuff that adds frown lines to that beautiful face of yours and tells you that you'll never be perfect. It's powerful enough to give you a string of failed relationships, a pattern in your life that you just can't seem to get out of – to never make the most of your Goddess given life's purpose and talents. Our old stories are enough to topple us and you know you're in one when you find yourself thinking – *no matter what I do, nothing really changes.*

Take a look back at what you've written lovely one. What comes up for you when you read it back? Remember, they were just doing the best they could with what they had back then.

OK, so you should have somewhere in there a sentence that describes your family's story. Underline it and you've completed your family's story. We've had to go back for you to go forward. Ready to go forward with me now? Is this a surer yes now? Good! Because it means you are already freeing yourself from your old story! Hurrah! You can't see me, but I'm holding pom poms (they're bright red) and I'm cheering you all the way. Yaaaay!

PART 2 – YOUR CURRENT STORY (soon to be old story) WHAT HAS IT BEEN?

1. What story do you tell yourself as to why you can't have what you want right now? Write out, "I can't have what I want right now because..." Finish that sentence Write it all out...

2. So, how do you treat yourself?

3. How do others treat you?

4. How do you treat others?

5. How much good can you let into your life under this current story?

6. Does your current story empower, or disempower you? It's a yes/no answer.

7. Are you your own best friend in this story?

8. Become your bestie and know it to step out of it. Take a fresh piece of paper and at the top write, "The 5 biggest things that tell me I'm in my story are" and list the emotional and physical things that tell you immediately you're in it.

E.g.:

⟳ I get this nervous fluttery feeling in my chest.

⟳ I doubt myself telling myself, "I can't do it."

⟳ I feel disempowered and small in my story.

⟳ I don't make decisions based on me and my true essence. I hide behind this one-dimensional story of me, the story of me that I'm rich, that I'm not good enough, that I'm a nice person, that I'm cool.

⟳ I always feel better than or inferior to the other person.

⟳ I believe that I'm not good enough to _____ so I don't...

⟳ My self-esteem is too low to ask for what I want.

⟳ I'm angry with the world and feel ignored by it.

⟳ I cannot get what I want from a situation.

⟳ I'm wrong and you are right.

⟳ If I don't look good, I won't have a good day.

If you had a saucepan and were going to boil all these bullet points down into one theme for your story: what would it be? For example: My current story is that I am never enough. My current story is that it's never going to happen for me. My current story is that I have to work hard for what I want. My current story is that I am invisible.

These bullet points and your boiled down theme are your particular triggers that tell you that you are operating from your old story. Yes, this is now your old story because this is the old you that disempowered yourself. But, no more! Write your own particular list; remember, nobody knows how it feels to be you when you are in your old story, but you, so stay true to yourself and if it makes sense to you then that's all that matters. For some amazing women I know, it's a colour. For example, I know I'm in my story *when I feel beige*. Underline the five biggest things that tell you you're in your story. Write these five points out nicely on a separate bit of paper and carry them in your handbag for the next few weeks. Some of my clients laminate their lists to make it handbag proof!

Look at this list each time you go to the bathroom, and ask yourself, "Am I in my story or out?" Especially look if you're not feeling happy. As soon as you look at this list and go, "Oh! I'm feeling angry with the world," then you know that you've slipped back into your old story and knowing this, it's enough to pop you out! Pop! You are free to be your best friend, hold your hand, and get the hell out of there.

What usually makes us slip into our stories is when we feel others are not happy with us. What do you do if you're in a conversation with someone and can feel yourself slipping back into your story and can't help yourself? Here is a cool four-step process I'd like you to tattoo on your brain for these moments! It will help you step out real quick. Here is what I want you to think:

1. They've just fallen off *their* happy horse.
2. I want to help you.

3. What do you need?

4. Appropriate action.

If you follow this, you'll step out of the story you are currently telling yourself and into a real relationship with that person. Out of story and into real relationships. For example:

Nic was well used to dealing with disgruntled clients, and by knowing that they'd fallen off their happy horse, it freed her from taking it personally. And it's here she begins to step out of her story, when she focuses on *I want to help you,* she takes the focus off her and onto them, which means she becomes of service. When you step into service, it becomes about what the other person needs and you become present to them. So, you ask them *what do you need?* Again, just hear them, so you can take the *appropriate action.*

Helping immediately gets you out of your ego and your disempowering story that makes the situation all about you and instead, makes it about them. You cannot stay long in your story, if you're focussed on helping another's heart. Try it. Try it with your children, with your husband, or with your boss. And when you jump out of your story? They are much more likely to jump out of theirs.

PART 3 – STARTING YOUR NEW STORY OF: YOU!

1. What new story would you like to tell yourself daily as to why you can have what you want right now? Write out, "I can have what I want right now because..." Write it all out.

2. So how do you treat yourself in your new story?

3. How do others treat you now?

4. How do you treat others in your new story?

5. How much good can you let into your life under this new story?

6. Does your new story empower or disempower you? It's a yes/no answer. * If it's a no, go back and re-create it until it's a yes.

7. Are you your own best friend in this story?

8. Become the bestest friend you ever had and create the kind of story that empowers you in every situation. Take a fresh piece of paper and at the top write "The five biggest things that tell me I'm in my new story are" and list the exact opposites of your old story. Emotional and physical. Underline your top five.

Then go find some paper you love, I like to use soft pink paper and write at the top with *a flourish:* The new story of: Me! Here, write those five bullet points that mean you are fully in your new story. How do you know you are? Because you feel the opposite: Empowered, taking up space, equal with the other person, good enough, at peace with the world, heard, I can get everything I want from any situation I find myself in, easily. Decorate this paper, if you wish. I like to sprinkle on glitter and then laminate it. Add it to your handbag and for this coming week look at it regularly to check in with yourself. Are you making decisions and living from this new story of yours? OOO, I am excited for you! This is the beginning of your new story: imagine a whole year of this? Scary, exhilarating, and exciting – Everything is possible here – you are ALIVE!

If you were to boil all these bullet points down into one theme for your brand new story: what would it be? Describe it in one simple sentence. How would you like to feel in it? What is possible for you in your new story? Take a fresh piece of paper and write it all out from the point of view that you are already living it *right now*. For example: In my brand new story, I am good enough because I was born that way! I live as if it's always going to happen for me because I'm me! What I want comes easily to me. My new fiancé (who's in love with me) is rustling up lunch, with just a loose pair of jeans on. Sigh. I love the way he moves... You get the picture.

**Live from this point, make decisions from this point.
When you're in your old story, you can only continue to build
more of your old story; When you're in your new story you
can only make new story decisions for yourself, thus building
more of your new life. Where do you want to spend
most of your life? Propelling yourself towards
your dreams or away? Far away?**

Now Goddess, you know – you know when you're residing in your old ethos, the one that doesn't serve you and you know that as soon as you know? Pop! You're popped out! You cannot be in AND out at the same time see? Knowing it is enough for you to be out. How long you are out is up to you.

To know thyself is half the battle, Goddess. Voilà! You have just created your foundation, your roots for your new story, which will become your new system a little later on in this book! Practice this for the next few weeks, noticing when you are in it and when you are out of it. In time, operating from your old story will happen less. Remember this is your new story and you can change it and tweak it as we go along. But for now, this is the beginning of it – so congratulations; you've just completed a very important piece of this.

Go celebrate, go treat yourself to something that makes you smile! And notice, what happens for you when you operate from your new story? What happens for you when you operate from the old? You might bounce between the two stories for a while, but eventually you'll stay in your new story for longer and longer stretches of time. The trick is not to beat yourself up, if you've slipped back. Sometimes we need to slip back to remind ourselves. And when you do? Heap on more love for yourself. It's just another excuse to love yourself more.

Chapter 8

Turn On Your Receiving Button

· · · · · · · · · · · · · · ·

W here art thou button that receives?
Me thinketh it's long gone;

But where, where to find it again?
Ahhh it's been in ye the whole time.

Oh if I squint, I can see yours. Ooo, ahh, but it's not pressed? How come? I thought that's what you would have wanted? Ever gone to meet your bestie? Who upon laying eyes on you immediately knows something is wrong? Like she can smell it? You wave it away with your hand and say, "No *I'm fine, really.*" But she knows. *She knows.* Not because she's some ace ventura super-slick detective, but because she knows you better than you do. In that moment, she recognises *your signs*. Your signs that tell her you need to receive. *Those ones.* You know the ones I mean, or do you?

You're gorgeous and I know you want the best for everyone. So, you give your time, your love, your brilliance, and yourself to your day as much as you can. You're like a giant sparkly gift, once you're up in the morning you give as much as you can. And, if you're like me, you give a lot.

**Us *Giver Lotters* are prone to Dry-out because we over estimate our energy levels; assuming they will be level for the whole rest of the day.
Ha! Not so.**

We are not built like this. Never have been. And we never will. But after a good nights' sleep, us Giver Lotters begin each day with a fresh list in our heads, amnesic to what occurred yesterday when we gave too much and with the steely resolve of an army, we say, "Today! Today I'm going to get it done!" Why do we overestimate our ability to give?

The wonderful men I meet don't seem to suffer from this affliction and it's not because they are selfish; it's because they know how to receive.

Um, I'll just say it again – no, I'm going to YELL it – THEY KNOW HOW TO RECEIVE.

We women, bless us, have a receiving button in us, too; it just needs to be found, dusted off, and switched on. Finding your receiving button tips the scales to evens, which means you are open to receiving as much as you are open to giving. How many women do you hear complaining that they do too much? How many women do you hear complaining that they receive too much? *You know why.* Because we Giver Lotters give freely, it's natural. And we constrict our receiving on a daily basis:

"Ooo, I haven't got time to meet her - got too much work on."

"I could do with a massage/holiday/blow dry/business coach, but that's too extravagant for me right now. I don't *really* need it."

"Sorry I'm late, I had too much to do!"

"I feel guilty if I spend too much money on myself."

"I do most of the cooking and cleaning because I only work part time."

Dolly was a 42-year-old woman, mum to three and married to a man she likened to a stone. Because getting anything out of him was like getting blood out of stone. She would regale us with stories of how bad he was at giving to her, so much so that she turned these stories into an art form. She called him *Stony Tony*. We would laugh, but deep down *Dolly* was real sad. Was she not good enough for this man? Why couldn't he give to her? What was wrong with her? Was she not pretty enough for him? She would be in turmoil travelling the subway on the way home.

No, there was nothing wrong with her husband, but there was something wrong with *Dolly*. She'd blamed him for not giving, but actually when she looked at what happened in the early years with him, *it was her* that started blocking him from giving to her. Early on, *she had set the tone* of cooking every night by asking him, "Tony, is it OK if you cook tonight? *I'm really sorry.* I'll be fine by tomorrow..." Early on, she said yes to sex when she didn't want to (guilt) and so faked orgasms like an Oscar winner. (I'd like to thank my ability to give and not receive...)

You, just like *Dolly*, are the privileged owner of a lusciously full, soft, and curvy body, which is perfectly made to capture what it needs from somebody. When you receive, you soften, you glow, lighting up the very next conversation you find yourself in. Things turned around for *Dolly*, but it was only when she *decided* to receive that they did. If she'd stayed focussed on only giving for another ten years, *Stony Tony* would have missed out on a very happy marriage.

This is why we have to find your receiving button and press it, so you can let all the goodies in that are always surrounding you. It's us who stop ourselves from receiving.

And why don't we receive what's around us?

We're out of the habit! We place more importance on doing, doing, doing and giving, giving, giving because that's what's going to get us "there" quicker, quicker, quicker! Trust me, I know you already give in so many ways. But if you're not receiving properly along the way, you're going to find your natural ability to give diminished:

You freely receiving = you enjoy giving & give more

You blocking receiving = you're too overwhelmed to give & you give less

When you don't allow yourself to receive, you'll find yourself not enjoying the journey of getting "there". While on your journey (i.e. life), you'll find your vibe kind of lowers along the way, you get more irritable more quickly, Dry-out creeps in, and obstacles seem to pop up and slow you down. The very time to take a holiday is when you don't think you have time to do so. And as you'll never get all your ducks lined up in a row, then it could be said that you enter into a life of constant doing with not much coming back to you. After all, there is always something to be done isn't there? You may think that after you become richer than rich, then you won't have as much to do – but you still have to talk to your assistant to fire the gardener on Monday, so...?

So, have you included any receiving for you on your to-do-list today? *I'm gasping*: is your to-do-list just that? Oh, Goddess! No wonder! You got to start right!

What if forever more you called it "My Receive & To-Do List" instead?

Has a nice ring to it doesn't it? One that suits you much better; it taps you on your shoulder at the very beginning of forgetting, which for you is the moment you begin writing your to-do-list – at your amnesic stage.

Sometimes when a woman gets busy, she can lose her own direction and ends up marching to the beat of *who needs her the most*. The antidote is to stop and receive immediately what is on her to-do-and-receive-list... if only for a moment, to remember who she really is; *so she goes in the direction she always wanted to go in.*

So Goddess, you were made to receive and give; just like your breathing.

If you were made to get high off *giving only*, then Saturday mornings would be like living the dream, man! You would get off doing the Saturday morning shopping, you would get so damn turned on by doing the washing, you would froth at the mouth at the very thought of running the kids to their soccer matches, netball, baseball, something ball; Darling you'd be as high as a kite cleaning your house, giggling profusely all the way to your dustbin.

But no.
Busy bee's need to get a BUZZ out of receiving
or they ZZZZZ flop! Receive, receive, receive,
so you can fly again!

So, fancy locating your receiving button to make your life easier? So you can receive the money you deserve for your talent, receive a man worthy of you, so that you do in fact receive every little detail of life that you desire? Otherwise, it's going to cost you; you're going to stay in the same place unable to move forward because you haven't received enough to do so. *And tho art nobody's slave.*

I want you to imagine you have a giant PINK receiving button inside of you: See, sense or imagine it. This is your indicator of how much you are allowing yourself to receive in this moment. Notice, is your receiving button turned on or off? Or is it part of the way turned on?

Want to know how I turn mine on? I know my signs, I have to; because I'm much more likely to give *to you* as a habit, *than give to me as a habit.*

HOW YOU TURN ON YOUR RECEIVING BUTTON QUICK AS A FLASH!

What tells you that you need to stop and receive? Recognise it. Make a list of your top indicators, including; what does your mood become? What, or who suffers? If I were to walk around with you in that moment, what would I hear you worrying about, thinking about, and feeling? What happens to you? Include below at least one emotion and one physical symptom. For example:

1. My happiness goes out the window, it becomes all about the task.
2. I'm always annoyed with him by the time he gets home.
3. I find myself sighing before the next thing to do.
4. Nothing inspires me – can't be arsed.
5. I worry that I won't have enough time so become mechanical and clinical; there's no time for emotion.
6. My thoughts are overtaken with lack: lack of time, happiness, money, and the lack of goodness in the world.
7. I haven't received in the last 2 hours.
8. I crave sugar.
9. My body is heavy with exhaustion.
10. I've created a to-do-list that does not contain an ounce of receiving.

Write yours out so that when you're in it, you will recognise them easily. Use your own words particular to you. I've created a really special video for you to stop feeling guilty about receiving and it's my gift to you. Use your special code TYOGoddess to access it at marinaj.net.

What is your real deep pleasure in life? Jot down at least five things that you love, love, love to receive when you've been doing too much. For example:

1. Self-pleasuring.
2. Walking for at least half an hour outside in whatever weather.

3. Chatting to my girlfriends on the phone.

4. Singing loudly and dancing to songs I LOVE.

5. Going to the SPA.

Welcome to your receiving signs! Let's use them today to turn that receiving button ON!

Step 1 – Recognise your signs.

Step 2 – Time to get SELFISH NOW. Selfish is the BEST thing about YOU.

Step 3 – Receive real deep pleasure NOW.

Step 4 – Repeat every hour until fully out of Dry-out.

Step 5 – Congratulations, you did it!

Step 6 – What can you put into your day to regularly receive, so you get to what you want quicker?

During your day when you don't, can't remember these six steps...

Here is your one and only step:

Step 1-6 – STOP. Receive what your heart needs.

Failure to listen to your heart is failure to live a life that pleasures you.

"I am good at receiving like a pro to get back into my delicious flow again."

Your Receiving Button is kind of like your healing button. You can place it all over your body to ask what this part of your body needs. So, if you're about to over-eat, then see, sense, or imagine your receiving button right over your belly and ask the receiving button, "What does my belly really want to receive?" If you're annoyed about a part of your body not doing what it should; for example, your arms, then place your receiving button over it and ask, "What do you really want to receive?" Your body is always talking to you.

Chapter 9

Turn On Your Sensuality

· · · · · · · · · · · · · · ·

Sensuality is innate to you; you were born with it. To operate from it is to live in a world full of wonder where everything gets the giddy chance to turn you on. To live apart from it is like tearing a toy away from a baby, you wouldn't dream of it. And yet, we do it every day. I see women walking towards me every day, who are living apart from their sensuality, and it makes me sad because I know they are missing out. And so often, these women are living apart from their sensuality because they've been taught, consciously and subconsciously, that there is *no room for it*. There is no room for it when you're running a meeting, when you're running after two kids, or when you're running through the park, hair stuck to your face and you just assume you look like a sack of shit.

What do you think is acceptable? That your sensuality only needs to come out in the bedroom? For you to place limits on your sensuality, to live without its effects is like living without your left arm; you can do it, you can compensate for the lack of it, but it's not natural that a part of you is missing.

What is sensuality? My answer to you is this:

Run your hands through your hair right now... how did it just feel to you on a scale of 1–10? 1 being OK and 10 being WOW! Now get really, really present, take yourself to this moment and then do it again, but this time take it slow and *feel everything*. Run your fingers through your hair now. How did it feel this time on a scale of 1–10? I'm guessing you closed your eyes too?

This is sensuality; it's fully receiving the NOW, and it's being fully present with all of your senses switched deliciously and tantalisingly on: seeing, hearing, smelling, touching, and tasting. It's fully taking *these words* in that I am saying to you right now without being distracted by that noise out there, or that you really should get dinner on. It's you fully switched ON. If you are somewhere else, you are never here in this present moment; and if you are never here, just like a woman who isn't home, both she and you cannot open the door to receive. So being sensual is in every moment – so when you receive from someone *you really allow yourself to receive.*

You being fully switched ON *is* where magic happens. It's the difference between living an OK existence and living the kind of deep rapturous life you thought only existed in the movies. It's what's happening to you NOW. The more you feel *your now,* the more exquisite decisions and connections to other people you will make.

You are made to receive your now.

Not later.

Delaying your now delays fulfilment.

Look down at your body as it's sitting or lying right now and you'll notice that you don't have many parts that stick out to produce, do you? That's because you and me are made to receive men for pleasure, we receive babies, and carry them. Yes, your beautiful body has been perfectly created to receive.

When the way that you live is not in sync with the way your body has been made, you lose vitality. You lose vivaciousness, charisma, charm, your fabulous flair, and your Goddessness. You lose the top notes and the deep sensual notes of life. You flat line. You are not a flat liner. You never were, if you're honest. Would you like to know how I can help you with this?

Let's begin with something you might not want to. Goddess, how much do you really know about your most sensual of centres?

DO YOU HAVE A STANDARD VULVA?

What does yours look like? Do you know? When was the last time you looked *down there*?

For many women, this is not the topic they bring up at the dinner table! (Like ever!) I mean have you ever discussed *yours* with a girlfriend? Has she ever discussed *hers* intimately with you? Yuck, oo-er, no? So, how about it Goddess? *Are you brave enough to get this sorted with me?* (I won't tell a soul, but you'll be very glad you did.) Trust me on this, you reading this chapter is the difference between a 6/10 turned on life and a 100/10 one. (Sorry about the math.)

So you know by now that the relationship you have with yourself sets the tone for every relationship you're ever going to have; and it's the same for that glorious part of you that you have down there. The relationship you are currently having with *her* sets the tone for every sexual and sensual encounter you're yet to have.

So we're going to go on a little journey me and you into your sensual depths and gorgeous richness. Imagine standing outside a dark cave. It's not where you want to be. It's dark, damp, and smelly and you have no idea what you're going to uncover when you explore inside. You're a bit repelled by it all, if you're honest. You don't even know what to call this place; you have no name for it. So I give you a little bit of light and you walk into the cave with your lamp illuminating one of the walls to its entry. "Oh!" you exclaim, "Look!" Smiling as you read this childlike writing which is scrawled across the wall are the words: *Vagina,* Kitty, Tinkle, Wee Wee, Pee Pee, Mini, Foo Foo, Front Bottom (my favourite) Coo Coo, Pee Centre, Gloria, VJ, Vjay Jay, yer Fanny, Vag, Rose Garden, Private Part, Fluffy, Willy. You realise these were the names Vulvas were called when we were children. You keep walking deeper into the cave and you see adult type writing now: Pussy, Honeypot, Cunt, Flaps, Slit, Twat, Hole, and then some. You realise it has to be society's wall of shame for this part of you. You don't like how these words make you feel. They don't make you feel good about this part of your body. Vulgar, hard, and ugly. You want to get past it, but somehow some of this energy sticks to you. Somehow when you think about this part of you, *light* doesn't come to mind. But dark does. Smelly does. A bit yuck does.

At the end of this tunnel is *a lot of light*. You see a throne. It's where a Queen would sit. It's where you would sit, if you brought light to this part of you.

You and I are going to get there, in this one chapter, and to do it we're going to start in a decidedly unsensual manner; we're going to shake off the darkness, the shame, the hatred, and the fear that's gone into your psyche; so, you're free to celebrate this light filled happiest of places in you. It really *is the happiest place* on earth when YOU become The Queen of your Vulva – rather than others taking that title and owning it. And owning YOU. You're going to reclaim it back! It's your Vulva and you're the Queen.

So it's here you're free to make friends with this part of your body. So you have the BEST time ever together! Right now, how much of a good time are you two having together? Do you regularly and easily enjoy her with deep orgasms or would you honestly not know what your Vulva looked like, or what a really good orgasm felt like? Do you like her? And if you already like her? Love her? And if you already love her? Love her even more? *Her.* Yes, I call her, *a her.* What do you call yours?

Did you just feel a splash of embarrassment just then? This might be a squirmy kind of chapter for you at first, but I'm going to walk with you through it, so you'll never see this part of you in the same nonchalant or ugly way, again. Try squeezing your face with me and squeeze your hand hard, so you get some of the yeurrrrgh out!

See, when most women were little, they were taught the wrong name for this part of themselves. And if you try and ask a girl *now* the name she uses for her Vulva? She'll probably tell you the wrong name. Because she's still being taught it.

Did yours have a name growing up?

Or was it just not mentioned at all? It was that thing *down there – she that shall not be named.*

And what you cannot name carries shame and embarrassment like an age old cloak that cannot be shaken off.

Or, if you've graduated from Wee Wee (well done), are you now calling yours a V*agina*? Well you are half right, though you are still doing a disservice to this part of you. I'll tell you why. The word Vagina comes from the Latin word "sheath" that which a sword slides into. Mmm yummy. Is that all there is to you? Something that is a holder for a penis? No. I thought not. So, the proper word is Vulva. Vulva encapsulates all of you, your vagina, your clitoris, urethra (the tiny opening your pee comes out of), your pubic mound (where your pubic hair grows, just above your outer lips) and of course your inner and outer lips. Vulva also evokes velvety indulgence in my mind and I much prefer it to the nasal "Vagina" that's normally associated with humour and embarrassment, rather than sensuality.

Did you know, as I'm typing this I just misspelled Vulva? Just then! I wrote vular missing the fourth letter out. Do you know what my auto-correct just offered me?? *In this order:* "Volar, Velar, Vulgar, Vulvar, uvular." Wow. Vulvar came in fourth and it's not how anybody I know spells it. Vulva has not been offered, and yet uvular has. Does anybody know what uvular is? Let alone a volar or a velar??

Conversely, I just misspelled the word breasts to test out my new little theory. Again, I missed the fourth letter out "brests", and the auto-correct just offered me "breasts" first! Do you think that auto-correct doesn't see "Vulva" appear too often?

What happens to a little girl if there is no name for her elbow? Or she's given the wrong name for it that even the adults seem embarrassed to use? One day, she falls down and hurts her elbow – what does she go running to the nearest adult with? "Mummy I've hurt my... my... my thing... you know my thing here on my arm." She has no understanding of it. She has no relationship to it. She has no connection to it. She learns from the adults to be embarrassed about it and she learns to be ashamed of it. Sure the adults can say "elbow," but look at the stack of emotion, embarrassment, and shame behind saying the word "Vulva". You can see why 100% of my clients grew up with the wrong name, or with no name. Yes, that's 100%, so far. Wow!

And yet, this is one of the most powerful and feminine parts of you and we've learnt to be ashamed about it? To not connect to it, but to let a guy connect to it? You cannot love something if you cannot connect to it. How powerful can a woman be when she is disconnected from her most feminine of parts and the giver of life? What happens to a woman who thinks her Vulva is smelly, wrong, deformed, ugly, and is embarrassed by it? And doesn't know if it's normal or not, because let's face it – yours is hidden and so is mine. We don't see them out and about parading themselves proudly in the street. You don't compare yours to your girlfriend and talk about the way yours looks to your girlfriend. The only point of reference most of us have (unless you're a doctor, nurse or bikini waxer) is porn and the way guys react to us. But, let's face it: Did your guy go to "How to pleasure a Woman Class" at school? No, he was behind the bike sheds with a bunch of boys pouring over porn with his friends. And what did he see?

Vulvas that are digitally altered. Did you know that Australian law requires Vulvas to be digitally altered for soft porn? The Australian Government's Guidelines for the Classification for Publications 2005 states: "Realistic depictions may contain discreet genital detail [,] but there should be no genital emphasis." And the term for this in the magazine industry is to "heal it to a single crease". So no inner lips, no clitoris can be shown to be hanging outside? Like a *neat little cream invite, folded to a single crease that invites you to a buttoned-up tea.* And what does it mean to "heal"? Heal implies it's sick, very offensive, ill, unbalanced, *not right.*

Is your very own Vulva not right if your inner lips and/or clitoris are daintily or unabashedly dangling, and swinging gaily past your outer lips?

Do we measure how much men's testicles dangle? Do men worry if they show through jeans? Can you imagine if men's penises were digitally altered in magazines and photos? What would that imply to you? That the real ones where not good enough? Wrong even? You'd have power over a man who thought his penis wasn't good enough, wouldn't you? He'd be vulnerable. Should men's testicles be healed to a "single crease"?

"To heal it to a single crease" is to show the Vulva of a child.

It's children, who have a "neat" Vulva.

It's pre-pubescent girls that don't have hair on their Vulvas.

So, what are our men being taught about beautiful you through these magazines?

That it's sexy to have a Vulva that looks like a child's?

That if you don't, you should be embarrassed, hide it, only let it out under the cover of darkness and consider a little op to lop off the offending protrusion?

In the scary explosion of child pornography over the last decade, has this been a factor? Is that why Brazilian waxes have become synonymous with being sexy?

Because pubic hair is actually meant to be there for a reason. It's meant to protect the very soft delicate skin of your Vulva; so your Vulva remains sensitive enough to reach you to the highest orgasm your body can produce.

Do men really want us to have child-like Vulvas?

Only if they've been educated by digitally altered Vulvas. And I have to say, this law isn't made by those people who run these magazines, nor from the men you know and love, nor is it coming from the men in the street. They love you, your Vulva, and the way you were made to look. No, these magazines are being forced by law. I wonder who these law-makers are? What are they trying to protect the public from?

I'm not sure what happens around the world, but I do know that surgery on Vulvas to make them "neat" is on the rise.

So, what is the benefit of having sticky outy inner lips and a sticky outy clitoris?

Well unless you are a child, by the time you hit puberty your labia minora (inner lips) have already extended and your Vulva has changed resplendently, lusciously, magnificently. If you find that your labia minora have extended beyond your labia majora (outer lips), then you still have a deliciously standard Vulva and are lucky some might say! I believe the more your clitoris and/or inner lips stick out, the more surface area is available for your pleasure and so the more likely you are in for a giant orgasm. OOO! Why shouldn't we want our Vulvas to be richly expansive pleasure centres? The more you feel, then the more you are likely to orgasm. And I believe that when your inner lips and clitoris protrude, it's like a hug for his penis because – there is more of you to massage the shaft and more of you to get massaged, deliciously right back!

And so how do we get our guys to realise that ours is NORMAL and those pictures that they have become accustomed to, are not?

By falling in love with your exact shape, size, and texture *is* leading the way for him. Having an "innie" or an "outie" Vulva, or being the proud owner of one inner lip that is rebelliously longer than the other are all *gorgeously standard* for Vulvas, and we need to lead the way, not governments and not magazines. Every man I have ever met LOVES the way women look down there. They get intoxicated. Now, it's your turn to love *yours*. Otherwise, how are you ever going to relax when he goes down on you and those bright lights are on...

1. **Decide** to fall in love with your Vulva. Because you're incensed with what I've been talking about, because it's going to free you up to feel relaxed during sex and because you're curious about having longer stronger orgasms. You want to take better care of this part of you because you realise you've never really thought about this part of you and want to deepen your connection to sensual pleasure. (It's going to suit you.) Btw, now is a great time to get yourself checked out for STDs and get healthy. Loving your Vulva is key to knowing how to receive a much higher level of pleasure than you're used to. Because to know her is to turn her on. So, would you like to make a simple, but profound decision for yourself? "I choose to fall in love with mine." Say it out loud and mean it. Is it your first time? Awww, you deserve it! It's time. And while you're at it, what can you thank her for? Orgasms? That OOOOOO feeling she gives you with the perfect touch? Birthing your children? Making the men you've played with deliriously happy just to be remotely near one?

2. OK, you're ready for the next bit. **Desire.** Do you want to reach your sensual potential this lifetime? This is impossible if you haven't met your velvety Vulva! "Oh, I do!"

3. Then let's **detox** yourself from what's in your way of seeing her as your happy place, full of light and loving her. Take a piece of paper and write at the top – Vulva Detox! Write out everything that's in your way, from stupid painful periods, to not having the birth you wanted, to your vagina being really hurt, torn, wounded during birth, painful sex, to being raped, hurt, disrespected, to hating this part of you, to finding it all a bit yucky if you're honest, to not ever experiencing an orgasm, to not really feeling anything down there, to your anger at how women are treated, and not

even having the education to use the right name! Let any shame and embarrassment come out. No matter how small, no matter how big. Write it all out till you are spent. Now burn it. Safely. I can talk you through this next process if you want, just use the special code TYOGoddess and go to marinaj.net. Close your beautiful eyes, the change is coming. Breathe into the deepest part of your belly. See, sense, or imagine you're at the entrance of a dark cave. I give you a lantern. As you walk in, you see a wall with the name that they called your Vulva when you were growing up. Or is the wall empty because there was no name? What name is there? Say it out loud. Or say, "There was no name for it." This might make you smile. It might make you sad. Maybe you feel nothing. Keep walking and come to the adult wall of shame. Stop. What has your Vulva been called by others? Or, by even you over the years? Notice the colour and shape of the wall. Is it pretty? What's the energy of it? Does it make you feel good about yourself? What name or names are there? Say it/them out loud. Breathe deeply again. You notice there are other things on this wall. Beliefs you've accumulated over the years scrawled all over it – what do yours say? Say them out loud. "I believe this place has been a source of pain and humiliation for me." "I'm scared of this part of me." "I've always believed I take too long to orgasm." And so on. Say them all out loud. Now, I want you to imagine that there is a Queen waiting for you and she wants to walk you to your throne to where the light is; however, in order to do so, you've got to forgive yourself for all this darkness you've imagined this place to be. For whatever hurt, injustice, or pain has been done to you, it's time to leave it in the past – if you're to ever have full light in this area. So out loud hear yourself say, "I forgive myself for being a participant in the way society has treated this precious part of me. I forgive myself for letting darkness in when all this part of me ever needed was my light. If I am ready now, I forgive this part of me to release me from the past. I forgive myself for these beliefs, they've only bought heaviness to me – I forgive myself. I forgive you, my Vulva. I choose to now move forward to a new future filled with happiness and light. I choose to have a new relationship with this important part of me. I choose to be kind. Love, respect, and pleasure surround my Vulva forever." You look at the Queen. You are ready. She guides you towards the light; light fills this cave like the brightest sunlight burning away any old, last bits of fear, and burning away all darkness. Ahhh, and so she motions and you sit on your throne. In charge of this part of you. In charge of your sensuality and your pleasure. You say who, you say what, you say when. You smile. You're ready to rule! Let light fill this whole area of your vuvla now. You are complete! Open your eyes... are you ready to do the external healing now?

4. Ready for external **self-love?** When was the last time you looked down there?

⚬ Take a warm bath or a hot steamy shower, so you're relaxed and warm.

⚬ Dry yourself and get comfy; take a hand held mirror and spread your lips apart with your first two fingers and take a peek! When was the last time you looked down there? I often hear, "Oh it's when I was worried I had a problem down there." Can you imagine if that was the only time you looked into the face of your beloved? What kind of relationship would you expect to have with them? Blimey! So, back to it: make sure you have good lighting, as it's often dark down there! (A client of mine recently purchased a mini mirror surrounded by fabulous mini lights just for this!)

⚬ You're going to see your clitoris, which looks like a little button, and your vagina, which sits just a little underneath this; your inner lips which hug around your clitoris, and your outer lips which protect everything. And you're going to see what shape you are and what colour and texture you are today. Like the lips on your beautiful face, your Vulva can be an entirely different colour to your skin colour. Take a good look and follow your shape with your eyes. Is yours cute? Queen like? Has character? No two are the same and this one's yours. If you were to name her, what would you call her? The more you look, the more chance and time you give yourself to get to know her and to fall head over heels for her. She's your best friend in pleasure; so keep looking at her until you love the exact shape and colour she is. It's up to you how long this takes. You might want to form a relationship with her over a few sittings.

Celebrate her. Draw a heart on your inner thighs with eyeliner or glittery lip gloss. The fabulous Amy Jo Goddard, author and Sexual Empowerment Expert says, "A woman's Vulva is her opulent doorway into her source energy, her sexual power, her true north. This exquisite part of her body is but a reflection of the natural world. It is her birthright." Celebrate your uniqueness, celebrate that she's the darkest brown, the lightest pink, purple, and every single colour in between, and *decide* to love her because she's yours. There is no right size, Goddess. She's the perfect shape and size to give you your perfect size and shape of pleasure. You just have to get to know her. Decide to love her; you'll relax more in exploring what turns you on, so you do reach your sensual potential this lifetime. And that lover by your side? Goddess, they won't question if they're with the right lover (See page 99, if you need reminding!)

Sing her song! Yes, she has a song! What's her energy now? We know the song she used to sing, but now? Would she be the most beautiful symphony? An opera? A darling pop song? Press play and DANCE her SONG – why not? Have fun with it!

- Buy some gorgeous RED silky knickers, and parade around in them all week! Red is the healing, very energising colour of your powerful base chakra, which surrounds this part of your body. The word chakra just means energy centre, and YES, this is your new energy centre!

- Walk around proudly all week. You're turning back centuries of shame towards women's Vulvas with your choices – thank YOU!

So Goddess, yes, you are made to receive more than you have been. And if you think that's impossible in your world, then I'm going to let you in on a little secret... when you decide to *receive as you are meant to*, your whole world externally *can and will* transform.

No matter how rich or how beautiful a woman is, if she is not good at receiving, she cannot be happy, and she cannot flourish; it's impossible to. I'm not talking about an hour here; I am talking about a day. If in that 24-hour period she has given, but has not received real sensuality, she starts to wane. She'll look to receive chocolate, or something of a lesser quality, something that is easier to attain, quick, and reliable: like food, shopping, internet surfing... but it won't be what her sensual self is yearning for.

What kind of sensuality are you yearning for right now?

How about a massage table arriving right where you're sitting for you to move onto and receive a warm oil massage, your hair being lightly pulled right at the end? Is it to feel that silky skirt of yours slide across your thighs as you walk down the street sans underwear tonight? Or, is it a deep sensual kiss you yearn for, the kind that lifts you off your feet? Do you crave to paint using colours that shout how you feel... with your fingers? Walk to an art gallery and become deliciously preciously absorbed by it all? Be surrounded by soft open flowers, as you deeply inhale the fragrant oils swirling in your bath? The list is endless, what matters is that you feed your sensuality daily. And it comes in all different shapes, sizes, smells, and feeling...

For some, it is their deep practice of yoga that arouses their sensuality, but for others, it's sex, figs drizzled with honey, applying a slick of lipstick, or swimming at the beach and drying naturally in the warm sun. What turns you on sensually? Big or small, make a list, and place one of these into your every day and just notice what happens to your natural ability to receive happiness, sensuality, and nourishment from your life. Does it feel easier for you to connect to what you want?

And so what turns you on *with him?* What do you love him to do for you? Ask him!

How about in the bedroom? Let him meet the Goddess in you. Create a sensual meeting between you both, like – a date with a Goddess. It's you bringing him into what turns you on.

Write or send him a little note inviting him to a *Date with a Goddess*. Tell him to knock on the bedroom door at 8:00pm tonight... Tell him enticingly that it's a sensual meeting between you both and that he should be showered and ready to learn about you and how you'd like to be pleasured tonight.

You're going to bring him into your world. If it turns you on, it will turn him on; whether he's into candles or not. Your satin negligée or not. This is all about you; heavenly and, sensual you.

This is a fresh start between you and him. You are setting the tone for him to worship and celebrate your beautiful feminine sensuality and so we begin with your bedroom. We need to clear the energy of old with a dash of Feng Shui. Clear your bedroom of clutter so he sees you, not the washing basket, and open the windows and put fresh sheets on the bed. When you've just come away from giving, you need to actively put yourself in the mood to receive. So, next, flick into receiving with a bath or a warm shower, and massage some gorgeously scented moisturiser into the whole of your body.

Play music that you love and light some candles, have some beautiful oils burning: like rose oil, sandalwood, something luscious. Have next to you a play box – just like when you were a child and had a dress-up box, this is your play box for today. In your play box have things you love to wear, lingerie, silks, scarfs, satin gloves; gorgeous frilly knickers that bring out the Goddess in you... put them on. In that play box, have some natural lubricant ready for you, a vibrator, playthings for the bedroom, a sensual book you'd like to read from, massage oil, chocolate, wine, champagne, strawberries, whatever turns you on, place them in your play box... Look around you, you've created a dreamy love nest for you both to discover each other with, as well as... you're safe in here to show him this side of you. The very sensual, Aphrodite Goddess in you, you're ready...

Oh, there's a knock at the door... It's him.

Invite him into the bedroom; tell him this is "your date with a Goddess" and that "you'll be showing him what turns you on tonight."
Then, show him how you want to be touched and pleasured this month.

Start by telling him that the next hour is about discovering new ways of pleasuring you and you are going to show him how. Start by sitting on the bed, go ahead, and show him how you love to be touched. Take his hand and run it up your arm in the exact length and pressure and slowness of this sensual movement. Then let him try. Then show him again. Take your time. Enjoy this. Show him how you want him to touch your face. Your lips. Your hair. Show him how you want him to caress all of you. Now, would you like him to massage you?

Remember your 3 Amigos – use these to get you started:

I love how you're touching me, or I love how you normally touch me

Would you touch me like this now? (Show him.)

Ooo, I love it... *that's turning me on*... that feels so good... yes... (This is your version of saying thank you when naked!)

Keep using The 3 Amigos to bring him up to speed. Remember,

if it's scrumptious and luscious for you to say it, you will lift him into a higher even more sensual state. You can use tonight to go all the way to orgasm or to really enjoy his touch on your skin.

You set the tempo, how far, and how much.

... You can tell him that next time he can have his sensual meeting with you, and he can show you what turns him on, keeping it oh so pleasurable for you both! But remember, tonight is just for YOU. Remember, you're the Queen. And YOU have the power to turn your sensuality on anytime you want.

Chapter 10

Turn On Your Pleasure...

· · · · · · · · · · · · · · · ·

...As well as your happiness, limitless joy, fun, giddy giggles, zest for life, and OOO the list goes on. When was the last time you threw your head back and laughed till you almost peed your pants? I hope it was only as far back as yesterday!

So, I declare today is *Revel In Your Sexiness Day!* What if we all walked around today knowing that we are sexy, alive, and beautiful? This is self-love; would every interaction today be better? More pleasurable for you?

What if *we all* did it today, not just you and me, would the world be a better place? And I have to tell you, I AM having a *bad hair day* today, but I don't care! You and me... we're heavenly and perfect just the way we are: LET'S GO REVEL IN IT!!

You're a lot of fun (that much I know about you), and how much fun you are being right now teeters specifically on two things:

1. How important fun and pleasure are (to you).
2. How friendly you are with your pleasure button.

Where on your body could you turn your pleasure button on and together become the best of friends... if you had *said button?* If you had a button that you could press right now (OOO!) that *turned on* your ability to receive pleasure, like you were born to? So you feel pleasure wherever you go today? (Especially, if it's a place you don't want to go to?)

And it's a little button that's made purely for your pleasure; *it doesn't do anything else.* It doesn't cook for you, it can't smell your baking smells that waft through the house, nor is it a fancy shape, nor is it obvious to the naked eye... and in between those pleasurable moments it's so fond of? It just sits there for you. And waits. It doesn't think like the rest of your body, it doesn't talk like the rest of your body, it can't taste that food you just whipped up and it can't help you do your taxes. (Although if yours can, do let me know.)

All it does is receive pleasure for you. Oh, what a job! Can you guess which area of you, I am talking about?

Your clitoris. The queen of pleasure. Your little innocuous button is quite simply, so full of pleasure receptors she is the centre of your pleasure universe.

How well do you know your teeny tiny button of pleasure? Do you press her often? Are you in love with her? The making of her is exquisite. Perfect.

Do you know how many receptors for pleasure she holds within this teeny tiny bud of a landscape? A hundred? Could a thousand fit?

Actually it's 8,000! Oh swing from the chandeliers, yes your teeny tiny clitoris carries 8,000 receptors just for receiving exquisite pleasure for you! Can you believe it? You hold a much richer capacity for pleasure than you're using and right now? *They're just waiting for you.* When I ask my clients this very same question it's met with a charged pause... they take a shot in the dark and almost always get it wrong. I mean really, who knew? I didn't when I was growing up that's for sure! Who knew about those 8,000 nerve endings just giddy with the possibility of receiving sexual and daily pleasure for you? And yes, you were born like this, and how divine! How lushly lucky...

Now, we've been talking about sensuality, but how well do you receive pleasure in life? Easily, or do you delay it – only allowing yourself to have it after hard work, or restricting it to certain times of the week? Do you receive the kind of pleasure that is your deep womanly birthright?

You were born and designed to receive. And you were born and designed to give. One could argue that the *giving parts of you* are your brain, arms, legs and heart, and I'm pretty sure you're already in touch with those parts of you. You know the name of them and you're not ashamed or shy to use them. In fact, you're proud and comfortable to use them. It's normal. Could you say the same about your clitoris?

I dare you to say this out loud, "My Clitoris is perfectly formed to outrageously receive my pleasure and I LOVE it!" Say it again!

Did you just laugh? Swallow your words a bit? Kind of embarrassed? Did you find yourself saying them in a little girl's voice that just came out of you? Or did you feel nothing, you just kind of shut off from the words? Did you feel flirty and sexy, as if suddenly flooded with your power? If you're not sure, I invite you to say it again, and this time notice that the way you say it is a signpost to your relationship to your clitoris right now; thus, your relationship with your ability to truly receive pleasure. And we want it to be a close, loving relationship!

Can you see the connection?

One part of your body is solely made for receiving pleasure.
If you're in touch with her, then you'll be in touch with what
turns you on. Both in the bedroom and... outside of it.
(Smiley face.)

And what about him? Is he built in the same way as you?

Well let's start with his body: does he have a special part of his body that *only receives* pleasure? And it doesn't do anything else? Well the most obvious one is the penis, but it does several different things for a guy: it urinates, it ejaculates. Hmmm, but what about a guy's nipple? Maybe, but some men don't like theirs touched, so... no he isn't built with just one area solely to receive pleasure.

So, let's go back to the penis. Could you guess how many nerve endings a man's penis carries for his pleasure? Answer = 4,000. Wow, yes, that's 4,000 nerve endings spread over a much larger surface area. What does that tell you?

That you'll have a bigger craving for pleasure than he does on a daily basis because you're made with twice as many pleasure receivers than he is.

HMMM... SO ARE YOU RECEIVING TWICE AS MUCH AS HIM?

Did you receive twice as much as the men around you this week?

No?

Our bodies *need* to receive twice as much as his because your body that you're in right now? *Does twice as much.*

Yep, not only are our bodies made to live life (just like men's), but our bodies are also made to create, house, birth a life, *and* to feed that life, too!

Well what does this really mean?

It means that you genetically need to receive more pleasure than men, daily, because *you nurture more than men.*

Every woman I have ever met loves to give and nurture: a child, a project, a belief, a way of life and a better future for this planet – look at us all – we're all doing it! And we often do it all at once; hence, our ability to juggle. And we're good at it! *We're made for it.* So, this is not just about you and I doing less*, it's about receiving more.* You cannot do your life's purpose properly on receiving half as much as you're meant to. So whatever *it is* that you are currently nurturing, *you are made to do it hugely, exquisitely.* And, very logically, you are also built to receive hugely, exquisitely. That's half the fun!

Here's how I know:

It's a well-known fact that in bed most women need more foreplay than men to reach orgasm.

We just need longer.

And, most of us need to receive *at least twice as much foreplay* than men and if you're anything like me and most of my friends; ten times as much is where is starts getting really groovy for us gals.

This is a good thing.

Why?

Well, think about it; the more time spent on foreplay for you, the more of your life is spent experiencing exquisite pleasure! And let's face it, when we die, we're not going to wish we'd worked longer hours. So, what if you dropped your annoyance at taking so long to "get there" during sex and instead, celebrate this rather wonderful design flaw of yours instead? This means you are forced to use a bigger chunk of your day being ravished and pleasured... so added up over a lifetime, *your perfect design* ensures you must spend *more hours* receiving than men! There's a reason why we live longer than men Goddess, I wonder if this is part of it?

Remember at the beginning of this book we found out that, "Women experience depression at roughly twice the rate of men." (From Mental Health America)

Is it possible that because we're built to receive twice as much pleasure *and don't,* that we're therefore twice as likely to slide into depression than men? It's possible isn't it?

And another thing; ever noticed that we need more comfort than him? More talking things through with our girlfriends than him? And more romantic gestures than him? I could give you a huge list right here, but it's quicker to say:

Imagine you're invited to stay at your friend's holiday house with your partner. She shows you to your room *and it's a single bed.* "Sorry," she says. "It's all we've got." Without missing a beat your guy races past you, launches onto the bed, and looks up at you grinning, and says, "First in babe, first get."

You can't believe it, what an idiot. As you take the floor that night, are you going to look up at him and feel romantic towards him? Especially, after an uncomfortable nights' sleep? Have you fallen ever so slightly out of love with this man? Or, in fact, hugely? *Yes, you need more comfort than him.* Imagine it's the other way round and you get the bed: will he be disappointed by that? Will he wake in the morning and fall out of love with you? No. You won't hear him moan either because – he loves that he's helped you receive and because he wants to make you happy. Plus, he doesn't need all the detail in the comfort that you do; for instance, all those bathroom products, or all those different variations on a pair of shoes. I mean why did you have to pack all those shoes? No, he doesn't get it, and he's not meant to. But if it makes you happy to have that extra pair of wedges, then he wants you to have them.

You would get so irritated at half that stuff he puts up with, like not as much wardrobe space, or you taking ages to get ready... he doesn't need to receive as much pleasure in quite as much thought out detail as you.

He loves to receive pleasure, but what gives him pleasure isn't necessarily what gives you pleasure. What makes him really happy? Write it out. Is that enough for you?

RAISE YOUR PLEASURE LEVEL GODDESS!

Have you been living to his pleasure level, or your own? Do you march to his daily rhythm, more than your own? You'll know by your inner glow – how much are you glowing now, as you read this? There's your answer. See – when we live to his level of pleasure, its fun, *it's nice*, but it's not in nearly *as many ways as we need it...* we need more variety than him and we need to immerse ourselves in richer feminine pleasure daily.

He quite rightly has fed himself to his level of pleasure. His masculine pleasure *is not* your feminine pleasure; *they are two entirely different things.*

Whereas for him, he might be happy meeting with his mates for a beer and comes home all content, I will not be entirely fulfilled coming home after just meeting my friend for a beer. But... add in dancing the night away in a venue with a fabulous vibe, with cocktails along the way, and I'm well on my way to reaching my 8,000 pleasure level! Your hankering for pleasure is bigger! Mine is bigger. Wanna stop living to his pleasure threshold? Because:

The men around you *cannot* add to you *unless they know what you want* – in those 4,000 *further* feminine ways that you need it. He'll never need those extra feminine ways, but he'll enjoy them. Let me explain:

Imagine you're seated at a sexy candle lit dinner and you want dessert. Mmmm – just the thought of that chocolate oozing out of that warm fondant turns you on. But he says, "Nah, let's skip dessert and head back. I've got a really busy day tomorrow." What do you do? Push your pleasure level down to match his?

Or,

Keep at your level, trust it, and bring him up to yours? It's way more fun to feed him some dessert with your spoon and seductively ask him if he wants to dance. (*You haven't danced in ages and you love this track!*) To which he mutters, "You know I don't like dancing in public."

What do you do? Push your pleasure level down to match his?

Or,

Smile at him anyway, bless him, *because he doesn't know what you know* and dance your way to the dance floor; OWN that dance floor! For without this, there is no real happiness for you! Yes, *you could* leave the restaurant at 10:00pm in a taxi feeling flat, or leave at 11:00pm laughing, wild, and free. And who's happier, him or you?

Ha! A trick question – it's both! Because he loves to see you happy and it makes everything he works so hard for, absolutely worth it. And his busy day tomorrow? Just got itself a little left over glow from the night before.

Your level of pleasure = raises his pleasure

Yes, your requirement for pleasure is bigger, and he actually knows this. It explains why you get more irritated than he does with certain things and why your standards are higher for the house and other things that he's happy to let slippety slide.

Remember the sketch we did earlier when he asks you, what do you want to do Friday night, and you just don't know or get irritated that he doesn't know? It's because he knows you can go higher than him, and that's why he asks you! And that's why he so easily agrees to whatever you say, which is why you get annoyed because he seemed to agree so easily and so you'll say, "Are you sure? You sure, that's what you want?" And that's why he gives you an angsty reply, "Of course, I wouldn't have said it, if I didn't mean it!!"

Huh! And so this is why you get so annoyed. It just feels flaky to you that he so readily agreed... until this moment. Oh, he was responding to a much deeper requirement, my pleasure level.

Why do I turn away from my pleasure, so easily?

A few reasons – let's see which you resonate with:

1. You've not been brought up to put your pleasure first and centre of everything.

2. At school, it was work first and play later; at work it still is – work first and play later. TV is full of pain, hospital dramas, police dramas...

3. If you're like most women, you've grown up with images, films, and conversations that show women putting men's pleasure first. If she puts her own pleasure first for too long, then she's bossy, selfish, and cold. Like not wanting to have children. Enough said.

4. You've been living to his pleasure level and not your own. You've just become used to it.

The world knows you are a Goddess, but do you?

When I first met my husband, I was already living at my high pleasure level and not his. Even though I was a single mum I was really reaching as high as I could go. And then, my edges rounded and I found myself dropping down my pleasure level to be in line with his. He got annoyed.

All my umming and ahhing and settling for what does not become me. *Settling*, now *there's* a word. That exhausts him. It wastes his time. It's not what he signed up for. He signed up for me to be me. Unreasonable, high maintenance, huge energy, vibrant, and highly sensitive which gives me no tolerance for violence, mediocrity, or films that make me cry. He worships the ground I walk on. I want that for you.

It happens when you're brave enough to share *who you really are* with everybody. The real you. You may wonder if there is room for you to do this?

Goddess, there has *always* been room for you, all of you; it's just that you haven't taken it yet. And don't look around you for inspiration – most women are not living at their pleasure level! Here is where my pleasure level really resides:

To grow a Marina, to maintain a Marina, so a Marina flourishes day in, day out needs a new kind of pleasure level that turns me ON. One that nourishes me right back. One that treats me to huge amounts of joy and teaches me how to have the biggest voice of all. One that leaves me no choice, but to run into the ocean with only my underwear on because I forgot my bikini and quite frankly, my day NEEDS me to have this level of JOY in my life. My 8,000 rich pleasure level needs me to dance and sing daily. I am WOMAN. I am sensuality. So I need this richness of pleasure daily. My feminine pleasure level requires that I listen to every little need I have, including the one I'm acting on right now, which is to slowly savour a piece of Willie's cacao chocolate as I write these words to you.

The feminine build of my body requires that I must have sensuality placed fairly and squarely in my day, every day to feel alive. Otherwise, a part of me dies every day. This may mean wearing my favourite "Nobody" dark skinny jeans with a champagne satin top that slides across my nipples all day. And asking for warm coconut oil to be dripped and massaged into my whole body from my husband's hands, even though he is tired from work on this cold Tuesday night.

If you truly lived to your natural 8,000 pleasure level – what might that look like? Would you only work in a job you truly loved? Would you only have people in your life that give you masses of joy and leave the rest? Would you ensure you reach your peak of pleasure more often wherever you want? Like really go for it? Can you expand that much? You might not be used to it, but I know it's in you. I know because you're all woman.

Would you raise your standards?

Would you receive a luxurious bath every night before bed?

Would you insist on and relax fully into 30 minutes of foreplay?

Try this – for the next 24 hours, notice, are you accepting his pleasure level and other people's pleasure levels as your own, or are you brave enough to go for your richer level of pleasure?

Introducing The Pleasure Barometer:

> ## My 8,000 Pleasure Level
>
> ▼ *Dry-out Zone for a woman* ▼
>
> ## His 4,000 Pleasure Level
>
> ▲ Functional Zone ▼
>
> ### Nil Pleasure Level

In my head, this lives as a rather sparkly visual barometer! Your 8,000 pleasure level at the top, the Dry-out zone for a woman below this, and his pleasure threshold at 4,000. When we operate below the 4,000 level we are at *function level* – and so we will feel functional. There is no glow here, just function. By contrast, your feminine glow gets unleashed between the 6,000–8,000 level. So if you find yourself having to deal with things that only need you at a functional level: like paperwork, doing your taxes, having to repair your car, fiddling with your damn computer, cleaning your house, buying or renting a house, then moving house, dealing with builders, calling up your insurance, nameless people in large corporations, etc. (I mean the list goes on...!) You can find yourself at that very flat and functional 0–4,000 level. But, if you decide that you deserve to reach your pleasure level everywhere you go (as nature intended) put a spin on it and chat to the service lady behind the counter. Play crazy good music or meditate while you clean (whatever floats your boat). Bring the 8,000 into your functional 2,000 meeting with your accountant by bringing cupcakes and gorgeous herbal tea, because that's just you and that makes you happy you little hippy. (That's me!) (Oh, and go with your special silky red knickers on.) Yes. That should do it. Goddess, it's HERE that your true HAPPINESS lives. You can make any situation an 8K situation! It may take another couple of minutes to 8K it, but Goddess, it is so, so worth it!

Take your pleasure level with you wherever you go. Remember, it's your natural feminine rhythm to receive more richly per hour. So ask yourself, am I living to his pleasure level, or my own? His level works for him and yours works for yours, and when you are brave enough to live to your level? Everybody wins! Bring your feminine pleasure to the restaurant, to a boring business meeting, to the food shopping, and to your exercise class. What would give you your 8,000 level of pleasure? Are you going to rise to your level *of your feminine glow,* or are you going to drop down to the level you are used to *and most of us were brought up* with? – His?

This also means not being afraid of standing out, so in the face of disapproval: do *you really want that much? OMG you are just too much! Surely, you want to go home now?* You smile a knowing 8,000 feminine strong smile in their direction and party on at your pleasure level. We will be partying with you, in spirit! Yes, you might be a bit too much for those living at that 4,000 level, which *of course you are* and you're meant to be! Celebrate your feline difference, "MEOW!" Proudly lead the way Goddess – we're smiling – are you brave enough to live at your natural pleasure level? Because there is nothing more to say; except... just that it really, really suits you! Goddess, you look gorgeous armed with this information!

Would you like to turn your Pleasure Button on to start living the way you were naturally created to?

HOW TO TURN ON YOUR PLEASURE BUTTON & REACH YOUR 8,000 PLEASURE LEVEL:

This is the best bit of Blisswork you're ever going to get! You just need time and the below ingredients.

Ingredients:
Natural lubricant, like Sylk
Lighting that turns you on

So, you're already the Queen of this part of you. You filled this gorgeous part of you with light. It's time to treasure her and introduce new levels of pleasure, new pleasurable sounds to you and your body. You're ready. Take a warm fragrant bath or shower and hop into bed. Pour some lubricant over your fingers and use your warm fingers to slowly, sensually turn yourself on. Your fingers are your pleasure creators, creating different pressures to turn you on, and whatever strokes that turn you on. To begin with, slide your pleasure creators slowly and up and down either side of your clitoris, as your pleasure button will often feel too sensitive to be touched directly at first. As you begin to turn yourself on, notice that your clitoris begins to swell and engorge with blood giving you more surface area for those 8,000 pleasure receptors to be touched and pleasured! Notice that your inner lips and your outer lips engorge and swell literally begging your fingers for more and more pleasure. Go with it and bring yourself to orgasm if it pleasures you or if it pleasures you not, do not! This is all about your pleasure, so compromising is not an option for a woman like you. Congratulations for taking yourself into pleasure, now notice what happens for you in the next 30 minutes – are you more likely to sit closer to your pleasure and choose more of it for yourself, or not? My clients find that the answer is a resounding yes, yes, yes and not just for that 30 minutes, but for the whole day. Goddess you've switched your pleasure button on and so you move from this turned on, 8000 pleasurable state.

You've got to turn yourself on to create *turn on*.

When your pleasure button is regularly turned *on,* your capacity for real rich pleasure gets bigger. A gorgeous client of mine, *Jasmine,* happened to drop me a little note; and it said, *"And, the sensuality part of my week? I think I have self-pleasured literally more times than I can count on one hand since our session! AND my brand new silver silk pajamas came in the mail yesterday just in time ;). I think it's safe to say that my sensuality and pleasure is ON! There is no going back now – it's something that I'll never turn off, thank you."*

You can't turn on 8,000 pleasure receptacles and not expect it to have a knock out effect... I mean you regularly turning your 8,000s on? Gives you a bigger affinity for pleasure in the whole rest of your life. And you want that. You have everything to gain with that and nothing to lose except your fear of the good things in life. And so *you knowing what you want* becomes second nature. Decisions become much easier. You choosing pleasure over pain in your life becomes a natural next step. Because you know what it feels like in your body. If I were to put my librarian glasses on, flick my hair and point a pointy thing at a diagram of your Vulva, I'd safely say:

Your vagina = the receiving part of you.

And your clitoris = the pleasure part of you.

Your ability to receive happiness in your life is the same ability needed to receive a mind-blowing orgasm. Did you know that? So the more you can say YES! YES! YES! to your pleasure and yes to laughing, yes to help, yes to support, yes to that facial, to receiving from life, the more likely you'll let more pleasure in. It's that simple. So, how much have you received today?

And what about now? Are you running towards your pleasure or away from it? Because you cannot be running in both directions at once. Are you running towards what is turning you ON, or to what is turning you OFF? It's either one, or the other.

Ditch the pain and reach for that pleasure because your life force depends on it!

And your life, your ability to orgasm, your body, your relationship with your lover all reflect how much you allow yourself to receive or how much you block it.

What you choose is up to you, and then – you are free!

FLIRTING TO TURN YOUR DAY ON

Goddess, other people are lucky just to be in the same room as you! Your wit, your beauty, and your spirit are just divine.

Flirting is essential to flourishing daily for a woman and it starts with you shining your light everywhere! Yet, why is it that you and I have, at one time or another, shied away from it? You might be shying away from it right now. Most women I know fall into three flirting categories: Those that love to flirt and can't live without it; those who like to flirt, but never at full volume because it amplifies everything they do including an amplified public rejection; and those who don't do it at all because they are scared of the power it holds. Which one are you relating to most right now? Most women who come to me for coaching fit into the third category – they don't want the extra attention it comes with because it scares them. It used to scare me. I'd cross the road to avoid even making the tiniest eye contact with the boys at the bus stop. Does it scare you? Have you diluted yours in the past, scared of its very power?

And what is flirting anyway and do we really need it? Surely, it's just a manipulative superficial way of talking to men, right? Have you used it in the past to get what you want? Do you relate flirting to that, or something cheap and desperate?

Most women I meet have an icky relationship to flirting – they like the power it brings, but are too scared and too "PC" to use it daily. It makes everyone look at you and you get embarrassed. So, this rusty joyride is wheeled out, only at parties and then it theatrically plays out with the woman batting her eyelids and flicking her hair... and not really relating to anyone else, but herself. Me, me, me. Look at me. It's a lonely game at the top, you, totally in love with you and not connecting to anyone else's heart. So, it's a long way to fall with nobody down there but you, you, you on the way down.

No, I'm talking about *real* flirting, the kind that takes the user and receiver to a higher, happier bubble. Real flirting is you being your charismatic best while being completely present with the other person. You're not diluting your charisma for the sake of the other person, or situation. It's you fully sharing your full charisma with the other person, and being present with them. And when you really see the other person? Really look and connect to them? You'll see their charisma too, peeping out at you. Hullo!

Your charisma + their charisma = flirting!

Even if they're not really showing theirs to you, talk to it anyway. It's way more fun than what you were about to do with them anyway! Welcome to Flirtsville, where real flirting makes the man in your orbit feel like a million dollars and its damn sexy. Try it!

Try it today with your bored, or not so bored husband, boyfriend, or girlfriend. In fact, anyone with a pulse who comes swimming into your orbit is yours to take higher. Don't wait for a good hair day, this little injection into your day will give you great hair, great legs and great teeth, all without grooming. Yes! It's just you shining your light and being present to theirs, no matter how dim theirs may seem at first. It's the most fun way to conduct a conversation with everybody. It's the most fun way to receive what you need and yes, it really will turn the most mundane day: ON!

Welcome To Flirtsville:

✻ Look deeply into the other's eyes and really see them first.
✻ Shine your light, Charismatic Girl; smile with teeth.
✻ Talk to the light in them, no matter how small.

Remember you're the Queen, you're the power, and you can turn your pleasure on, any which way you want today!

Chapter 11

Turn On Your Beauty

· · · · · · · · · · · · · ·

You can turn your beauty on, or off like a switch. Live with it turned on and everything wonderful is possible for you. Live with it turned off, and your light diminishes *no matter how unimportant you think beauty is.* You were made beautiful.

The shape your body makes is so lovable. Did you know that? And the exact shape of your face is very beautiful. And most people know it, *except you.* Are you rolling your eyes at me? "Well, I used to be beautiful when I was younger," "But I don't like my jaw line," "I've put on a lot of weight, so this doesn't really apply to me," and so on. I know, I know – talking about your beauty has the power to turn your happiness on, or off right now. Have you truly fallen in love with the exact way your body *looks*? And yet, we can both fall in love with our children's beauty, we might not have looked at *him* twice in the street, but now we're married to him, he's grown on us, and now we find him sexy! In fact, we're pretty damn good at appreciating his looks – we use the word *rugged* to mean *rough looking, so we find him sexy.* The same standard isn't used to describe us women is it when we're peering into the mirror... "God, I look rough," Ha! Why can't you find yourself sexy when you're looking rough? In fact, we've become rather good at putting conditions on ourselves in order to feel remotely attractive. How conditional is your beauty?

Conditional Beauty:

- My hair and my clothes have to be right, so that I can walk out the door...
- If I don't use concealer on my under eye circles/blemishes...
- Only once I've defined my brows, so my face is framed...
- When I've popped a slick of mascara on...
- A dash of red lipstick just lights up my face...
- And so on...

Do you see? This isn't love; *this isn't beauty*. This is conditional beauty. You feel beautiful on the condition that you're wearing something beautiful, or that you've at least had time to put a dash of mascara on. It's very limited isn't it? Conditional beauty grinds us down into Dry-out before we've even walked out the door in the morning. It stops us from feeling on top of the world; it stops us from feeling worthy of everything. And:

Conditional Beauty:

- ages us
- repels love
- makes us judgmental of ourselves in a big way
- makes us judgmental of every other woman we meet too
- shackles us
- stops us from taking risks
- is exhausting (all that getting ready)
- is inhibiting
- gives us conditional confidence
- is ugly.

And yet...
You chose your face,
And you chose your body,
Before you came to be.
What if your choice was in fact perfect?
And that's all you need to be?
Rocking your beautiful face as is,
And rocking that body of yours,
So that *all he can do*
Is come into agreement with you.
... The choice is YOURS!

Conditional Beauty vs Unconditional Beauty

When your beauty is without conditions, you are free. Free to wear makeup, or not. Free to feel beautiful and take all the accolades that come with that even though your skin's broken out again, even though you're having a bad hair day... even though... God I'm bored already – isn't it boring to be so conditional on how much we love ourselves? Isn't it? To love your face unconditionally, is to accept it just the way it is. I'm going to throw down the gauntlet and say you have it in you to do this! And you do. You are important enough to have your beauty voice LOUDER than photos of celebs/the beautiful people, films, other people's selfies, and social media making you feel like you're not polished enough, beautiful enough, pretty enough. You are. Take your attention off of looking at everyone all the time and thinking that your voice isn't the correct one. It is.

And here's how you find it:

Each woman is born a particular way, with a particular type of beauty only specific to her. To ignore it and try to look like someone else or to cover up your "wrongness" is to hide away this beauty from the world. And if you are doing this right now, the world will never have and will never see this particular beauty again. It misses out. Stop missing out on rocking yours. You have a particular specific type of beauty. I wonder what yours is? Shall I tell you what mine is? I have beautifully shaped "pouffly" lips that take over my whole face when I'm happy and light me up. I also have firm smooth skin, which combined with my long hair and long legs make me very beautiful. Falling in love with my beauty didn't happen because of what anyone said, or because I look classically beautiful. I actually don't. I think I look unusual.

Let me explain:

Whilst I was busy being 18 years old in London at University, my best friend Mike and I were talking about a guy I liked, so – I asked Mike *if he knew if this guy David, liked me?* He said somewhat thoughtfully: "Well Maz, you're the kind of girl that polarizes men, half find you stunning and the other half don't find you beautiful at all. I don't find you the slightest bit attractive, but David definitely does." A shocking answer to a plain question really, but it underlines what I'm saying. We each have a brand of beauty and it's up to us to fall in love with it. For every beautiful model you see in a magazine, there will always be a guy who will say she's got the body of a 12-year-old girl – "YUCK, no thanks!" Who is right?

Imagine you have an orange sitting happily on your kitchen countertop and every morning you greet the orange by telling it how beautiful it is. "My, what perfectly pocked orange peel you have and your shape, wow you are the most beautiful orange I have ever seen." The orange preens, and it blushes. "Oooo, I'm beautiful!" she thinks. One morning you storm into your kitchen cross and angry and the orange looks at you, and waits to receive a compliment on its new peel dress, and... and; in a fit of anger you say, "Look at you! You're not the orange you used to be, you're a lemon, and I don't find you attractive anymore." The orange is shocked. What? "But, but, I thought you said I was an orange and you thought I was beautiful." "No," you say, "I never said that. You've always been a lemon and I'm sick of you."

The orange has no internal approval of her beauty; she has not fallen in love with her beauty, so she *has had* to rely on outside validation of her.

So she goes up and down like a yo-yo depending on who in the outside world is complimenting her, loving her, and giving her the most attention.

But when she and you fall in love with your beauty? Well let's ask. What do you think would happen in your world if you became utterly beautiful? What would you *have more of*? Take a breath and hear the answer. Write it down. Just notice how you think the world will respond to you now? When I ask the most classically beautiful woman this and an unusual looking woman this (like me) I get ingenious answers! Here are some of my favourites:

- I would earn more.
- He wouldn't look at other women.
- He'd give me more attention.
- He'd give up sport all day Saturday and want to be with me.
- I'd be more desirable.
- I could do it with the lights on.
- I'd have a better grade of friend.
- I'd have a more glamorous lifestyle.
- I wouldn't have to work.
- I'd go to more beautiful places to eat and be seen.
- I'd have a much better wardrobe.
- People would be nicer to me.
- People would give me stuff.
- I'd be more popular.
- I'd like myself better, so I would look after myself more.
- It would be easier to eat cleanly and increase my self-love.
- I'd walk differently.
- I'd have no restrictions.

⟳ I would be more successful.

⟳ I'd be happier.

⟳ He wouldn't have left me.

What did you come up with?

Curious to see if you've got what it takes to fall in love?

We're going to turn your beauty ON by taking the fabulous steps to decide, desire, detox, and take self-love action. There's the most fabulous beauty party taking place at a rooftop terrace near you and it's filled with women of all different shapes and sizes and ages who have all fallen in love with their different shapes, sizes, and ages so much so that they ooze beauty, they are luminescent. And when you walk in? You are swept high and you are reminded of *your stunning luminescent beauty.*

You may already be there with a glass of bubblies in your hand throwing your head back in beautiful laughter. You may be feeling *what's the point of all of this*? I'd rather be a good person, or I'd rather trade on my brains. Yes, this is the right way to feel for *where you've been* so far with your beauty. But, if you genuinely want to be at peace and loving towards your body, then I invite you to dip your little toe in and see how many goodies you are willing to receive:

Decide what I don't want:

Write out everything you are done with in the area of your beauty. For example:

I'm done with peering at myself in the mirror looking for problems.

I'm done hiding my legs with jeans.

I'm done with clothes that don't make me feel beautiful.

I'm done with ignoring my feminine beauty.

I'm done with having to put on a full face of makeup, just to go to the store.

And I desire to make a strong life-long decision:

Yes, decide that you are beautiful, *unconditionally*. Just like that! Beauty can *only be* your decision. If you don't decide, then you'll let others decide for you. *You're only going to believe him, if you've decided.* Can you decide that you are beautiful right now? Mirror, "I am beautiful" until you know. Turn this coal into a glittery diamond for you.

Remember the orange? It doesn't matter what anyone else has said about your face, or your body. It doesn't matter what you have said about your face, or your body. It matters not that you think you are too tall or too short, that you are hugely overweight, model like, feel your boobs are too big, too small, or just perfect ma'am! It just matters to me that you are willing to decide that you, just as you are right now are completely beautiful. Without condition. It's going to take you being brave, you suspending your beliefs that might be shrieking obscenities at you now and you making a stand for the body and face you chose. Yes make no mistake, you chose your body and your face – why would you not love it?

Because you've been taught to. Or you've been too lazy to.

So what's the point in deciding that I am beautiful?

When I was 13 years old, I asked my mum if I was beautiful. I was worried my nose was too big. "Beautiful? No, you're not beautiful," she said. "But attractive? I'd say you are attractive." I remember going to the bathroom cabinet immediately, which when opened up, you stared into a mirror front on, with mirrored doors either side of your ears. There. Was. My. Nose. In. All. It's. Glory. I stared at it for a long time. Was it beautiful? Was it too big? Was it, gulp, ugly? I stared at it for the longest time and couldn't be sure. So, I went to that mirror again and again, most nights for 6 months, and just stared at it. I got to know my profile, with all its depths and movements. I got to know my nose and how it fitted into my face. And I came to the conclusion at the 6-month mark. My nose, while larger than what I wanted it to be, was actually the perfect size and fit for my face. It gave me gravitas, power, and an unusual kind of grace that I hadn't seen on magazine covers. I decided there and then that my nose, profile, and face was beautiful. And you know what? I really must have decided because I have not ever needed to go back and check on my profile. I made my strong decision then and have never needed to re-do it. Deciding is that powerful.

*So I have to make a little side note here, my mum is absolutely brilliant by the way! She made a wee mistake as we all do as parents and I know I've made many myself and will continue to do so, but what happened was absolutely perfect for me because I used it to create an internal approval of my beauty. And that now forms the basis of what I do today with my clients, so thank you mum!

So, when Mike said what he said to me at 18, it didn't undo me because I'd already decided that I was beautiful *unconditionally* and funnily enough every man I've ever dated has found me beautiful. That's not to say that every man will, but does it matter? No – then how wonderful, I'm free! I want this for you, too. So go ahead and decide for you, go on; decide to fall in love with your beauty now. And take those conditions that you have put on yourself and CHUCK THEM OUT! You deserve to! Have any of the other ways lasted for you? I'm thinking not, so you have nothing to lose and so much love to gain.

Your life force rises hugely when you approve of how you look. When you approve of how you look, you will have higher standards for yourself. When you have higher standards for yourself, you will allow yourself to receive the highest love from men and from everyone around you. In turn, this lifts the planet up. Can you imagine women everywhere loving how they look? Do you think there'd be less eating disorders, and more mums inspiring their daughters to walk tall? Do you think then that your average teenage boy surrounded by a culture of women practising a high level of self-respect is being educated the right way? You hold the power and the key to your beauty. No one else.

Detox

Let's start with a fabulous internal detox. Take a piece of paper and at the top write "My Beauty Detox". Underneath, write everything you feel about your own brand of beauty, both positive and negative, until you have emptied out your mind. Like an empty chalice waiting to be filled up with goodies! Too often, my clients think they love their beauty. Then they read back to me what they've written and oh, goddess! Their sentences are littered with little self-hate jabs at themselves disguised as beauty remarks. They howl with laughter sometimes as they read theirs out, but it's also painful. And what if you really don't fit the norm? What if you think you used to be beautiful, but now you've slipped? What if you're thinking you're too spotty, fat, and old to be beautiful anymore? Detox it out NOW. Trust this process more than your mind.

Here is a super short example to give you:

I hate the back fat that splurges out from my bra. Yuck!

Though I do like my breasts, they could be perkier, if I'm honest. I like my nipple colour and the smoothness of my skin here. There always seems to be something wrong with my body. When I was younger, I wanted bigger breasts, but now I'm older I want a flatter stomach. I detest my "bat arms", the extra wingage that seems to fly each time I move my arms when I talk. I dress to hide the bits I hate. I'm too tall. I adore the colour of my eyes and my eye shape.

After you've written your beauty detox, read it back to yourself and notice if you're more pro or against your beauty?

Close your eyes, breathe and ask yourself, *how old was I when I decided I wasn't beautiful?* Why? What was happening to you at the time?

Imagine you're looking in the mirror you usually do your makeup in/ or look in first thing – what does your conditional beauty voice say to you? Open your eyes and write them down. *Eyes are looking really small today... Oh God there's another wrinkle...*

What do you feel when you are saying these things to yourself? Sad? Annoyed? Less than? Not good enough? Ugly? You're slipping? You don't care?

How does that make you feel?

Want to stop feeling this way?

Imagine you are looking at yourself in that mirror and you are loving yourself unconditionally. What does your unconditional beauty voice say to you? Open your eyes and write them down. *Oh I'm lovely, I'm so beautiful... if you have never had this experience before, imagine it and write down what you think she'd say.*

How do you feel to say all these things to you? Do you feel empowered or disempowered? Does it feel nice? Want to feel more of this?

Have the unconditional beauty voice talk to the conditional beauty voice until you can turn the volume up on your unconditional beauty to a "10".

Here is what you might say to help you along;

Unconditional Beauty talking to your conditional beauty:

You know you've always been beautiful, it's just that when you put conditions on it, you know like you have to have clear skin and like you have to have the perfect looking hair, your beauty immediately shrinks and you become so much smaller than you actually are. You don't need to do this anymore, it doesn't become you. (Keep going, what else does your unconditional beauty want to say to your conditional beauty part to open her eyes as to how naturally beautiful you are?)

Now, let's accept your conditional beauty, once and for all and be at peace with her. What gift has conditional beauty given to you? For me, it's honed my ability to blow dry my hair, and to create (sometimes) strong eyebrows that frame my face. What's yours? Good. Thank your conditional beauty and now turn her volume down to a "1". You've got the gift, so you don't need to keep wheeling her out.

You know the gifts your unconditional beauty are going to give you, so turn her volume up to a "10". What would she like you to do this week to feel and to know you are 100% beautiful?

> "There was a point in my 40s when I went into the bathroom with a bottle of wine, locked the door, and said, 'I'm not coming out until I can totally accept the way that I look right now."
>
> *– Sharon Stone, actress*
> *Vanity Fair*

And for the days when you look into the mirror and you're really not feeling it? That's where your unconditional love comes in – wrap your arms around yourself, look into the mirror, and say out loud, "I'm worth loving today" – and love yourself with all your might.

I DESIRE TO TURN MY OWN BRAND OF BEAUTY ON

Take a warm bath or shower and as you soap each part of your body, I want you to say to it out loud, "I'm sorry for not loving you, please forgive me." Say it to each part of your body and just notice how each part of your body responds. Do you breathe differently, do you feel softer, or are you still choosing to feel nothing at all? There is no right or wrong here, just notice where you are at.

Walk into a warm room that only you will be in; light some candles and slip all your clothes off. With gusto face a full length mirror and gaze at the lines and curves your body makes. Can you love the exact shape your body makes? From the top of your head to the tips of your toes? This is the shape your body is wanting to make. Don't look at the bits in between, just focus on the beautiful curve of your neck down to the beautiful curve to your bottom. Imagine seeing yourself as a painter would like Botticelli, where he would paint you as the most beautiful woman. What kind of line does my body make? A wibbly wobbly one? A smooth one? How would he paint that? Opulently, heavenly...

Choose to find this beautiful. Decide to find *that beautiful*. What's beautiful about your brand of beauty in this area? Don't imagine what you would prefer to look like, *look at what is*. Stay looking until you know. Most of us don't look at our body for very long. So, I want you to spend time gazing, getting to know you, just as you are, right at this minute. Look at the lines your legs make. This is your special shape for your leg right now, Goddess choose to fall in love with it just as it is. Because it's you. I cannot think of a better reason.

Then after you've decided that your lines are in fact beautiful, start at your head and work your way down. Use an eyeliner to write "love" onto each body part. What could I find beautiful about my hair, forehead, eyebrows, and eyes, then ARE YOU BRAVE enough to make the decision that you are in fact beautiful? Because beauty is just that, it's a *beautiful decision* made by you.

Ask a girlfriend who wants to own her beauty to join you: Each morning for 7 days in a row, take a photo of yourself bare faced with your phone and send it to your girlfriend. She then sends you the three most beautiful things about you. Then you do the same to her photo AND yours! I did this with a group of my clients, so we each posted up a no makeup selfie on the private page of my website for 7 days. None of us wanted to do this because selfies can be the least flattering of them all, but by day 3, we all got into it and the results were astounding! *Jessica* said: "I'd already owned my beauty, but after doing this it took me to a whole new level of love for me. I can now go to the store with no makeup on! This morning I didn't hide myself when I saw my crush, instead

I flirted with him mischievously and now I'm going on a date with him tonight! Hello new power and confidence!"

Self-love Action

Are you treasuring yourself like a beautiful woman would?

1. Detox your wardrobe and chuck out anything that does not make you feel beautiful when you wear it. Include shoes, handbags and jewellery. They have no place in your cupboards anymore. If you haven't worn it in a year, it's time to go! This will leave room for real beauty to enter your wardrobe. Stop hanging onto things just in case. Beautiful women only keep things in their wardrobes that make them feel and look like a Goddess.

2. Celebrate your beauty! Do you have a beautiful haircut? Treat yourself to a beautiful haircut that highlights the structure of your face, change hairdressers if you need to. The mark of a great hair cut is you walking out of there feeling like a million dollars. Do you have makeup that accentuates your colouring and beauty? Each year, our skin and our eyes change a little. Book yourself into a makeup session at a department store, or find a makeup artist to play with. It's their job to enhance you, so let them! Throw out your old nail polishes and only have the colours that excite you!

3. Beautify your outer world. Your car, your house, throw out anything that doesn't feel beautiful to you and add in what does. It's time. One of my clients beautified her car by plugging in a mini oil burner into it, always having the music she loves ready at hand, and bought woolly car covers for her bottom. Warm, soft and beautiful.

4. Beautify the plain and beautify the ugly. A beautiful client of mine had had a double mastectomy resulting in a scar across her chest. She was due to see her doctor the next day for "boobie replacements" as she put it! She was terrified of going in to the hospital again, as it brought up old memories, so we beautified

the ugly appointment. We packed her a beauty bag consisting of fragrant frangipani hand crème (because hospitals do not smell of flowers), a beautiful book to read and strengthen her during the wait, and where the "ugly" scar was? She drew two glitter eyes above it to make the scar into a smile. By the time she walked into the hospital, she was strangely excited. And when the doctor peeled up her top? He burst out laughing! "I wish all my patients were like you, you've made my day!" he said. He then drew out where her new breasts would go and added a couple of eyebrows to her beautiful scar face. *There!* The appointment and those after it became fun, beautiful, and poignant. A real ode to her beauty. She said she glitter dotted on those eyes each morning until her operation and it changed the way she felt about herself. She is now the proud owner of a beauty scar. What can you beautify that is plain, or ugly in your world?

5. Walk, move, think, and hold yourself beautifully: how are you sitting right now? How are you thinking about yourself right now? Yes, you are beautiful. Live from this deep knowing and you alert everyone around you that they have a Goddess in their midst.

Adore your brand of beauty and watch the world follow suit for the rest of your life.

Chapter 12

Turn On Your POWER

· · · · · · · · · · · · · ·

With your very own system to flourish, flourish, flourish in! This book gives YOU your power BACK. Now, we're going to take it up a notch and it's your turn to take what you like from this book and from other things you've learned, and make it into one big beautiful system that ONLY fits you!

Are you going to follow my system completely, or add in some glittery bits of your own? (Who doesn't like glitter?) Remember that NO ONE knows you like you do, minute to minute, second to second so – you know what I'm saying, let's listen to your inner voice...

... This is the greatest gorgeously glittery gift you could give yourself.

And... let's have fun with it, Glitter Goddess...

Dance to feel your true essence:

Without further ado, pop some music on and dance, dance, dance to the full track, singing as you go! Dance exactly how you feel, happy, sad, high as a kite, feel your essence, *feel you* exactly as you are right at this moment. How magnificent are you? = VERY!

Then, go find yourself something you love to drink, some delectable nibblies and make sure you are really comfy. I'm drinking a black chai tea and have a sweet pea and geranium candle lit. (I won't eat while I'm talking to you.)

Now as you know, *you* were made to receive what turns you on this lifetime and if you live away from the way you were made you... Dry-out. What an anti-climax. This proven system has powered you up, lit you up, I tell you! And we've immersed ourselves in it up until now. Together, we now build your own system that takes into account all the gorgeous details about you that I cannot possibly know. (This is the bit where your heart sings to you.)

So here we're going to create your very own system that takes you out of Dry-out AND stops you from going back in. Every. Single. Month. But, it needs to be inserted into your month. To help you, download your help sheet with me talking you through creating your very own delicious system! Oh I'm excited for you! Use the special code TYOGoddess at marinaj.net.

Once you've downloaded your free sheet, press play on my audio, and let's do this together.

OK, you're now hearing my voice talk you through creating your very own system (told you I wasn't eating!)

Glitter Bits:

Hop to each chapter now and sweetly extract what you've learnt from this book *and* from your own life, pull it altogether and fill out your help sheet. Make a little list of what you personally need in your system each day to flourish. This can take 15 minutes (but don't make it longer than an hour or you won't do it). Here are some questions to help you:

Add each answer below into YOUR system for flourishing!

- **What is important for me in this life?** So what do I *make time for*, each month? Might be to have an artistic outlet daily, or to really find out what life's all about, or to reach my highest potential this lifetime.

- **What is important to me in my relationship?** So, what needs to happen/change/be maintained? What regular habit do I drop into each month for us?

- **What makes me/us particularly happy?**

- **What pleasure is non-negotiable for me daily?**

- **What will keep me healthy at work?**

- **What heals me when I'm (tired, annoyed, etc.) at the end of a long day?**

- **What makes me flourish?** Think *ways* to invest in yourself and make yourself happy that I couldn't possibly know about you.

- **What three things are really good for me that keep me grounded, happy, and flourishing?** For example, mine are sleep, yoga, being outside daily.

- **What turns me on?** List everything here, this your Personal Turn On List. Trust it. Follow it.

- **What turns me off?** Again, only you know. You don't have to show it to anybody, but trust it and take baby steps towards limiting these.

Once you've made your notes, it's time to add in the details that are the opposite. The ones that *personally derail you* on a daily basis and only you know what those are.

My personal derailments are:

Add these into your help sheet. Here are some questions to help you:

Q: Are you the kind of woman that says yes too quickly only to regret it moments later? If yes, then in your system answers, you could add:

A: My answer to any question is always, "Can I get back to you on that?" Because I need time to make sure this thing adds to me.

Q: Would you like to make quicker better decisions?

A: To maker quicker and better decisions I ask, "Does this add to me or take away?"

Q: Can you trust yourself with the munchies at night?

A: Just as I reach for the munchies, I yell, "STOP!" And ask myself "What do I need to receive instead?"

Q: Are you the sort of person that hates to be rushed?

A: I am to give myself 10 extra minutes in my diary for everything.

Q: What do you need to stay on track with your wants for the day?

A: I am to set my phone alarm to go off every hour for me to check in with myself. I ask, how close am I sitting to my desires right now?

Q: Do I forget about my needs and myself, until it's too late?

A: I am to set my phone alarm to go off every hour until putting myself first becomes natural to me. So to train myself, each hour I ask myself, "How kind am I being to myself right now?"

Q: Do I enjoy my mornings?

A: I am to commit to a new morning ritual for myself that I will not budge on for toffee BECAUSE I AM IMPORTANT.

Now pull all this information about yourself together and write; *My New Personal System is* – and just spell it out for yourself deliciously.

Feel it, trust it, write it, and create it because your very own system will fit you perfectly. So you can navigate each situation from your own internal compass. You can do it. You can trust yourself and you do know what to do. Own it. And then go play it large in the outside world each day, each month, and each year. And it will take discipline. But it will keep you strong, true and to your dreams, with less roundabouts and U turns to go through. I've given you examples in the rest of this chapter to help you.

Once you've created it, it is here in this book that you come to strengthen YOU. Especially, if you've given yourself away. You'll know you've done this, if you know more about what someone else is thinking, needing, or you are worrying more about their reactions than your own.

Take your new personal system complete with fairy lights and pop it into a beautifully bound book just for you. Make sure there is space for you to add in extra glitter bits over time. This is the beginning of your new fabulous life – you've just created the foundations for it to now grow. Hurrah and well done!

EXTRA INSPIRATION FOR YOU

Do you want to see what my personal system is in condensed form? Sharing is a great way to get inspiration – well of course, I've put a lot of mine into this book:

I use the 3 Ds to navigate all situations:

1. Decide what I don't want.

2. Desire what I do.

3. Detox what's in my way.

4. Self-love action.

And I regularly ensure these feminine parts of me are turned on:

5. Best friend.

6. Receiving.

7. Sensuality.

8. Pleasure.

9. Beauty.

10. POWER.

My favourite question that snaps me back, if I start to lose myself is:

"I am a Goddess – am I treating myself as one?"

And I so choose to LOVE the sticky! I mean, what part of me is it trying to switch on? So, I *make time* each month to heal the sticky, sometimes it takes 10 minutes, a couple of hours; I always make time for it because this is key to me flourishing. I am so sensitive that I must in my personal system *make* time to heal. So, I close my eyes, go inside, and use one of the processes in this book because almost always it's an INSIDE job to heal the OUTSIDE.

I keep my standards high (because I am a Queen), and if I forget, I've surrounded myself with souls who are invested in me and my happiness. For instance: my dad is the first one to tell me if I should be aiming higher, my mum will not let me drop out of my power, my sister and her partner believe in me 100%, and my husband keeps the standard so high for my happiness, that he was part of the inspiration for this book. My daughter is the first to have compassion for me and reminds me to do the same. Do you know where the rest of the inspiration came from to write this book? YOU! Because when I see what happens to you when you create your own system? Nothing else matters, I've done my job.

My spiritual ethos

My spiritual ethos is that I am a Goddess. This means some of my time is focussed on having a divine relationship with myself between waking and sleeping. To live the life of a Goddess is to truly reach my potential this lifetime. It means that I am God; I am Goddess; and because I also feel the same way about you; I see you as God and as a Goddess. Whether you treat yourself as one or not is up to you, my deepest desire is to treat you as the God and Goddess you are.

I also believe in God and the Goddess. Yes, those ones *up there*. I believe that I have great power to do great things and great power to do bad things. So being a Goddess and believing in God and the Goddess (*up there*) also carries great responsibility. And it's one that I relish because we are incredible beings and the more we trust our God and Goddess given power, then the less we will abuse it.

I believe *we only ever need to abuse* because we are busy believing in lack, which is the exact opposite of being a Goddess.

If we trust our God and Goddess given power, then we will have more than we will ever need; and so who needs to abuse power if we're already fully nourished?

So how does this look in practice?

Let's say, you need to receive more support from your husband. How do you go about it?

The first thing I do to create delicious transformation *in any area of my life* is to apply the 3 Ds.

Decide what I don't want.

Desire what I do.

Detox what's in my way.

Self-love action.

Transformation always begins with a decision. What does it take for you to decide once and for all?

Will you need a much stronger desire in you *to decide what you don't want; more than your current attachment* to your situation? YES! it's like saying, "Enough! I'm done."

So, how does this look? You would be clear with yourself:

- I *don't want Tom expecting dinner at 6:00pm on the dot anymore.*
- I desire to have dinner on the table loosely between 6:00–7:30pm.
- I detox what has been in my way up until now by going to the detox chapter.
- I implement this self-love by taking action on this: I ask *Tom* for what I want in a powerful way that makes me happy to say it. And

each time he enjoys eating at a loose time, I'm mentally high fiving myself. I did it! I JUST TURNED AROUND 7 YEARS OF HABIT!

COMMON SCENARIO QUIZ

Let's do a little quiz and see how your new system is working for you! Make your decision based on your new system with some common scenarios below:

1. You've agreed with someone to do something at a certain time. But now you don't feel like doing it. For example, you said to your husband, "Yes, I'll meet you at 9:30am." It's now 9:00am and you've just meditated, and received a lot of information about that project you've been creating.

Do you:

a) meet him anyway and ignore the tug of your new information?

b) jot down the basics and meet him late at 10:00am?

c) call him to cancel? You gotta surrender to it!

In your new system: What turns you on and how brave are you to follow it?

2. It's 8:30pm and you're about to watch a movie. In your new system, you eat foods you love, that love you right back. *But it's the end of a hard week,* you hear yourself saying, *you deserve to relax.*

You go to the fridge and:

a) pull out that slightly hardened chocolate cake from Tuesday; if you squirt some cream over it, it'll do.

b) virtuously start with raisins and nuts, and then graduate to the hard stuff. S'mores, melted chocolate on top. By 9:45pm, you are feeling sick, sleepy, and food hanger-overy. *(I know this is not a word, but 'tis perfect.)

c) in a coup d'état, you pull out the old story you laminated back in chapter 7: Hmmm, bullet point No. 2 says, "You are not kind to yourself when you're stuck in your old story." So *in a world first* you stop and ask yourself, if I was being kind to myself right now what would I give to myself? The answer comes to you: A phone call to my best friend deeply discussing the films' leading man while we're both watching it *while also* soaking my feet in a warm bowl of Epsom salts. *Optional: Stuffing face with homemade popcorn.

In your new system: What dollops of love can you drop into your day, so you are not toast by the evening? Would you create a little care pack for yourself especially for your evenings? E.g. think Epsom salts + bowl + magazine + delish healthy nibblies waiting on the couch for you.

3. The guy that broke your heart wants you back.

Do you:

a) answer his call, let his words sway you? Shit, and now you're seeing him tonight. How did that happen?

b) answer his call and say, "No," but let him set the tone for another phone call to happen?

c) not answer the call? This is the man who was not invested in your happiness then, and he isn't now. Text him back, "Please don't call again." That's it. No need to over answer, or analyse and you don't ever need to answer his calls or texts back again. Minimum time wasted. You are free, remember? You don't owe him anything; you set the tone, not him!

In your new system: What do you have in place to remind you NOT to say yes to people who drain you? It might just be a special quote you put on your phone.

4. This is your bit! What scenarios stop you from flourishing? Jot them down, and then write what your new system is, so you come prepared for your week! You're going to flourish!

Yes, you are. Turn on this brilliant system within you *that works for you to create a life that turns you on.* One that is shaped exactly to fit your heart.

Would you like to create a top and tail ritual for your day? Here are some ideas:

New System 15-Minute Morning Ritual

Close your eyes:

Decide to create a day that turns you on and hug yourself! 10 seconds.
Desire what you want for today? Visualise for 30 seconds.
Detox anything that's in your way, do a quick process. 7 minutes.
Self-love Action Choose one: Green juice it, dress beautifully, yoga, dance, stretch it out, self-pleasure it out, run it out, laugh it out, take a hot shower followed by a cold one, OOO!

For example, sometimes I just wake up *tired.* I know you do too. So, I love to desire the kind of day that is *easy on me.* If you wake up needing this too, then say to yourself:

"Today, I desire that everything comes easily to me. I have way more energy at the end of today than I do now, thank you!"

New System 5-Minute Evening Ritual

Stop. Receive exactly what you need to get back into delicious alignment again for at least 10 minutes, no compromise.

Go ahead and jot anything else down in your beautiful bound book that you rather like.

In case you're sitting on that fence about creating your new system...

... What if you made your happiness important? You were not put on this planet to say "not now" to your happiness. You are not designed to delay your happiness. That just delays your LIFE!

So, repeat after me out loud:

"It's always the right time to treat myself like a Goddess."

Chapter 13

You've Turned Yourself ON!

. . . .

Ahhh we're floating together towards the end of this book – and it's here that we can quickly turn ourselves ON:

To become the woman, *the Goddess,* you were born to be, is to be the QUEEN of your decisions, of your desiring, detoxing, and self-love:

Turn on the 3 Ds:

1. Decide What You Don't Want.

2. Desire What You Do.

3. Detox What's In Your Way.

4. Self-Love Action.

And

Turn on these feminine parts of you, your:

5. Best Friend.

6. Receiving Button.

7. Sensuality.

8. Pleasure.

9. Beauty.

10. POWER.

ON!

When you take your 3 Ds with you to the next situation you find yourself in? You stand in your fabulous power, Goddess, and you will THRIVE.

Choose to THRIVE today rather than make do.

And you have! You are the Queen of your turning yourself on. You know how to turn your sensuality on *whenever you want it*, you know how to turn your deep self-healing on *whenever you need it* and yes, you know how to turn on your self-love... because your happiness is everything!

Because when *you turn on the most feminine* and *delectable parts* of you, you can only FLOURISH. YOU can turn them on and YOU can turn them off! When you greet your husband at the door with a fetching yellow tracksuit on, *and* with your beauty turned firmly on inside of you; that's what he's drawn to. When you strut down the hallways at work, owning and rocking how brilliant you are at what you do; *you do* get noticed by *those who want to promote you*. When you turn on your ability to self-heal, you gain the kind of confidence most women your age don't have.

The way we are requires us to receive twice that of men. If you and I live *away* from this set up? We shall Dry-out to a crinkle crisp!

And we don't want our marriages to Dry-out, we don't want our light to get dim. And, the only way out is to live from a system that we created just for us that turns us on, takes us out of Dry-out, AND stops us going back in. The world may not be doing it but WE ARE!

When I started writing this book, I knew I had a lot to say to you:

If you are a woman, you were born a Goddess.

Which means you are beautiful beyond words.

You are designed to receive,

And created, only to have a divine relationship with yourself.

It's what you were born to do.

It's so much easier than Dry-out, because you're,

Ripe, and lush, you are L.O.V.E incarnate.

With a mere flick of a smile you can move this earth,

Astonish those lucky enough to be in the same room as you,

Blind me with your sheer magnificence.

The world needs you turned ON,

And living from this point.

Without meek apology,

Strutting your stuff.

Because when you're turned ON, you turn this world ON.

Go ROCK the day with you Goddess, we're cheering you
all the way!

WOOOOO!

So, ta daaaaaaa, you've turned yourself on – I love it when you're feeling fabulous! Your own natural system for flourishing is now ON – can you feel it? How brilliant are you?

I've loved sitting by your side supporting you to use this system because it powers you up from the inside. It gives you your amazing power BACK! Just like brushing your teeth to keep them shiny, this is *your system* and it only works when you use it. Find some women to share it with and go through it together! Community helps you stay disciplined, join ours, and find women just like you; along with some little gifts I've created for you at marinaj.net. Don't forget, you'll need the special code, TYOGoddess, to access them ☺

Once you've finished this book, look at the detailed contents at the beginning of this book like you'd look at a delicious box of chocolates – which one would turn me on now? Here's a quick flirt with it!

QUICK TURN-ON:

1. Decide what you don't want

To come out of Dry-out, make a stand for yourself and decide. What's turning you off? Be honest. This will always lead you to make the best decisions for yourself. So, start here and decide with your whole body. Yes, you deserve better, yes your standards need to lift, and yes it's safe for you to decide. You are fully supported to do so. Never be a slave to anything, you are a Goddess. Or, have you forgotten?

2. Desire what you do

How close are you sitting to your desire? Want. Deserve. Desire. Have you read them recently? What would turn you on right now? Sit close to raise your life force. Make your desire bigger than the hurdle in your midst. Want it; *don't need it.* How much have you allowed yourself to pirouette from worry to what you want today? Align, ask, and appreciate.

I trust that good giggly things are always coming my way, even if I can't see or feel them yet.

3. Detox what's in your way

Become a Detoxing Diva – let nothing come in the way of you healing fully to set yourself free. LOVE the ugly today. It's OK to feel the ugly feelings, the more honest you are about the way you feel, the deeper you heal. YOU are totally and utterly normal for feeling the way you do. Turn on your self-healing this month and LOVE every single feeling, whether you love it or hate it, because each *feeling* is always bringing you back to self-love. You can heal anything 100%. When we also choose to fall in LOVE with each *part of ourselves...* then we know what real love is. Each part of us becomes our friend and has no power over us anymore. What do you need to heal this month to stop you from sliding back into Dry-out? People are always responding to the *real* relationship you have with yourself, never towards what you do, or say. So use the outside as your mirror and ask yourself, "Have I slipped?"

4. Self-love action

Self-love is you being kind to yourself. How kind are you being to you right now? *Being kind to me makes it natural for me to be kind to others.* Your self-love is the warmest blanket on the coldest of days. Wrap yourself up in it and remember - you have to implement it for it to be self-love!

5. Best friend

Are you being a best friend or a toxic friend to yourself? What tells you that you're in your old toxic story? Remind yourself, "Am I in my old story or my new one?" Voilà! In a second, you've just become that wonderful friend to yourself because it takes a brave woman to step out of her disempowering story, and a brave one to step into your empowering new one, but that's exactly who you are!

6. Receiving

Too much doing and not enough receiving will make any good woman become dull, tired, pissed off, angry, and just plain OVER IT! So, you gotta receive, right down to your teeny tiny toes to get back to being happy again. So you have to know your signs. What are they again? Receive what you need today to simply FLOURISH. You are WAY too gorgeous not to!

7. Sensuality

Fully receive the NOW: breathe, feel the fabric touching parts of your body right now. You are a sensual being, have you allowed yourself to be sensual today? Invite him to a *Date with a Goddess* tonight. If it turns you on, it will turn him on. Celebrate your Vulva whenever you can – sing it! Trá lá lá lá lá... put what you're doing down, have a sensual moment *all to yourself*, play music, sway your hips, feel your sensuality – it only takes a moment to turn the sensual Goddess in you ON!

8. Pleasure

Are you receiving twice as much as him? Turn your pleasure button ON regularly, to open you up to receiving, like the Goddess you are. Whose pleasure level are you living to: his or yours? 4,000 or 8,000? You don't want to slip into Dry-out today, so what pleasure do you have lined up for yourself? What would turn you on today? Finding the bliss where you are is not for the faint hearted. And Goddess? Are you running towards your pleasure or very far away from it?

9. Beauty

Don't wait for your hair to be right, go straight to the mirror and blow yourself a kiss for all that you are, and all that you are not this very minute! Gorgeous gal, YOU are beautiful just the way you are. Decide that your brand of beauty is beautiful and let the day go no further without you using every hallway, and every moment as a celebration of your unique beauty.

10. POWER

You yes YOU. You are important, have you invested in your health, business, or happiness today? The system you created gives you your power BACK! Have you let it support you today? Repeat after me, "It's always good where I am because the party starts with me! I thrive when I keep deliciously high standards for myself and it is *always* the right time to treat myself like a Goddess!"

Your turn-on helps me turn on. Your self-love teaches me self-love – teaches you self-love – teaches the world *how to love.*

You change the cells in your body; you change the very biology of your body and you show your daughters, mothers, friends, colleagues, community, and neighbours what's possible for every woman out there.

Treat yourself like the QUEEN you are and watch others remember who they really are too.

An inner belief that is not shakeable seems to settle in a woman's body when she pays attention to what turns her on – she is able to ask her husband to cook, even though she said *she would* because she needs to finish this book! And he is only too happy to do it because he loves making her happy. Is he exhausted? Yes. But is it more exhausting to come home tired from your day and be around a woman who is so turned off that you have no idea how to make her happy? So it becomes a weight you'd rather not come home to? Yup.

You making you happy and him making you happy is your birthright. You cannot hope to nurture a project, a baby, a child, and your life's purpose, without receiving what you need to do it. And if it doesn't turn you on: don't do it! Because you choosing what will turn you off, like saying yes when you mean no – will turn YOU off. And we can't have that!

Come out of Dry-out, and stay disciplined enough to stay out of it.

This is you turning yourself on, so you LIVE the life that you knew all along was yours. It's yours now. Guard is safely. Treasure it. Decide what turns you ON. And Stick to it. Don't dare try to receive *any less than you were born to...*

And then you've become the Goddess you were born to be, see?

You're the Queen. You're the POWER.

YOU Turn Yourself ON!

Yipee!

Here are some questions to ask yourself, so you snap back to flourishing – the very same ones that help shape my life and thousands of women around the world. I hope they add to you as much as they have to me.

My love to you,

1. Does this decision add to me, or take away?

2. Did I shrink my light to fit yours?

3. Am I the Queen of this situation?

4. Have I turned my power ON here?

5. How kind am I being to myself right now?

6. My feelings are right for me and yours are right for you; what's the gift?

7. Who is setting the tone here: me, or you?

8. Am I running towards my pleasure, or away from it?

9. Have I received *enough* today?

10. My wellbeing is all around me: how much of it am I letting in?

11. What if I didn't abandon myself today?

12. What part of me is this situation trying to turn on?

13. Am I treating myself like a Goddess?

The Gorgeous End

Thank you

. . . .

Thank you so much to the delectable Alicia Freile for your dedication, love and pure brilliance. Without you my book would not be what it is, so a million thank-yous and a million kisses; you have been fantastic to work with, an über professional of the highest order.

A MASSIVE thank-you of immeasurable proportions to the very special Pam Mountfield (pammountfield.com; she is brilliant, so please go check her out). I love you very much. You are exquisite magical fabulousness! You're like stardust! Thank you for holding my hand in the most powerful way possible. For caring so deeply about me and my message and my future. I could not have done this without you. I am in awe of you, R.G. You are simply spectacular.

To my beautiful daughter Maya, thank you for your kindness, smoothie bowls, spot-on intuition AND for your exquisite design addition to my book cover. I trust you implicitly. You are talented and wise beyond my years. I am very blessed you chose me to be your mummy. I love you. x

To my beloved Paul, I've never met anyone like you. I could be in the gutter with you and still have the BEST time ever! Thank you for chocolate brownies, real love, and for believing in me from the first time we met. Without you, this book would have been at least another 2 years away. That speaks volumes about the kind of man you are. I love you. xx Thank you.

A gushy thank-you to my beautiful sister Suzy Jacoby – your reaction to my book brought tears to my eyes (for all the right reasons!). Thank you for believing in me – and then some! Thank you to the legend that is James Ruddick; your razor sharp mind and suggestions were so valuable to me. Thank you both of you; I love you both very much.

A deeply heartfelt thank-you to my wonderful parents, Juliette Jacoby and Ben Jacoby; your faith in me and your love are everything. I love you both very, very much.

Thank you to my grandfather Hans Jacoby and my grandmother Marianne Jacoby for passing on the family tradition. Granny, we all used to say you should write a book and you never did. I wrote this for the both of us; I hope up there you've got a copy and you like it! MWA!

Thank you so much to the super-talented, super-special Katia Twyford. Your love, talent and amazing vibration when you work took me higher than I could alone and you brought me back with cherries on top each time, thank you!

To the gorgeous Jen Boxer, designer extraordinaire; thank you for putting your heart and soul into designing some special bits in this book. You're absolutely brilliant at what you do! Thank you for always being there for me.

And sparkly sequinned thank-yous to the fantastic Ian McDonald, the fabulous Naomi Lee, the beautiful Nicole Bednarek, and the magical Cleopatra.

A big thank-you to Darryl Nixon for your big heart and big guidance. Huge appreciation. To Joseph Emnace, you read my mind with my book cover and I absolutely love it – thank you sooo much!

A HUGE thank-you to Mike Bluett for your wonderful feedback, Anna Truman for lending Mike to me, and Sarah Knapman for YOUR brilliant feedback and Matt Knapman for lending your Sarah to me! THANK YOU! To the very special Ginny Bain, you are just D.I.V.I.N.E. Thank you.

To my beautiful clients, thank you for creating amazing lives worthy of the Goddess. You amaze me every single day and I'm so grateful you chose me to get you there. You're just FABULOUS!

And to you reading these words right now, thank you for reading my book. My wish for you is that you become the Goddess you were born to be. I'm wishing you a gorgeous moment... um right now actually! You deserve it AND the best life ever! Because your happiness is everything. And your happiness is my happiness!

Some fabulous authors you might like to explore:

Hans Jacoby – *Analysis of Handwriting:*
An Introduction into Scientific Graphology

Debbie Ford – *The Dark Side of the Light Chasers*

Marianne Williamson – *A Return to Love*

Doreen Virtue – *Archangels & Ascended Masters*

David Deida – *Blue Truth*

Amy Jo Goddard – *Woman On Fire*

Regina Thomashauer – *Mama Gena's School of Womanly Arts*

John Gray – *Men are from Mars, Women are from Venus*

Christiane Northrup, M.D. – *The Secret Pleasures of Menopause*

Steve Bodansky & Vera Bodansky – *Extended Massive Orgasm*

Eckhart Tolle – *A New Earth*

About the Author

• • • • • • • • • • • • • •

Marina J teaches women one of the most important skills of all: How to turn your power on and get your fabulous back after upset with him, with her, or with life in general – because your happiness is everything! She does the deep stuff and the sparkly, gorgeous stuff.

A relationship expert, best selling author and speaker, she has helped thousands of women around the world live the life they always knew they were meant to be in. And she wants this for you too.

Known as The Relationship Goddess, she deliciously focuses on YOU and the relationship you have with yourself because this sets the tone for every success, and every relationship you'll ever find yourself in.

Marina is the creator of The Turn Yourself On System: A powerful program for women who want fast, deep transformation and healing. Marina comes from a long family history of psychotherapists and authors, and trained to become a life coach whilst being a single mum, with her work strongly founded in Jungian psychology. She started out as a yoga instructor almost 20 years ago, and had her own line of yoga wear (sold internationally). She loves to write regularly as a contributor to magazines, newspapers and websites, and has been known to do the odd interview on TV and radio! She is married to the love of her life and lives with their daughter by the beach near Sydney. She can be found at marinaj.net, Facebook and Twitter.

The crown fits!
(Knew it would.)

Would you like extra support and fabulous energy sprinkled into your day? Then come join me on:

f Facebook @MarinaJCoaching
🐦 Twitter @MarinaJGoddess

Like my page and make yourself known to me, I'd love to meet you!

And because I know how determined you are to live a life that turns you on? I've created a gift you will use time and time again!

Go to marinaj.net and pop your name and e-mail where prompted so you can have access to it immediately.

And shhh... don't forget you also get private access to that secret page because you bought this book! You know what to do — MWA! X